The Question of John the Baptist and Jesus' Indictment of the Religious Leaders

The Question of John the Baptist and Jesus' Indictment of the Religious Leaders

A Critical Analysis of Luke 7:18–35

Roberto Martínez

☙PICKWICK *Publications* · Eugene, Oregon

THE QUESTION OF JOHN THE BAPTIST AND JESUS' INDICTMENT OF THE RELIGIOUS LEADERS
A Critical Analysis of Luke 7:18–35

Copyright © 2011 Roberto Martínez. All rights reserved. Except for brief quotations in critical publications or reviews, no part of this book may be reproduced in any manner without prior written permission from the publisher. Write: Permissions, Wipf and Stock Publishers, 199 W. 8th Ave., Suite 3, Eugene, OR 97401.

Pickwick Publications
An Imprint of Wipf and Stock Publishers
199 W. 8th Ave., Suite 3
Eugene, OR 97401

www.wipfandstock.com

ISBN 13: 978-1-60899-459-5

Cataloging-in-Publication data:

Martínez, Roberto.

The question of John the Baptist and Jesus' indictment of the religious leaders : a critical analysis of Luke 7:18–35 / Roberto Martínez.

xiv + 232 p. ; 23 cm. Includes bibliographical references and indexes.

ISBN 13: 978-1-60899-459-5

1. Bible. N.T. Luke—Criticism, interpretation, etc. 2. John, the Baptist, Saint. 3. Jesus Christ. I. Title.

BS2456 M2 2011

Manufactured in the U.S.A.

Dedicated to

FR. FELIX STRUIK, OP, SSD

Ἐργάτης ἀνεπαίσχυντον, ὀρθοτομοῦντα τὸν
λόγον τῆς ἀληθείας

(2 Tim 2:15)

For his many achievements as a biblical scholar and as a tribute to his almost thirty years in the formation of priests, religious, and laypersons

Contents

Acknowledgments / ix

List of Abbreviations / x

List of Tables and Figures / xiii

1. Luke 7:18–35: A Historical Survey / 1
2. The Origin, Redaction, and Literary Function of Luke 7:18–35 / 42
3. A Narrative-Critical Interpretation of 7:18–28 / 80
4. A Narrative-Critical Interpretation of 7:29–35 / 124
5. Conclusion: A Narrative-Critical Interpretation of Luke 7:18–35 / 168

Bibliography / 197

Index of Subjects / 207

Index of Authors / 211

Index of Scripture and Other Ancient Writings / 215

Acknowledgments

This book is a revised version of my 2010 Catholic University of America doctoral dissertation. I wish to acknowledge my gratitude to those people who have encouraged and assisted me in my studies. To Felix Struik, who first opened up the treasures of the Bible to me while I attended graduate school at Study Center of the Dominicans of the Caribbean. His enthusiasm and reverence for the Sacred Scriptures were a source of inspiration and motivation. I also owe a debt of gratitude to Frank J. Matera, under whose experienced and studious guidance I was fortunate enough to complete my doctoral dissertation. To my professors at Catholic University of America, especially Raymond F. Collins, Francis J. Moloney, Christopher T. Begg, Francis T. Gignac, and John P. Heil, from whom I have learned so much and whose methodical and careful approach to the study of the Scriptures I can only aspire to emulate. Thanks also to Joseph Mindling, whose meticulous and helpful suggestions allowed me to improve the original manuscript of the dissertation. I would also like to thank the library personnel at the Evangelical Seminary in Puerto Rico, especially Sonia Arrillaga Montalvo, Milka Vigo Verestín, Carydis Gabriel Franco, and Lyda Alvarado Cardona, for providing me the space and resources necessary for completing this project. Thanks to my religious superiors Fr. Alberto Figueroa and Fr. Francisco García for their continuous support and encouragement throughout these years. To my parents Edwin (RIP) and Elsie Martínez, whose love and unconditional support have been the cornerstone of my vocation, thanks. Thanks also to Constanza Arena for talking the time to help me proofread the final text of this book. Finally, I want to thank Wipf and Stock for their assistance and guidance in the publication of this work.

Abbreviations

AB	Anchor Bible
ABD	*Anchor Bible Dictionary.* Edited by D. N. Freedman. 6 vols. New York, 1992
ABE	Asociación Bíblica Española
ANTJ	Arbeiten zum Neuen Testament und Judentum
BCR	Biblioteca di Cultura Religiosa
BDAG	Bauer, W., F. W. Danker, W. R. Arndt, and F. W. Gingrich. *Greek-English Lexicon of the New Testament and Other Early Christian Literature.* 3rd ed. Chicago, 2000
BDF	Blass, F., A. Debrunner, and R. W. Funk. *A Greek Grammar of the New Testament and Other Early Christian Literature.* Chicago, 1961
BETL	Bibliotheca Ephemeridum theologicarum Lovaniensium
BH	Bibliothèque Historique
Bib	*Biblica*
BS	Biblische Studien
Bsac	*Bibliotheca Sacra*
BZ	*Biblische Zeitschrift*
BZNW	Beihefte zur Zeitschrift für die neutestamentliche Wissenschaft und die Kunde der älteren Kirche
CBQ	*Catholic Biblical Quarterly*
CBQMS	CBQ Monograph Series
CC	Corpus christianorum
CCS	Cambridge Classical Studies
CTM	*Currents in Theology and Mission*
CUF	Collection des Universités de France
DJD	Discoveries in the Judaean Desert
DJG	*Dictionary of Jesus and the Gospels.* Edited by Joel B. Green and Scot McKnight. Downers Grove, IL, 1992

EBib	Etudes bibliques
FC	Fathers of the Church
FCBS	Fortress Classics in Biblical Studies
FF	Foundations and Facets
FRLANT	Forschungen zur Religion und Literatur des Alten und Neuen Testaments
GBS	Guides to Biblical Scholarship
GNS	Good News Studies
HB	Herder Biblische Studien
HTKNT	Herder theologischer Kommentar zum Neuen Testament
HTS	Harvard Theological Studies
ICC	International Critical Commentary
JBL	*Journal of Biblical Literature*
JSNT	*Journal for the Study of the New Testament*
JSNTSup	JSNT Supplement Series
JSPSup	Journal for the Study of the Pseudepigrapha Supplement Series
JTS	*Journal of Theological Studies*
KEK	Kritisch-exegetischer Kommentar über das Neue Testament (Meyer-Kommentar)
KBANT	Kommentare und Beiträge zum Alten und Neuen Testament
LCBI	Literary Currents in Biblical Interpretation
LCL	Loeb Classical Library
LEC	Library of Early Christianity
LNTS	Library of New Testament Studies
NC	Narrative Commentaries
NICNT	New International Commentary of the New Testament
NIGTC	New International Greek Testament Commentary
NTOA	Novum Testamentum et Orbis Antiquus
NTS	*New Testament Studies*
NTT	New Testament Theology
NovT	*Novum Testamentum*
PBM	Paternoster Biblical Monographs
PD	Parole de Dieu
PL	Patrologia Latina
PTS	Paderborner Theologische Studien

PRS	Perspectives in Religious Studies
RB	*Revue biblique*
RNT	Regensburger Neues Testament
SBB	Stuttgarter biblische Beiträge
SBS	Stuttgarter Biblestudien
SBL	Studies in Biblical Literature
SBLDS	Society of Biblical Literature Dissertation Series
SBLMS	Society of Biblical Literature Monograph Series
SBLWGRW	Society of Biblical Literature Writings from the Greco-Roman World
SBS	Stuttgarter biblische
SBT	Studies in Biblical Theology
SBTFS	Studies in Biblical Theology, First Series
SHS	Scripture and Hermeneutics Series
SJLA	Studies in Judaism in Late Antiquity
SNTSMS	Society for New Testament Studies Monograph Series
SNTSU	Studien zum Neuen Testament und Seiner Umwelt
SacPag	Sacra Pagina
TBS	The Biblical Seminar
TDNT	*Theological Dictionary of the New Testament.* Edited by G. Kittel and G. Friedrich. Translated by G. W. Bromiley. 10 vols. Grand Rapids, 1964–76
WMANT	Wissenschaftliche Monographien zum Alten und Neuen Testament
ZNW	*Zeitschrift für die neutestamentliche Wissenschaft*
ZS	Zacchaeus Studies

Tables and Figures

TABLES

1. Matthew 11:2–6 and Luke 7:18–23 / 45
2. Matthew 11:7–15 and Luke 7:24–30 / 48
3. Matthew 11:12–15 and Luke 16:16 / 54
4. Matthew 11:16–19 and Luke 7:31–35 / 57
5. Annotated Translation of Luke 7:18–35 / 83
6. Matthew 11:12–15 and Luke 16:16 / 126
7. Matthew 21:31b–32 and Luke 7:29–30 / 130

FIGURES

1. The Immediate Context of Matthew 11:2–19 and Luke 7:18–35 / 66
2. Jesus' Galilean Ministry (4:14—9:50) / 71
3. Possible Redactions/Sources of Matthew 11:12–15 and Luke 7:29–30 / 125

1

Luke 7:18–35: A Historical Survey

INTRODUCTION

LUKE 7:18–35 (// MATT 11:2–19) contains one of the longest fragments of traditional material dealing with John the Baptist in the NT. Many contemporary scholars attribute this material to a source no longer extant, commonly referred to as Q. Since the patristic era the Lukan passage has attracted the attention of interpreters who have sought to respond to the problem echoed by the question of Algasia to Jerome: "Why does John send his disciples to the Lord to ask: 'Are you the one who is to come or should we wait for another?' since he himself had previously said: 'Behold, the Lamb of God, who takes away the sin of the world?'" (Hieronymus, *Epist.* 121.1).[1] In other words, how are we to make sense of the fact that in the Gospel of Luke the Baptist seems to question the identity of Jesus, while in the Gospel of John he had already identified Jesus as the "the lamb of God" (John 1:29–34)?

Although this apparent contradiction has been one of the major concerns of the passage for commentators, other important issues are addressed in the pericope. For instance, what is the relationship of the Baptist to the kingdom of God in light of Jesus' praise that "among those born of women, no one is greater than John; yet the least in the kingdom of God is greater than he" (7:28)? Of no less significance for understanding the relationship between the Baptist and Jesus, and the relationship of both "to the people of this generation" (7:31), is the comparison that Jesus makes between the Baptist and himself in the parable of the children in the marketplace (7:31–35). The interpretation of these and other issues have influenced the way in which commentators understand the

---

1. Translation mine.

role of John the Baptist, the identity of Jesus, and the relationship between them.

OBJECTIVE AND METHOD OF THE PRESENT WORK

Historical-critical methods have dominated the study of this pericope in recent times. The purpose of the present work is to investigate the function and meaning of this passage from a narrative-critical perspective. I analyze how literary aspects of the passage such as setting, character, and plot function within the whole of Luke-Acts. Although narrative criticism is the main approach of this investigation, the exegesis also takes into account historical-critical and redaction-critical observations to gain a fuller understanding of the passage. The study begins with a *Forschungsbericht* in which I present a historical overview of some notable interpretations of the passage, beginning with Origen and concluding with contemporary scholars. In the second chapter, I study the origin and redaction of the passage in comparison to the parallel material in the Gospel of Matthew 11:2–19. In the third and fourth chapters, I make a narrative-critical exegesis of the pericope, paying particular attention to the function of this passage within the Third Gospel and the Acts of the Apostles. In the fifth and final chapter, I summarize my findings and discuss their implications for the interpretation of the passage as well as for other issues related to John the Baptist within Luke-Acts and the other Gospels.

LUKE 7:18–35: A *FORSCHUNGSBERICHT*

From the Patristic Period to the Reformation

One of the first authors to address the pericope in his homilies on the Gospel of Luke was Origen (185–255). While commenting on the birth of John, Origen states: "'Greatest among the sons of women' [7:28] he was evidently worthy of a greater upbringing."[2] Origen emphasizes the greatness of John and compares him to Moses, who lived in the desert and "spoke to God."[3] Yet, he considers the Baptist greater than Moses, because he associated himself with angels in preparation for his role as precursor of Jesus. In the eyes of Origen, the Baptist received an upbringing that made him worthy to be the forerunner of the Lord. Origen does

2. Origen, *Luke*, 43.
3. Ibid., 43, 46.

not dwell on the meaning of the Baptist's question to Jesus (7:19–20), but he limits his remarks to note that "a question about Jesus arose."[4] Rather he points out that the Baptist taught even while in prison and that with the response he received from Jesus he was "armed for battle." Origen is convinced that, strengthened by these words, the Baptist believed in Jesus and affirmed his faith in him as the Son of God.

Ambrose of Milan (339–97) is another early Christian author that addresses the passage in his commentary on Luke.[5] For him it is impossible that the Baptist would have not recognized the identity of the person whom he had already identified, according to John 1:34, as the chosen one of God: *Non cadit igitur in talem prophetam tanti erroris suspicio* ("therefore, suspicion of so great an error does not fall on such a prophet").[6] Since Ambrose views the Baptist as a representative of the Law, he interprets John's question as a way of allowing his disciples to obtain the fullness of the Law, which is Christ.[7] For Ambrose, the question of the Baptist had to do with John's difficulty to accept that the "one who is to come" had to face death.[8] The greatness of the Baptist is directly related to his relationship with Christ, whom John saw, befriended, and baptized, but who is subordinated to Christ for two reasons: (1) John was born of a woman whereas Jesus was born of a Virgin; and (2) the Baptist is human and Christ is divine.[9] Jesus' remark about the Baptist's subordi-

---

4. Ibid., 113.

5. Like other patristic writers, Ambrose presumes the historicity and integrity of the passage. He occasionally interprets the pericope along allegoric lines. For instance, Ambrose (*Lucam*, 166, 168) views the two disciples of the Baptist as representatives of the Jews and the Gentiles who came to understand the OT through Christ and are witnesses to his contemporaries of the power of Christ. He also interprets in allegorical terms the reference to the fine clothing in 7:25 as representing the human body by which the soul is clothed (171). Ambrose also uses particular elements of the passage as a springboard for his moral exhortation. Hence, he uses Jesus' question about what the crowd had "come out to see" (7:24–26) to hail the Baptist's moral stature and contrast him to the fickle morality and worldly pleasures of those represented by the reed and those dressed in fine clothes (169–71).

6. Ibid., 165. Henceforth, when no English version is available, all Latin translations are mine.

7. Ibid., 166.

8. Ambrose (ibid., 167) considers the incredulity of the Baptist as *Non igitur fide, sed pietate dubitavit*, ("therefore, not the faith but his loyalty hesitated") and *Pietatis adfectus, non indevotionis est lapsus* ("the loyalty of his affection, not lack of religiosity is sliding").

9. Ibid., 172.

nation to the least in the kingdom of God is related to his subordination to the heavenly angels. God is wisdom (7:35), and the forgiveness of sins through the baptism of John is the reason for which the people and the publicans, the children of wisdom, justified God (7:29, 35).[10] In commenting on 7:31–34, Ambrose identifies the children of the parable with the Jews who frustrated the plan of God through their unbelief.

Cyril of Alexandria (378–444) deals in three separate homilies with each of the three main units of the passage (7:18–23, 24–28, 31–35).[11] In a hortative style, Cyril interprets the episode in light of other OT and NT references, repeatedly acknowledging the stature of the Baptist. Alluding to the Baptist's remarks in John 3:28–31, Cyril is convinced that the Baptist knew who Jesus was but asked the question about the identity of Jesus to lead his disciples into a deeper understanding of him.

> [B]ut to produce a firm and steadfast faith in Him, in those, who as yet were halting, nor thus far convinced that He is the Christ, he puts on the appearance of ignorance, and so sends to Him certain [sic] to ask Him, saying 'Art Thou He That cometh, or do we wait for another'? . . . I said then, that he puts on the appearance of ignorance purposely, not so much that he might himself learn—for as being the forerunner he knew the mystery—but that his disciples might be convinced, how great is the Savior's superiority, and that, as the word of the inspired Scripture had announced before, He is God, and the Lord That was to come.[12]

Jesus' characterization of the Baptist as the "greatest among those born of women" means for Cyril that John represents a type of Jewish righteousness, which Jesus uses to exemplify the superiority of the kingdom of God over the Law.[13] Jesus praises the Baptist not only to illustrate how faith surpasses the righteousness of the Law but to show that those who have received the faith are greater than those who have been born of women.[14] The qualification of Jesus regarding the "least in the kingdom of God" is not made to diminish the status of the Baptist

---

10. Ibid., 175–76.

11. Cyril, *Luke*, 156–69. Cyril glosses over 7:29–30.

12. Ibid., 158.

13. Cyril (ibid., 162) says: ". . . [T]he blessed Baptist is brought forward as one who had attained the foremost place in legal righteousness and to a praise so far incomparable. And yet even thus he is ranked as less than one who is least [in the kingdom of God]."

14. Ibid., 163.

but to underscore the superiority of the gospel way of life.[15] Regarding the episode of the children in the marketplace (7:31–35), Cyril points out that the Jews failed to discern properly between good and evil and regarded the actions of the Baptist and Jesus as wicked, whereas in reality they were holy.[16]

Another early commentator on the passage is Bede the Venerable (672–735).[17] For Bede it is out of envy that the disciples of John bring him the report about the power of Jesus.[18] Along the lines of other previous authors, he interprets the question about the "one who is to come" as a pedagogical device of the Baptist to help his disciples appreciate the glory of Jesus. Bede paraphrases many verses of the passage and explains a number of its elements (e.g., the reed shaken by the wind) in the form of petty moral exhortations.[19] Thus when he comments on the eating and drinking habits of the Baptist and Jesus, Bede says:

> *Et iustificata est sapientia ab ominibus filiis suis, ostendit filios sapientiae intellegere nec in abstinendo nec in manducando esse iustitiam sed in aequanimitate tolerandi inopiam et temperantiam per abundantiam non se corrumpendi atque oportune sumendi uel non sumendi ea quorum non usus sed concupiscentia reprehendenda est* ("and wisdom is justified by all her children; she reveals to the sons of wisdom the understanding that there is no justice neither in abstaining nor in eating, but in bearing need with patience, in not letting temperance be corrupted by abundance, as

---

15. Ibid., 164.
16. Ibid., 165–69.
17. Bede (*Lucae*, 163–64) also presumes the historicity and integrity of the passage. He refers constantly to NT and OT texts, including psalms and prophets, to support his interpretation. For instance, in his comment about the wisdom of the playing children's metaphor, Bede recalls the book of Psalms (*Ex ore infantium et lactantium perfecisti laudem* ["out of the mouths of babes and infants you have perfected praise"], Ps 8:3) and the prophet Joel (*. . . convertimini ad me in toto corde vestro in ieiunio et in fletu et in planctu et scindite corda vestra et non vestimenta vestra* ["return to me with your whole heart, with fasting, and weeping, and mourning and rend your hearts, not your garments"], Joel 2:12–13).
18. Here, Bede (ibid., 159–60) recalls the Gospel of John 3:26: *Rabbi qui erat tecum trans Iordanen cui tu testimonium perhibuisti ecce hic baptizat, et omnes veniunt ad eum* ("Rabbi, the one who was with you across the Jordan, to whom you testified, here he is baptizing and everyone is coming to him").
19. Bede (ibid., 161) interprets the reed shaken by the wind symbolically as the weak *carnalis animus* ("carnal intellect"), which he contrasts to the moral uprightness of the Baptist.

well as in taking or not taking things of which only the carnal desire, not the use, is to be rejected").[20]

For Bede, the Baptist's greatness lies in his moral compass, and John's subordination with respect to the kingdom can be interpreted as referring either to the eschatological kingdom of God or to the Church.

Bonaventure (1221–1274), one of the most renowned writers of the Middle Ages, interprets this passage in his commentary on Luke. Although Bonaventure follows the interpretations of some of his predecessors, he approaches the passage more thoroughly and with a more organized methodology.[21] Following Bede, Bonaventure remarks that it is out of envy that the disciples of the Baptist report to him the works of Jesus.[22] He regards the question about the identity of Jesus not as a doubt but as a way by which the Baptist helped his disciples to understand the "truth" about Jesus more fully.[23] Bonaventure interprets Jesus' remarks about those who might be scandalized as a warning against those who have not acknowledged his divine status.[24] Jesus' praise of the Baptist allows Bonaventure to emphasize the virtues and austerity of the life of John. He contrasts the Baptist's spiritual life, his constancy, and his abstinence with the inconsistency and preference for worldly pleasures of sinners.[25] For Bonaventure, the humility of Jesus makes him "the

---

20. Ibid., 164.

21. Bonaventure makes a systematic theological exegesis of the passage, dividing and subdividing the different sections of the pericope and explaining the meaning of each particular statement. He makes frequent use of Scripture to support his interpretations, quotes previous authors, and allegorizes certain elements of the passage. Bonaventure also presumes the historicity and integrity of the passage and occasionally harmonizes some of its statements with other passages of Scripture. For instance, when commenting on 7:26, where Jesus identifies the Baptist as a prophet, Bonaventure recalls John 1:21, in which the Baptist rejects such characterization. But Bonaventure solves the apparent contradiction by stating, "Neither is there some contradiction here, but rather harmony. For a prophet foretells what is future and not present, but a voice openly declares what is present" (Bonaventure, *Luke*, 613).

22. Ibid., 596.

23. Ibid., 596–99. In a sense, Bonaventure implies that the disciples of the Baptist have taken as a question what was really a statement about the identity of Jesus. "*Or shall we wait for another?* As if to say: If you are the one, there is no need for us to wait for another, lest perhaps in expecting another, we receive not Christ but the anti-Christ" (598).

24. Ibid., 606.

25. Ibid., 609–12.

least in the kingdom of heaven" and therefore greater than John.[26] He attributes 7:29–30 to Jesus, underlines the soteriological significance of these verses, and regards them as a commendation of John for having proclaimed Jesus.[27] For Bonaventure the last verses (7:31–35) are an injunction against the Pharisees for their "infidelity, hardness, detraction, and blasphemy."[28] They contradicted the wisdom of God, who is Jesus, and the behavior of his children, who are the apostles.

John Calvin (1509–1564) is one of the most important Reformation authors to comment on the passage. He dismisses as "foolish" the suggestion that the Baptist doubted the identity of Jesus and regards as speculation the proposal that, sensing the proximity of his death, the Baptist's question was really an inquiry about what message he should carry to the deceased fathers.[29] Calvin proposes that the Baptist knew that Jesus was the Christ, and he sent his disciple to him so that they might be "aroused from their sloth."[30]

Calvin also uses the passage to address his preferred moral issues.[31] According to him, Jesus quotes the prophet Isaiah "to teach all his followers the first lesson of humility, and partly to remove the offense which the flesh and senses might be apt to raise against his despicable flock."[32] Calvin interprets Isaiah's quote (7:22) ecclesiologically and soteriologically, as a reminder that the poor are those who are "qualified to appreciate the grace of salvation."[33] He interprets the statement about scandal as an exhortation to remain firmly rooted in the faith of the gospel in the midst of offenses.

For Calvin, Jesus' question about "what they had gone out to see" is an exhortation to remember and apply what they had learned from the

---

26. Bonaventure also suggests another possible interpretation for the "least in the kingdom of heaven": the blessed (= angels) (ibid., 617).

27. Ibid., 617–20.

28. Ibid., 620–25.

29. Calvin, *Commentaries*, 4.

30. Ibid., 4.

31. For instance, when commenting on the Baptist's delegation of his disciples to be instructed by Jesus, Calvin (ibid., 4) says: "Besides, the pastors of the Church are here reminded of their duty. They ought not to endeavor to bind and attach disciples to themselves, but to direct them to Christ, who is the only Teacher."

32. Ibid., 5.

33. Ibid., 6.

Baptist.³⁴ Calvin does not understand Jesus' words about the "fine garments" as a condemnation of extravagance but rather as an affirmation of the austerity of the Baptist. He is aware of the tension between Jesus' prophetic identification of the Baptist in 7:26 and the Baptist's denial of that category in John 1:21 and finds the preeminence of the Baptist in being the "herald and forerunner of Christ."³⁵ Calvin takes Jesus' words regarding the "least in the kingdom of God" as referring to the ministers of the gospel. "Again, the teachers who were afterwards to follow are placed above him, to show the surpassing majesty of the Gospel above the Law, and above that preaching which came between them."³⁶ In Calvin's opinion the remark is not a personal comparison between John and the "least in the kingdom of God" but a comparison of "offices." He interprets 7:29 as a denunciation of men's tendency to judge the gospel by human standards and as an invitation to acknowledge that everything that comes from God is just and holy.³⁷

The parable of the children in the marketplace is for Calvin a reproach of those who have rejected the Lord despite the diversity of ways by which he has tried to draw the Jews to himself.³⁸ He understands the last clause about "wisdom" as implying a contrast between the true children of wisdom and the "bastards." Those who act with obstinacy are illegitimate children but those who remain steadfast in the faith of the gospel are her true children, who render appropriate praise and support to wisdom.³⁹

In sum, the commentators surveyed above are aware of the apparent contradictions between portions of Luke 7:18–35 and other accounts in the Gospels and show an effort to harmonize these various reports. These commentators tend to exculpate the Baptist from any real doubt and explain his subordination to Jesus in a way that is benevolent to John. They also interpret the rest of the passage along moral lines for the benefit of their ethical exhortations.

---

34. Ibid., 8.
35. Ibid., 8–9.
36. Ibid., 9.
37. Ibid., 13.
38. Ibid., 14–15.
39. Ibid., 16.

Luke 7:18–35: A Historical Survey

From the Modern Period to the Present

The development of new critical methods of biblical exegesis during the modern period allowed scholars to implement a number of different approaches in the interpretation of Luke 7:18–35. These hermeneutical developments have resulted in the publication of a vast literature, in which many have taken to task the interpretation of the passage. In what follows I will examine the interpretation of Luke 7:18–35 in some of the most important historical studies on John the Baptist, commentaries, and specialized studies.

HISTORICAL STUDIES ON JOHN THE BAPTIST

When the interest of scholars in the search for the historical Jesus turned to John the Baptist, Luke 7:18–35 began to be examined in search for reliable data that would help to recreate an accurate portrayal of the Baptist's life and ministry. One of the first studies on John the Baptist was the work of Martin Dibelius. For Dibelius the pericope has essential elements of an old tradition, but one which the early Christian community has edited in order to preserve the sayings of Jesus about the Baptist in a single collection: "[M]an wollte die Herrenworte über den Täufer zusammenstellen, um durch solche Komposition das christliche Urteil über Johannes zu fixieren—das legt die Annahme nahe, daß in diese Weise die ganze »Rede« aus Sprüche zusammengestellt ist, um jenem Bedürfnis zu genügen."[40]

In the question put to Jesus by the disciples of John, the final warning forms the conclusion and point of the story, which is that the old hope of the people finds its fulfillment in Jesus. The meaning of the

---

40. Dibelius, *Johannes dem Täufer*, 7. However, because the words of Jesus seem to lack uniformity, Dibelius wonders whether they are based on a historical memory rather than the result of editorial composition. The proof of this redactional work is that both in Matthew (11:7–19) and Luke (7:24–35) these sayings, which in the original form belong to another place and form, have been framed in a different context (ibid., 6–7). Dibelius expresses doubts about the use of the title ὁ υἱὸς τοῦ ἀνθρώπου (7:34) because it is used to depict Jesus in his daily life rather than in its original apocalyptic meaning. Similarly the use of the phrase τῇ βασιλείᾳ τοῦ θεοῦ (7:28) brings the authenticity of the verse into question because it appears as an end or a gift rather than as a fully realized state. For Dibelius, a saying in which the citizenship of the kingdom is presupposed reads not as coming from Jesus but as coming from the church. Therefore, only 7:28a can be considered an original saying. Dibelius doubts that the followers of the Baptist would have used the statement to assert the primacy of the Baptist over Jesus if the actual restriction would have been present in the current form (13–19).

answer is that the kingdom is near and the Messiah has no need for a speech. Only his final word in the form of an indirect warning is necessary: Blessed are they who recognize in the signs of the times, the fulfillment of the above promises (the coming of the kingdom of God).[41] Jesus gives the Baptist an answer that is both personal and prophetic. The experience of a new time has begun, and Jesus is in the middle of that messianic era. According to Dibelius, the question of the Baptist is ambiguous, and this suggests that he had not yet developed a definite relationship with Jesus.[42]

For Dibelius the Baptist's praise of Jesus indicates that Jesus had witnessed the rise and fall of the people's enthusiasm for John and was now trying to assess the meaning of the Baptist's ministry for those who did not have vain or unreal expectations about him. For Jesus, John was more than a Prophet. What is certain is that Jesus was impressed by the greatness of the Baptist.[43] Finally, in the parable of the children in the marketplace what is important is not the type of game that is envisioned but the argument of the children who do not want to play.[44] The parable reflects the misjudgment of the people regarding the ministries of Jesus and the Baptist.[45]

Maurice Goguel's reconstruction of the life and ministry of the Baptist focuses on the historical reliability of the passage.[46] Goguel highlights that nothing in the pericope indicates the reaction of the Baptist to the reply of Jesus. Moreover, the presentation of an apocalyptic Messiah rather than a historical one contradicts the messianic idea that Jesus would have had of himself. For Goguel, elements like these argue against the historicity of the episode. Consequently, the narrative attributes to the Baptist an attitude of reluctance, which must have been the same defiance or hostility that the group of the disciples of John would have shown against Jesus and the Gospel. The passage must have been used in the polemic against the followers of the Baptist in an effort to show that their master had refused to accept the messianism of Jesus as manifested by his mighty deeds.

41. Ibid., 36–37.
42. Ibid., 38.
43. Ibid., 15.
44. Ibid., 17.
45. Ibid., 19–20.
46. Goguel, *Jean-Baptiste*, 63.

The tribute paid by Jesus to the Baptist can have only one possible explanation for Goguel: "[E]lle consiste à admettre que la tradition a voulu concilier le témoignage éclatant qu'elle prétendait avoir été rendu à la messianité de Jésus par Jean-Baptiste avec le fait connu aussi bien des chrétiens que de leurs adversaires que ni Jean ni ses disciples ne s'étaient ralliés à Jésus."[47] For Goguel one thing is clear despite the editorial activity that makes it almost impossible to determine the exact sense of the passage: an abyss has been created between the Baptist as the representative of the old economy and Jesus, who heralds the beginning of the messianic era.[48]

In his biography of John the Baptist, Carl H. Kraeling examines the text to see what can be extracted about the relationship between John and Jesus.[49] Kraeling also questions the historicity of the reported encounter between the emissaries of John and Jesus, dismissing it as an "anti-Baptist polemic."[50]

> Again, therefore, the historicity of the reported encounters is questionable, the importance of the stories for us being rather to highlight an ancient conviction that the meeting of the two men was not fortuitous but continuous, having a profound significance for them both, and that had John lived to witness the later events in the life of Jesus and of the early Church he would have given his personal allegiance to the new Christian faith.[51]

Thus, for Kraeling the story of the delegation sent by the imprisoned John to Jesus has no historical value to assess the relationship between John and Jesus. It is only a foil for the Christians' own conviction in an effort to reconcile the tension between the Baptist's conception of a fiery-like Messiah with the appearance of a wonder-working preacher of the kingdom.[52]

With regards to the rest of the pericope, Kraeling partially accepts the authenticity of the encomia of Jesus on John (7:24–30) because the

---

47. Ibid., 64.
48. Ibid., 68–69.
49. Kraeling, *John the Baptist*, 11–13.
50. Ibid., 127–28; 178–79.
51. Ibid., 128; Besides Luke 7:18–23 (// Matt 11:2–6), Kraeling includes in his assessment here the reported contacts between the Baptist and Jesus in Mark 1:9–11 and John 1:29, 36.
52. Ibid., 129–30.

historical circumstances would have scarcely allowed the early Church to have created such words.[53] He considers the phrase about "the least in the kingdom of God" (7:28b) an emendation made by a later generation which did not understand the meaning of the original statement and saw it as a threat to the primacy of Jesus. The authenticity of the remaining phrase confirms Jesus' affirmation of the true prophetic character of John, who fulfilled the eschatological role of Elijah.

Jacques Dupont is one of the first authors to isolate and comment on the first part of the pericope (7:18–23).[54] Glossing over many of the contemporary critical issues, Dupont deals with the *sense* of the passage, which, for him, is based on an ancient and excellent tradition.[55] Dupont reviews some of the most common interpretations that have been given historically to the question of John the Baptist: fictitious doubt; real ignorance (both of which he considers extreme interpretations); and—a third one with many nuances—hesitation, astonishment, and impatience.[56]

After examining the meaning of the phrase "the one who is to come" within the context of the Baptist's preaching, Dupont concludes that the Baptist understood his mission as the precursor of the eschatological agent. The only possible meaning of the question is: "Es-tu celui dont j'annonce la venue, le Juge redoutable qui condamne les impies aux supplices éternels?"[57] Regarding the answer of Jesus, Dupont focuses on the mighty deeds. The wonders performed by Jesus are characteristics of a typical messianic activity and thus manifest his messianism.[58] Rather than responding with a simple "yes," which would have identified him with the "stronger one" that John awaited, Jesus makes the messengers relate the story about his benevolent activity. Jesus sends the messengers with precise terms, purposely chosen to evoke the prophetic descriptions of the messianic time in the book of Isaiah, to inform John that he

---

53. Ibid., 137–40.

54. Dupont, "Jean-Baptiste," 805–21; 943–59.

55. For Dupont (ibid., 805), the differences between Matthew and Luke are insignificant and they exist more on a literary level than in substance. Dupont is not very concerned with historical or literary remarks, some of which he considers hypercritical: "Toute notre attention peut se porter sur le sens de la question posée par Jean et celui de la réponse que Jésus lui donne" (805, see also n. 3)

56. Ibid., 806–13.

57. Ibid., 821.

58. Ibid., 945.

was fulfilling the messianic promises.[59] According to Dupont, this was an aspect to which the precursor had not probably paid enough attention. The first part of the response affirms that the messianic age has begun and the final beatitude places the person of Jesus in the center of the eschatological age. Salvation is tied to the person of Jesus.[60] The potential scandal against which Jesus warns the Baptist may come not from the messianic claim of Jesus, but rather from the way in which he manifests that role.[61] The challenge for John is to recognize the Messiah not as a fiery judge but as a compassionate and merciful envoy of God.

Charles H. H. Scobie's quest for the historical John provides another example of how the pericope has been interpreted. Scobie recognizes that the traditions on the Baptist may have been preserved and adapted according to the life and activity of early Christian communities.[62] However, he attempts to restore the factual reliability of the passage by arguing that the material belongs to the Q source and enjoys historical credibility.[63] After acknowledging the apparent dilemma posed by the question of the Baptist in 7:19 and his previous recognition of Jesus as the "coming one" during his baptism, Scobie rejects previous attempts to solve the problem that denied the historicity of the passage.[64] What caused some authors to doubt the authenticity of the account (i.e., the lack of reaction from John) becomes for Scobie its most important sign of legitimacy: "Jesus' refusal to give a direct answer and the way he leaves John to make the leap of faith bears all the marks of authenticity."[65] The passage provides reliable information about the lifestyle of John, his habitation in the wilderness (7:24, 33), and his ascetic eating habits.[66]

---

59. Dupont (ibid., 951) points out that the book of Isaiah has no shortage of oracles that insist on the arrival of the threatening end of time, where the wicked would suffer punishment for their sins, but Jesus only keeps the oracles of consolation, those that preach that God will take pity on his people and will send a merciful Savior.

60. Ibid., 955.

61. Ibid., 958.

62. Scobie, *John the Baptist*, 13–17.

63. Scobie (ibid., 17) concludes his discussion of the sources stating: "From all these considerations, it would appear that the Q source is the most reliable: it is the earliest, it contains the greatest proportion of material concerning John, it has the highest estimate of John, and it contains the clearest evidence of Semitisms."

64. Ibid., 143–44.

65. Ibid., 144.

66. Ibid., 41, 47, 134–35, 160.

Jesus regarded John as the greatest of the prophets, the eschatological prophet.[67] But, although John is the greatest of the prophets, he belongs to the old dispensation and therefore the members of the kingdom of God are superior by their privileges.[68]

Another study that deals with the history of John the Baptist is the work of Walter Wink. This author sets out to "examine the manner in which each evangelist has used the traditions about John in proclaiming the good news of Jesus Christ."[69] According to Wink, 7:18–23 is a passage that places limitations on the esteem that should be accorded to John.[70] He discusses the challenges that have been leveled against the historical plausibility of the passage. Wink views the origin of the question not in the historical Baptist but rather in the early disciples of John who, now as Christians, sought to justify their faith in Jesus as Messiah.

Without completely rejecting the possibility of a historical origin of the Baptist's delegation, Wink contends that the report would still have been modified for apologetic purposes in dealing with the followers of the Baptist.[71] For Wink, Luke seeks to clarify the relationship of John to the kingdom. In qualifying the high esteem that Jesus expresses for the Baptist, the church engages in "evangelistic maneuvering": "Unwilling to suppress Jesus' high regard for John, a regard which Jesus had already in his ministry defined eschatologically, the church simply hedged Jesus' enthusiasm with qualifications which made clear their perception of the fundamental distinction between still awaiting a Coming One and accepting Jesus as the Messiah."[72] John occupies for Luke a soteriological place of honor, which can neither be compared to that of the previous prophets nor to the apostles of his time. He is the prophesied forerunner of the Messiah.[73] According to Wink, the passage does not suggest that there is an *ongoing* polemic with the disciples of John but rather an effort to limit the role of the Baptist in order to guarantee the uniqueness of Jesus.[74]

---

67. Ibid., 126.
68. Ibid., 157–58.
69. Wink, *John the Baptist*, xii.
70. Ibid., 23.
71. Ibid., 23–24.
72. Ibid., 25.
73. Ibid., 54.
74. Ibid., 82–86.

One of most thorough inquiries about a portion (7:18–23) of this passage dealing with John the Baptist has been undertaken by Santos Sabugal. After reviewing the history of the interpretation of the Matthean and Lukan versions, Sabugal analyzes the redactional work of both authors. In his opinion Luke has faithfully transmitted—although not without modifying his source through his characteristic vocabulary and style—the traditional material received from Q. Sabugal, like other authors, suggests that the historical circumstances that lie behind this source are the controversies between the sectarian disciples of John, who regarded him as the Messiah, and the early Christian community which had similar claims for Jesus.[75] Sabugal reviews many of the arguments that have been leveled for and against the veracity of the account and decides in favor of its historic reliability.[76]

After examining the different layers of tradition (Q and the Matthean/Lukan redactions), Sabugal concludes that at the core of the story lies a specific historical event, which has been fashioned by the particular theological interest of each evangelist, and not a fiction of the primitive Christian community.[77] The text records Jesus' attempt to reaffirm the faith of the Baptist, who harbored a different expectation about the "one who is to come," and John's sectarian disciples regarding Jesus' messianic dignity. Through the manifestation of eschatological signs that evoked the arrival of the kingdom of God, Jesus "halfway answers" the inquiry of the Baptist in a passage in Q that preludes the subordination of John to Jesus.

Josef Ernst is another author who begins his analysis of the traditional material about John the Baptist with a study of the pericope.[78] This author underscores the secondary setting of the passage and its historical growth, which, in his opinion, is difficult to trace beyond some obvious editorial changes.[79] Ernst wonders what would have guided the early

75. Sabugal, *Juan el Bautista*, 114, 193–94.
76. Ibid., 9–27; 141–46.
77. Ibid., 141–202, esp. 159, 191, 194. "Resumiendo los precedentes análisis, podemos decir: El relato de Q sobre la embajada mesiánica del Bautista no es composición cristiana. Ningún indicio literario objetivo favorece la interpretación contraria. Sí refleja, por el contrario, varios semitismos, algunos de ellos característicos del lenguaje de Jesús" (159).
78. Ernst, *Johannes der Täufer*, 55–80.
79. Ibid., 55. Ernst underscores the difficulty of the analysis, saying: "Letzte Sicherheit ist wegen der nicht eindeutig erkennbaren Redaktionstendenzen kaum zu erreichen"

community in their use of the traditions found in the sayings source and suggests that a question about the meaning of Jesus' mighty works could have been exacerbated by the tensions between the young Christian community and those who were still following the Baptist.[80] He sees the controversy (but not a strong rivalry) in the alleged "Son of Man" Christology reflected in the phrase "the one who is to come." Ernst finds in the passage a "literary reflection" of the Q-community's christological consolidation of Jesus, the "Son of Man," and the Baptist's eschatological judge.[81] Ernst thinks that this happened in the early Palestinian mission when people who had adopted the call to conversion had not yet taken the last step of faith in Christ.[82] The early captivity and beheading of the Baptist would have prevented a greater confrontation with Jesus but also resulted in a certain ambiguity regarding the historical relationship between Jesus and the Baptist.[83]

For Ernst, the meaning of 7:24–28 is that the Baptist cannot be classified in any traditional category.[84] The passage portrays John as the *Zeitenwende* man who initiated the coming of the reign of God, which had not yet been officially proclaimed by Jesus. Ernst also highlights the ecclesiological orientation of the passage that reflects the role of the community of Jesus in the process of the proclamation of the kingdom in Israel.[85]

After discussing the redactional difficulties of the parable of the children in the marketplace, Ernst interprets it as referring to the increasing opposition that the community behind Q experienced in its missionary efforts.[86] In his view, the competition between the disciples

---

(56). His analysis is heavily indebted to Paul Hoffmann's *Studien zur Theologie der Logienquelle*.

80. Ernst, *Johannes der Täufer*, 58.

81. For Ernst, Luke has exonerated the Baptist from his insecurity through the artistic construction of the pericope (ibid., 317).

82. Ibid., 59.

83. Ibid.

84. Ibid., 62.

85. Ibid., 63.

86. Ibid., 73. Ernst discusses some of the distinctions that have been made since Dibelius and Bultmann between the original parable and the attached meaning including: (1) the allegorical and artificial interpretation of the children's cries; (2) the inversion of dance and grief; (3) the lack of correlation of images and facts; (4) the final remark on the *sophia*; and (5) the fact that an explanation had to be attached to the

of the Baptist and the disciples of Jesus is transferred to the present controversy with the Judaic contemporaries: "Der Gegensatz zwischen Johannes und Jesus einerseits und 'diesem Geschlecht' andererseits ist also der Gegensatz zwischen ihnen und dem Volk Israel, zugleich auch der Gegensatz zwischen der Kindern, die der Weisheit Recht geben, und den launischen Kindern, also zwischen den Gemeinde und Israel."[87]

Among the works that apply a social-scientific approach to the investigation of John the Baptist, Robert L. Webb's analysis of John within the context of Second Temple Judaism occupies a prominent place. Webb accepts for the most part the historicity of passage.[88] Although his research is focused on the ministry of the Baptist prior to the baptism of Jesus, Webb examines the implication of the Lukan episode for his social analysis. For Webb the question of the Baptist (7:19), which besides its explanatory notes and minor variations differs little from Q, helps to identify Jesus as the expected figured previously announced by John and the one who resolves the eschatological tension set forth by the Baptist's proclamation.[89] In the pericope, Jesus legitimizes the prophetic role of John as the greatest among all human beings and implicitly identifies him as Elijah *redivivus*.[90] Jesus also condemns the people for rejecting his message and that of John, and forecasts the vindication of their ministries by the acknowledgment of their wisdom.[91]

In a short but scholarly presentation of the Baptist, Carl R. Kazmierski deals with the question of John and the testimony of Jesus. Recognizing that the tradition received from Q has been shaped by the theological interest of the evangelists and the underlying situation of their communities, Kazmierski nonetheless defends the overall historic-

---

parable (ibid., 73–74 nn. 153, 154). Ernst observes that other scholars warn about a rigid interpretation and distinction between parable and meaning, given the metaphorical character of the passage (74 n. 156).

87. Ibid., 79.

88. After discussing the adaptation process that the traditions about the Baptist experienced, Webb (*John the Baptizer*, 88) points out: "These general observations substantiate as a working premise that the synoptic accounts are generally reliable sources for information concerning John the Baptist. They should therefore be taken seriously, though at the same time they need to be taken critically, in recognition of their limitations mentioned above." See also ibid., 278–82.

89. Ibid., 49, 65–66.

90. The term "Elijah *redivivus*" characterizes the Jewish expectation that a reincarnated Elijah would return to assume an eschatological role (ibid., 50 n. 11; 70 n. 66).

91. Ibid., 50, 65–66.

ity of the account.⁹² Applying a social-scientific approach that focuses on stereotyped role-playing or labeling theory, Kazmierski explains that the text reflects the historical concerns of the people to identify the Baptist and Jesus within the context of their prophetic messianic expectations.⁹³ The passage also depicts the struggle of the early church to understand the Baptist's role in the plan of God and his relationship with Jesus.⁹⁴

Another author who examines the passage in a historical reconstruction of John the Baptist is Joan Taylor. Following the lead of many other investigations, Taylor accepts that the traditions about the Baptist in the NT are overlaid with an ongoing Christian polemic regarding Jesus' superiority, but at the same time, she argues that the NT material is historically valuable.⁹⁵ Taylor discusses the possible links of the Baptist to the Essenes, and his role as teacher and prophet as well as his relationship with the Pharisees and Jesus. Taylor appeals to 7:18–35 as a witness to John's ascetic lifestyle and highlights his role as teacher with a group of disciples.⁹⁶

Taylor cites 7:29–30 in her discussion about the relationship between John and the Pharisees to support her claim that they were not necessarily at odds despite the harsh assessment of the Pharisees in some passages.⁹⁷ For Taylor, in the delegation of his disciples to Jesus, John was trying to find out whether Jesus was the expected prophet, that is, Elijah. Moreover the question indicates that John was still alive at the time Jesus began his public ministry.⁹⁸ In dealing with the relationship between Jesus and the Baptist, Taylor concludes that Jesus seems to be saying that John, as the greatest man that ever lived, enables people to enter the kingdom of God but, by virtue of a new order, the members of this kingdom become greater than he.

> The point does not really concern John at all, who remains 'more than a prophet': there is still no one greater than him. The point is about the radical inversions of the kingdom of heaven, in which someone as insignificant as an innocent little baby may be con-

---

92. Kazmierski, *John the Baptist*, 42–66.
93. Ibid., 51–52, 58, 88.
94. Ibid., 49.
95. Taylor, *Immerser*, 5–8.
96. Ibid., 32–43; 102.
97. Ibid., 201–3; 211.
98. Ibid., 288–94.

sidered 'greater' than John (who is still part of the kingdom, and no doubt the greatest one in it); the innocent little baby is the paradigm of excellence."[99]

In Taylor's assessment, 7:31–35 is a protest of Jesus against the people who rejected his and John's prophetic call.[100]

John P. Meier's critical analysis of the historical Jesus examines the pericope in discussing the relationship between the Baptist and Jesus.[101] In outlining the secondary nature of the exact narrative setting, Meier discusses the complex tradition history that would have influenced the placement of a similar saying of Jesus in different contexts (Matt 11:12–13 // Luke 16:16).[102] He presumes "certain points" generally accepted by most scholars regarding the authenticity of the Baptist tradition and repeatedly argues in favor of the historicity of the account.[103] Meier downplays the often heard claim that most of the pericope has been developed by the early church in its polemic against the Baptist sectarians. According to Meier, the Baptist seems to be revising his previous view about the "coming one" given the shift of emphasis in the message of Jesus. "John's question is therefore a genuine, tentative probe, allowing that he might have to revise his hopes in order to avoid giving them up entirely."[104]

In Meier's opinion, the indirect answer of Jesus and the concluding beatitude is a tacit exhortation to John to recognize in him the realization of the plan of God.[105] Jesus balances his appeal to John with a high praise that extols the Baptist as more than a prophet and the greatest of those born of women with a statement that may hold a veiled contrast to Herod Antipas, who executed John.[106] For Meier the main focus of the entire unit is the relationship of John to the eschato-

---

99. Ibid., 303.

100. Ibid., 304–5.

101. Meier, *Marginal Jew*, 130–81.

102. Ibid., 130–31.

103. Ibid., 131, 135, 139, 143–44. "While recognizing secondary and tertiary additions on the levels of both Q and the evangelists, we have seen that the substance of these three pieces of traditions fulfills various criteria of authenticity, and so the substance has a good claim to come from the historical Jesus" (154).

104. Ibid., 133.

105. Ibid., 135.

106. Ibid., 154–55; 205 n. 116.

logical message of Jesus.[107] The thrust of the pericope shows respect for John, emphasizes a new eschatological situation, and draws a parallel between John and Jesus.

Ulrich B. Müller also addresses portions of the passage in his presentation of John the Baptist. For him, the words of Jesus about the Baptist belong to an old tradition.[108] In his praise of the Baptist, Jesus shows his solidarity with him, who as an eschatological messenger breaks with the scheme of OT prophecy, but remains subordinated in regard to the new order.[109] Müller grants considerable historical credibility to the words of Jesus: "Das ganze Wort ist so sehr von Jesu Verständnis von der mit der Gottesherrschaft anbrechenden eschatologischen Heilswende geprägt, dass hier keine nachösterliche Gemeindebildung vorliegt, sondern der historische Jesus selbst zu Worte kommt."[110] The words are missionary in character, but not of a later date.

According to Müller, during the life of the Baptist, or probably shortly after his death, Jesus was trying to persuade the people to accept the message of the kingdom of God.[111] In the proclamation of Jesus, the admiration for the Baptist is relativized by the broaching of the kingdom of God. For Müller the introductory parable of the children originally belonged together and formed a unit with the words of Jesus about the Baptist. In this parable the similarities and differences between Jesus and the Baptist are underscored. Both are rejected by their contemporaries, but both messengers of God stand in contrast with each other: the Baptist is the ascetical preacher of conversion and Jesus the proclaimer of the message of jubilation.[112] Luke portrays the Baptist as a significant prophet, but without saving efficacy.[113] John is for Luke the precursor and forerunner of Jesus.[114]

---

107. Ibid., 154.

108. Müller, *Johannes der Täufer*, 67.

109. Ibid., 68–69.

110. Ibid., 68. He recognizes, however, the last verse in the parable of the children in the marketplace (v. 35) as an addition to a source saying that exceeds the defined framework (70).

111. Ibid., 67–69.

112. Ibid., 71.

113. Ibid., 136.

114. Ibid., 156.

Recently, Catherine M. Murphy has also undertaken an analysis of the passage in her investigation of the life and ministry of John the Baptist. Murphy seeks to decipher the role of John by taking into consideration the purification movements in first-century Judea and their notions of "purity and pollution." She studies the redaction of fifteen different vignettes, four of which are part of Luke 7:18–35.[115] Although in her analysis Murphy weighs the possibility that Jesus' affirmation of John may be a process of reflection in the early church rather than Jesus' own words, she ultimately accepts the historical reliability of the account.[116] For Murphy, the episode recounts the concern of the Baptist, who has not seen the fulfillment of his messianic prophecy of judgment, regarding the healing and preaching ministry of Jesus.[117] The testimony of Jesus about John means that the Baptist stands between the Law and the Prophets on the one hand, and the kingdom of God on the other. Based on the awkwardness of the statements from the point of view of the early Christian community and on the attribution of the tradition to Q, Murphy also accepts the authenticity of the parable of the children in the marketplace, which she uses to establish the ascetic lifestyle or lack thereof in the lives of the Baptist and Jesus.[118]

To summarize, the historical studies of John the Baptist raised new questions regarding the reliability of Luke 7:18–35. Greater awareness about the origin and diversity of the Synoptic accounts regarding the role of the Baptist results in a protracted debate about the authenticity of the story. Consequently, fewer commentators resort to harmonization in order to explain the apparent contradictions between the passage and other testimonies in the Gospels. They are also less constrained at attributing real ignorance or doubt to the Baptist, and eager to find in the prehistory of the text echoes of the controversies between John's followers and the early Christian community. Many of these authors emphasize the difficulties that Jesus' contemporaries faced in understanding the role of the Baptist in light of the messianic expectations of Second Temple Judaism.

---

115. In Murphy's book (*John the Baptist*, 65–69), vignettes 7, 8, 9, and 15 deal with Luke 7:18–35.

116. Ibid., 65–69.

117. Ibid., 66.

118. Ibid., 130, 142.

COMMENTARIES

The new perspective brought about by modern methods of exegesis in commentaries is exemplified by Paul Schanz's interpretation of 7:18–35 in his commentary on the Gospel of Luke. Schanz, whose commentary represents a greater scholarly awareness of the Synoptic problem, believes that Luke has taken the language of this passage from Matthew.[119] For him the episode deals with the relationship of Jesus with different classes of people, particularly the Pharisees, and serves to characterize the unresponsiveness and the opposition of the Jews.[120] Neither the delegation of the Baptist nor the testimony of Jesus about John can be described as favorable recommendations, because the answer of Jesus is not clear and his speech about the Baptist is in response to Jews' rejection. John, along with the rest of the Jews, expected another movement and other messianic signs, because they anticipated a different manifestation of the kingdom.

According to Schanz, John is the forerunner and stands as such over all the prophets. However, as a forerunner the Baptist also stands behind the members of the kingdom. Schanz regards 7:29–30 either as a Lukan addition or an insertion based on Matthew 21:31–32, because the speech overrides the preceding address of Jesus that resumes in v. 31.[121] The people and toll collectors who recognized their sins and obtain the mercy of God gave honor to the justice of God by recognizing the baptismal requirement as a condition for entry into the messianic kingdom.[122] Despite the opposition, John and Jesus are justified by all the children of wisdom, i.e., those who have recognized and acknowledged the wisdom of God.[123] Schanz proposes that by substituting Matthew's phrase "the works" (11:19) by "all her children" (7:35) Luke has gone beyond the earlier evangelist to stress the inclusion of all the faithful

---

119 According to Schanz (*Lucas*, 13 n. 3), who subscribes to the Griesbach hypothesis, Matthew shows more antagonism against the Jews in general than against specific sectors of the Jewish community (e.g., scribes and Pharisees). Regarding the style of the passage, Schanz indicates that Jesus' speech is already an example of his easy and compelling eloquence. Moreover, questions, images, and parables interact with one another to captivate the audience.

120. Ibid., 240–45.
121. Ibid., 243.
122. Ibid., 244.
123. Ibid., 244–45.

disciples in the kingdom of God in opposition to the Pharisees whose admittance is not contemplated.

With an acknowledgement of the notorious difficulty that the passage has posed since antiquity, Marie Joseph Lagrange argues against what he considers the most radical opinion of his time, i.e., that John is questioning here for the first time whether Jesus might be the Messiah.[124] According to Lagrange, such a claim would be contrary to the thought of the evangelist, who had previously professed the greatness of Jesus. Even the dialogue between the disciples of John and Jesus suggests that the Baptist must have had previously some sort of messianic expectation of Jesus. For Lagrange, the doubt of John dealt rather with what type of Messiah he had hoped for.[125] The question of John denotes that he was impatient with Jesus' messianism, and the episode reflects the historical difficulty that was entailed for the Baptist to understand the mission of Jesus: "Nous avons ici une leçon sur la difficulté—toujours actuelle—de comprendre l'œuvre de Jésus."[126]

Although for Lagrange it is possible that Jesus' praise of John could have been delivered in different historical circumstances, he accepts the integrity of the discourse because nothing here indicates a change of situation. The point of the speech is not so much to praise John as to correct the errors concerning his role. Despite his greatness, the role of the Baptist is subordinated to the role of Jesus. The ancient order is inferior to the new, and John is less than the members of the kingdom. His exclusion from the kingdom is not a matter of sanctity but of historical circumstance, and Jesus does not reproach him for this.[127] In commenting on the parable of the children in the marketplace, Langrange discusses the possibility of interpreting it either as an allegory or a simple comparison. In either case the parable results in an indictment against the Pharisees and the scholars of the Law. They have refused the baptism of John and have followed their own ideas. But the wisdom of God disposed that his baptism would prepare for the kingdom inaugurated by Jesus and that those who have been docile to the plan would be the true children of wisdom.[128]

---

124. Lagrange (*Saint Luc*, 213) mentions Harnack, Dibelius, and Loisy.
125. Ibid., 214.
126. Ibid.
127. Ibid., 221.
128. Ibid., 223–26.

In his commentary on Luke, Alfred Plummer regards the question posed by John's delegation as a sign of impatience.[129] For Plummer the Baptist was probably disappointed by the lack of progress shown by Jesus or by his failure to act more decisively against Herod and Herodias. Jesus' ministry had become for the Baptist a cause of stumbling. Through his mighty works and reply, Jesus rebukes as well as encourages the Baptist to overcome this temptation.[130] Plummer considers Jesus' comments about the Baptist as a "panegyric" similar to a "funeral oration." But despite the high praise, Jesus subordinates the Baptist to the members of the kingdom of God. Plummer regards 7:29–30 not as a parenthetical remark of the evangelist but as a statement of Jesus that contrasts the different ways in which the people and the hierarchy received the preaching of the Baptist.[131] He attributes the complaints of the children in the marketplace at the end of the pericope to the Jews, who on the one hand wish the Baptist to ease his severity and on the other want Jesus to be more sober.[132] Despite the rejection of the Jews, a faithful minority has welcomed the wisdom of God in the message of the Baptist and Jesus.

Although for Alfred Loisy the Baptist's question in Luke 7:19 could reflect John's original preaching, the designation "the one who is to come" is almost a sacramental formula that denotes the secondary character of the report.[133] The response to the delegation of the Baptist is a redactional fiction: "Mais la notice n'en est pas moins, au point de vue rédactionnel, une interpolation, au point de vue historique une pure fiction."[134] The text reflects the struggle among the factions of the Baptist and Jesus. Each verse represents what each sectarian group claimed to have heard from its hero.[135] Thus, Jesus' speech about the Baptist is completely neutralized by an apologetic interest. In it one can find the Christian thesis regarding the inauguration of the kingdom of God by Jesus opposing the thesis of the Johannine circle concerning the emi-

---

129. Plummer, *Luke*, 202.
130. Ibid., 203.
131. Ibid., 205–6.
132. Ibid., 207.
133. Loisy, *Luc*, 222–28.
134. Ibid., 223. Loisy questions the claims that this text has been influenced by the Mandean literature (224).
135. Ibid., 224.

nent role of the Baptist.[136] Likewise, the verses that deal with the way in which the preaching of John was received by Pharisees and publicans (7:29–30) reflect the Christian community's apologetic concern for justifying the role of John.[137] The parable of the children in the marketplace is a retrospective apologetic look at the role of John and Jesus made by the Christian tradition against the Jews.

Heinz Schürmann's commentary on Luke represents another example of the passage's interpretation. Schürmann examines a diversity of proposals regarding the integrity and the composition of the pericope and makes a host of redaction-critical observations. He notes that in the acts of compassion of Jesus as well as in the proclamation of his message, the prophecy of Isaiah is fulfilled and the eschatological visitation of God comes to pass.[138] The answer of Jesus, in which the narrator and the community become one, accomplishes a missionary task by affirming all those who recognized the Baptist as a messenger of God.[139] In connection with Luke 3:16, the question serves to clarify whether the Baptist's eager expectation is now fulfilled. For Schürmann the passage witnesses to a conflict that originates from the supernatural-eschatological picture of a savior and judge vis-à-vis the historic appearance of Jesus.[140] The redaction of Luke clarifies the messianic and eschatological character of the wonders of Jesus. The paradox of the historical/eschatological Messiah, created by the proclamation/expectation of the Baptist, is highlighted by the possibility of the "scandal" in the final warning. This warning manifests the difficulty of the question.[141]

According to Schürmann the narrative is missionary: it tries to promote the significance of the ministry and preaching of Jesus as well as his eschatological message of jubilation.[142] The answer is a kind of "propaganda" evidently directed at the circle of the Baptist's followers, who had not yet accepted the message of Jesus. Schürmann speculates about the historical circumstances that underlay the pericope.[143] He views the

---

136. Ibid., 225–26.
137. Ibid., 227.
138. Schürmann, *Lukas*, 406.
139. Ibid., 407–8.
140. Ibid., 409.
141. Ibid., 411–12.
142. Ibid., 412–13.
143. Ibid., 414.

second part of Jesus' testimony about the Baptist (7:28) as a later addition, formulated by the post-Easter community, aimed at discouraging the misinterpretation that believers should remain simply as disciples of John—salvation is only available through Jesus.[144] Schürmann regards 7:29–30 as a *Lagebericht* about the success and failure of God over Israel. The verses support the following parable by suggesting that the official representatives of the Jews, i.e., the Pharisees and scholars of the Law, are the ones whom Jesus reprimands. Meanwhile, the people of Israel, including toll collectors and sinners, are given the good judgment to recognize in the works of the Baptist and Jesus the wisdom of God.[145] In the parable of the children in the marketplace, the "people of this generation" are indicted for not heeding the call to conversion of the Baptist nor the message of jubilation of Jesus.[146] They are the unhappy children of the parable. Schürmann proposes for this parable a post-Easter scenario in which Israel has collapsed and its recovery is hopeless; there is only hope for the "children of wisdom."[147]

I. Howard Marshall dedicates a substantial portion of his remarks on the passage in his commentary on Luke to questioning whether particular verses of the passage should be regarded as interpolations or authentic.[148] Marshall acknowledges that Luke, like Matthew, relied on a common source (Q), which Luke has expanded. He finds no serious reasons to question the historicity of the account. For Marshall, John has doubts about whether Jesus is the expected "coming one" because the final judgment is absent from Jesus' ministry. In response, Jesus replies with a combination of OT allusions that depict him as the eschatological prophet who ushers in a new era of salvation. "The saying is thus an invitation to John to consider the scriptural significance of Jesus' ministry, and hence to attain to a deeper, and lasting, faith in him."[149] Correspondingly, Jesus praises John as the "greatest among those born of women" only to restrict his importance in relation to the kingdom and in doing so subordinate the Baptist to him.[150] The parable of the children

---

144. Ibid., 415.
145. Ibid., 420.
146. Ibid., 424.
147. Ibid., 428.
148. Marshall, *Luke*, 287–304.
149. Ibid., 292.
150. Ibid., 293.

Luke 7:18–35: A Historical Survey

in the marketplace is a verdict upon those who have not responded to the ministries of both John and Jesus, who nonetheless are vindicated by those who are wise, i.e., the children of wisdom.[151]

In his commentary on the Gospel of Luke, Joseph A. Fitzmyer points out that the pericope delineates the relationship between John and Jesus in relation to God's plan of salvation as well as the reaction of the disciples of John and their contemporaries to Jesus.[152] Fitzmyer discusses the modifications, omissions, and transpositions of the Lukan redaction that at times makes him more faithful than Matthew and at other times less so to the Q source. For Fitzmyer the question of the Baptist and the answer of Jesus reflect a historical statement recalled within the context of a later controversy between the disciples of John and Jesus.[153] According to Fitzmyer, the Baptist's view of Jesus as Elijah *redivivus* is reversed by Jesus, who casts John in that role as someone greater than a prophet.[154] For him, the testimony of Jesus about the Baptist serves to support the Lukan portrayal of John as the precursor of the Lord.

The parable of the children in the marketplace, which Fitzmyer derives from Jesus' own ministry, represents the Baptist, Jesus, and their followers, who have called their Palestinian contemporaries to join them only to be rejected.[155] Wisdom is personified, and John and Jesus are the children of that wisdom whose divine message is vindicated by all the people and toll collectors.

For John Nolland the historicity of the account is beyond doubt, even though he is aware of the redactional work of Luke, the diversity of its elements, and the secondary setting of some of its parts.[156] According

---

151. Ibid., 297–304.

152. Fitzmyer, *Luke*, 1:662, 671.

153. Ibid., 663. Besides his commentary on Luke, Fitzmyer also deals with the passage in his presentation of the Lukan portrayal of the Baptist as the precursor of Jesus; see Fitzmyer, *Theologian*, 86–116. Jesus' answer to John's question highlights the difficulties that the Baptist encountered in molding his preconceived ideas to the message of Jesus (ibid., 97–99).

154. Fitzmyer, *Luke*, 1:664–65; 1:671–73; see also Fitzmyer, *Theologian*, 97–99; 109. Fitzmyer stresses that John's portrayal as the precursor does not imply a presentation of Jesus as the Messiah.

155. Fitzmyer, *Luke*, 1:677–79.

156. Nolland (*Luke*, 327) argues: "But whatever explanation is to be given for those texts, they can certainly cast no doubt upon the historicity of the present episode." Among the literary elements that Nolland finds in the pericope are a pronouncement story (7:18–23), a summarizing editorial comment (7:29–30), a parable (7:31–32), and a wisdom saying (7:35).

to Nolland, Jesus' answer has an eschatological orientation but is not as cataclysmic as John may have had expected. He notes that Jesus responds to the question of the Baptist affirmatively, but with an emphasis on the graciousness of God rather than on his vengeance.[157] The final beatitude in Jesus' reply is a challenge that presumes a positive answer from the Baptist even when there is a potential for stumbling.

In Jesus' testimony about John, the Baptist is presented with unprecedented importance and unsurpassed greatness. Yet, the arrival of the kingdom, which he has heralded, has overshadowed his status.[158] Nolland finds that Jesus both exalts the Baptist as the supreme figure of human history and sets limits on his greatness with respect to the little ones of the kingdom, a view that agrees with Jesus' preference for the lowly and the poor members of society.[159] In the parable of the children in the marketplace, Jesus presents John and himself as signs of the coming kingdom of God and criticizes the lack of comprehension of their contemporaries. He also proclaims the final vindication of God in those who are open to his wisdom.[160]

Another author who in his commentary on the Gospel of Luke looks at the passage is François Bovon. He notes that Luke has arranged his sources (Mark, Q, and his special material) to alternate between words (6:20–49; 7:18–35; 8:4–18) and deeds (7:1–17; 36–50).[161] Regarding the history of transmission of the pericope, Bovon highlights the secondary character of many of its parts: 7:23, an early Christian prophetic saying; 7:27, a later effort to clarify the cryptic answer of Jesus; 7:28, evidence of a cultic activity of an early Christian prophet; 7:29–30, an editorial introduction; 7:33–34, an early interpretation of a parable (7:31–32); and 7:35, an independently circulating saying. He mentions that the passage has an interest in clarifying the role of the Baptist but not necessarily a polemical intent. Historically, John searched for a precise knowledge of the eschatological salvation (cf. 1 Pet 1:10–11) and Jesus answers with an implicit "yes" that actualizes the prophecy-fulfillment scheme of Isaiah.[162]

---

157. Ibid., 331–33.
158. Ibid., 334–35.
159. Ibid., 339.
160. Ibid., 341–48.
161. Bovon, *Luke*, 277–81.
162. Ibid., 281–83. Bovon also notices the similarity between the present pericope and John 20:24–29: "What is true there of the resurrected Jesus is here true of the 'mes-

But the question of the Baptist also reflects the uncertainty of the followers of John toward the emerging Christian movement. The absence of the Baptist's reaction, which has generated so much discussion, means for Bovon that the disciples of John remained distant from the emerging movement and were not able to rise above their reservations.

For Bovon, Jesus' testimony about John emphasizes the relationship of the crowd to him.[163] The status of John as the forerunner is restricted by being at the threshold of the reign of God. With a redactional summary (7:29–30), Luke prepares a final prophetic accusation against the "people of this generation" for having missed a historical moment.[164] They have rejected the benevolence of God, which, however, has been recognized by a contrite remnant of Israel among whom the Baptist and Jesus are included as children of wisdom.

Joel B. Green's commentary on Luke is one of the commentaries that look at the entire Gospel from a narrative-critical perspective.[165] For Green the pericope revolves around the ministry of Jesus, his identity, and the reaction he generates. It also recapitulates and interprets how Jesus is God's agent of salvation.[166] Green indicates that John, whose character had been cultivated in previous parts of Gospel, is brought to the fore once again to emphasize his role in the salvific plan of God. Green underscores the importance of John's question, which deals with the "fault line between his eschatological expectation and the realities of Jesus' performance," in relation to the host of negative reactions that Jesus has received up to this point in the narrative.[167] Jesus' response is a redefinition and confirmation of his messianic role.[168] Green points out

---

sianic' Jesus. Someone doubts; to defuse the tension in the situation Jesus decides to act" (281).

163. Ibid., 283–84.

164. Ibid., 284–88.

165. Green, *Luke*, 11–20. In explaining the particular focus of his approach Green states: "After all, this commentary is not focused on the identification of Luke's sources, nor on how Luke might have transformed the traditions available to him in the process of generating his Gospel, nor on whether each episode he records approximates what actually happened.... Our reading of the Third Gospel is concerned above all with the 'narrative' side of this equation—that is, with the sequencing of events and the interpretive aim that weaves its way forward through the narrative, surfacing here and there while lurking beneath the story elsewhere" (14–15).

166. Ibid., 294.

167. Ibid., 295.

168. Ibid., 296.

that the concluding beatitude in which Jesus warns about the possibility of scandal echoes other reactions to his ministry.[169]

In Green's evaluation the testimony of Jesus about the Baptist is consonant with Luke's previous presentation of John in 3:1–9.[170] Nevertheless, Jesus' remarks go beyond that passage to underscore how John is the agent of God who prepares his way not only by proclaiming his message but also by showing a positive response to the good news. Jesus' homage of John along with the language of the kingdom is an exhortation to the people to put away conventional expectations regarding the plan of God and adopt the perspective advanced by Jesus. With the positive assessment of John in 7:29–30, Luke provides "firm canons" to guide the reader in determining the profile of those who reject and accept the plan of God.[171] The response of the people to this plan of God is further illustrated by the parable of the children in the marketplace, in which those who are aligned with the world fail to recognize this plan while the children of wisdom recognize in John and Jesus the manifestation of God's divine purpose.[172]

Hans Klein's commentary on the Gospel of Luke provides a more recent example of the passage's interpretation. For Klein the *Sitz im Leben* of the entire pericope is the defense of Christianity against the disciples of the Baptist.[173] Within Jewish Christian circles, this results in the handing down of a tradition that places the words of Jesus within a new framework.[174] Klein assumes that the section has been taken from Q and highlights the Lukan redactional tendencies as well as the possible layers of Luke's editorial work. For Klein the passage deals with the relationship between Jesus and the Baptist and the relationship of both with Israel.

---

169. As examples, Green (ibid., 297) cites 4:48–49; 20:18; 22–23.

170. Ibid., 298–99.

171. Ibid., 300.

172. Ibid., 303–4.

173. Klein, *Lukasevangelium*, 44, 282.

174. Klein considers 7:24–26.28a, which deals with the evaluation of the Baptist by Jesus, the oldest and more historical part of the section. For Klein (ibid., 280–89) some of the redactional tendencies are the repetition of the Baptist's question in 7:20 and the comparison of the Baptist with Jesus. He considers the answer of Jesus in 7:22 and the Scripture reference in 7:27 nonhistorical. The parable in 7:32 may also be attributed to Jesus, but neither its introductory verse (7:31) nor its following interpretation (7:33–35).

Luke 7:18–35: A Historical Survey

To recapitulate, commentaries address many of the issues that studies about John the Baptist discuss but within the broader interpretative context of the Lukan work. Claims that the episode reflects missionary and/or apologetic concerns amid the struggles between the factions of the Baptist and Jesus vie with affirmations about the reliability of passage's historical reminiscences. Some of these authors emphasize how Luke's editorial work seeks to clarify the relationship between the Baptist and Jesus as well as John's soteriological role to the kingdom of God. While some underscore the modification of the sources and the secondary setting of the passage that sought to restrict the Baptist's role to that of the precursor of Jesus, others highlight the Baptist's historical struggle to reconcile his messianic expectations with the manifestation of Jesus' messianic signs.

Specialized Studies

Since the beginning of modern biblical exegesis a number of studies dealing with a variety of NT topics have presented their own interpretations of Luke 7:18–35. One example of such interpretations is the pericope's assessment by Julius Wellhausen in his introduction to the Synoptic Gospels.[175] To support his claim that Mark was the primary source for the teachings of Jesus and that Q represented a secondary version, Wellhausen turns to the passage that deals with John the Baptist. For Wellhausen the pericope suggests that the Baptist was not a disciple of Jesus. The Baptist remains a hybrid between the old and the new era, while Jesus holds a superior religious view. Jesus is the present Messiah, who already establishes the reign of God on earth, and the future belongs to him.

According to Wellhausen, Matthew and Luke are in substantial agreement regarding the relationship between the Baptist and Jesus. In their final analysis Matthew and Luke have transformed into a close relationship what in Mark was only a weak analogy that occurred at the conclusion of the eschatological speech (Mark 1:7–8). Jesus identifies himself as the "Son of Man" in a messianic sense and becomes the "Lord." For Wellhausen, these changes evidence Luke's Christianization of the original sources. In comparison to Mark, this speech represents a more

---

175. Wellhausen, *Einleitung*, 83.

coherent composition of Jesus addressed to his disciples and aimed at the church for which Jesus was already the present Messiah.[176]

Ernst Percy is another author who focuses on the passage in his study about the mission and message of Jesus. For him, Jesus' reply to the delegates from John seems far better understood from Jesus' own historical situation than from that of the early community.[177] Percy discusses whether the reports about the mighty deeds of Jesus could have been historically based on the evidence of Mark 6:14–16.[178] He also ponders how John could have come to the conclusion that Jesus was the "expected fiery-judge-Messiah." However, the tone of the final beatitude as well as the oblique manner in which Jesus' answer is delivered convinces Percy that this answer is original. The question of the Baptist itself may have originated not with John but with his disciples. Percy interprets Jesus' response to John as proof that the prophesied time of fulfillment has arrived.[179] The mighty deeds to which Jesus alludes announce the kingdom of God, because although they do not speak explicitly about the kingdom, the mighty deeds cannot be differentiated from it.[180]

Rudolph Schnackenburg examines the passage in his investigation of the meaning of the kingdom of God in the preaching of Jesus.[181] Schnackenburg cites the passage to support his claim that Jesus' message of salvation centered on the divine mercy of God and that this message, even to the amazement of his contemporaries, included the outcast members of society (7:34). For Schnackenburg the wonders of Jesus (7:21–22) also show that a new era of salvation—the fulfillment of the Deutero-Isaian prophecies—is already present and operative, although not fully realized. The passage plays a fundamental role in Jesus' messianic claim because in the close relationship of his preaching and wonders the coming of the reign of God was manifested.[182]

---

176. Ibid., 84.

177. Percy, *Botschaft Jesu*, 232.

178. Ibid., 231–33.

179. Ibid., 187–88.

180. After considering the textual data and its difficulties, Percy (ibid., 188–90) suggests that the mighty works mentioned were meant as metaphorical expressions. Moreover, he points out that the reference to the message of salvation being preached to the poor (7:22) may have been an addition by an author that shows particular interest in the poor.

181. Schnackenburg, *God's Rule*, 87–89.

182. Ibid., 119–21.

Luke 7:18–35: A Historical Survey

In his "History of the Synoptic Tradition," Rudolph Bultmann refers to Luke 7:18–35 as an apothegm (7:18–23) to which sayings about the Baptist have been added.[183] He considers the question of the Baptist as a "community product" that "belongs to those passages in which the Baptist is called as a witness to the Messiahship of Jesus."[184] The composition of the passage took place amid the arguments between the disciples of Jesus and those of John, who denied the messianic character of the mighty works.[185] The difference between the Lukan and Matthean forms of this apothegm must be attributed to Luke's habit of expanding traditional material that does not appropriately fits in his redactional context.[186]

The episode about the delegation of the Baptist to Jesus is the first "parable" that Joachim Jeremias deals with in his work on the parables of Jesus, which also treats the parable of the children in the marketplace.[187] Jeremias places the former into the category of parables that proclaim "now is the day of salvation," while the latter is treated as a parable that announces "the imminence of catastrophe." He does not discuss the historical circumstances surrounding either of them, because in outlining his ten "principles of transformation" he presumes that many of the parables have been modified from their original form and setting by the experience of the primitive church.[188] Jeremias seems, however, to admit the authenticity of both accounts, although he avoids discussing its editorial trajectories.[189] The parable of the delegation of the Baptist is for Jeremias a reply of Jesus in the form of a free quotation from Isaiah in which he announces the salvation of God with the proclamation of the arrival of a new age. Meanwhile, the parable of the children in the

---

183. Bultmann, *History*, 23.
184. Ibid.
185. Ibid., 24.
186. Ibid., 336.
187. Jeremias, *Parables*, 115–16; 160–62. Jeremias uses the term "parable" in the broad sense of the Hebrew *mašal* or the Aramaic *mathla*, which include parables, similitudes, allegories, fables, fictitious persons, examples, themes, arguments, apologies, refutation, and/or jests; see ibid., 20.
188. Jeremias (ibid., 23–114) explains the ten principles of transformation of the parables in the second chapter of his book.
189. "The question whether the Baptist's Messianic enquiry could have taken place before Peter's confession, is of no importance in our context, since we are only concerned with Jesus' logion" (ibid., 116 n. 6; 160 n. 37).

marketplace is an announcement of judgment, a warning against those who failed to heed the call to repentance and rejected the proclamation of the gospel.

Werner Georg Kümmel discusses part of the pericope to illustrate the contemporary difficulties affecting the methodology of research for the historical Jesus.[190] Kümmel surveys the contemporary development of critical biblical scholarship and the growing skepticism that led to the assertion that nothing can be known about the personality and life of Jesus. This is formulated in the expression *"vita Christi scribi nequit."*[191] Kümmel discusses the outcome of the research that led to a wider awareness of the relative historical value of the Gospel and a greater realization of the influence that the post-resurrection confessional statements of the primitive community had on the traditions. He points out the methodological flaws and erred assumptions upon which many historical-critical investigations formulated their conclusions. Kümmel advocates the possibility of extracting certain facts from the kerygma and faith reflected in the Gospels, and outlines a series of methodological criteria that should guide the use of the sources in the search for the historical Jesus.[192]

Kümmel rehearses the arguments advocated by many researchers, especially those of Dibelius and Anton Vögtle,[193] concerning the secondary character of Luke 7:18–23, summarized in the following objections: (1) given his eschatological messianic expectation, the Baptist could not have formulated the question to Jesus; (2) the involvement of the Baptist's disciples shows that this is not a conversation between Jesus and John; (3) the lack of response from the Baptist shows that the entire report has been formulated for the sake of the final warning.[194] Following

---

190. Kümmel, *Jesu Antwort*, 5–6.

191. The phrase, quoted by Kümmel, was formulated by Adolf von Harnack half a century earlier.

192. Some of these are: (1) the assumption that early Christianity had a fundamental interest in preserving the memory of the earthly Jesus; (2) the claim that the burden of proof for the historical value of a particular text lies with the researcher has to be rejected; (3) a "critical sympathy" toward the text that is not *a priori* and without compelling reasons overly skeptic; (4) paying greater attention to the underlying Hebrew and/or Aramaic language in the Greek text; and (5) whether the report about the behavior of Jesus is in line with his words and vice versa (Kümmel, *Jesu Antwort*, 18–24).

193. Vögtle, "Wunder und Wort," 219–42.

194. Kümmel, *Johannes den Täufer*, 25–28.

his own principles and criteria, Kümmel evaluates whether the redaction of the report in Luke 7:18–23 can be consulted for the historical reconstruction of the earthly Jesus. He concludes that the second and third objections can be dismissed if one approaches the passage with "critical sympathy," because in light of other NT texts what is reported in the passage is entirely possible and natural. Regarding the first objection, Kümmel notes that it would not have been unusual or impossible for the Baptist to have used the expression about the "coming one," since it was common among the Jews and similar to other modes of expression of the Baptist himself (cf. Matt 3:11).

In Kümmel's opinion, it is difficult to affirm with certainty that the Baptist did not waver in his end-of-time expectation given the limited information that we have about the relationship between John and Jesus. Kümmel underscores that the question of the Baptist (7:19) bears Semitic (Aramaic) characteristics. The origin of the answer in the primitive community cannot rely on the claim that it is based on an Isaian text and therefore not authentic because the passage bears the characteristics of a freely redacted Semitic statement.[195] On the other hand, Jesus' answer agrees with a similar tradition in Luke 10:23–24 and makes the challenge of its authenticity problematic. Moreover, the proclamation of the good news to the poor fits with Jesus' announcements to the poor elsewhere (Luke 6:20; 10:21). Therefore, the final warning of the pericope is completely appropriate because the friendly attitude of Jesus toward groups despised by the Jewish people (e.g., toll collectors and sinners) would have ignited opposition against him.

Another author who approaches the passage in his study of the narrative unity of Luke-Acts is Robert C. Tannehill. He focuses on specific roles in the story and, by detecting many of the complex internal connections, seeks to highlight their function within the broader context of the narrative.[196] Tannehill notes that the statements of Jesus about the Baptist in 7:26–27 depict him as a prophet who prepares the way of the Lord.[197] This portrayal has been foreshadowed in the words of Zechariah (1:76–77), which are a forecast of John's role in Luke. Tannehill points out the rhythmic form of Jesus' response to the question of the Baptist

---

195. Kümmel (ibid., 31–32) accepts the quotation of Isaiah as authentic words of Jesus.
196. Tannehill, *Luke-Acts*, 1–9.
197. Ibid., 23–24.

and discusses the purpose of its Isaian allusion, which signals that the salvation promised in those texts has arrived.[198] He notes the connection of the passage to previous parts of the narrative related to the Baptist (e.g., 3:16) and points out that the response of Jesus helps to integrate his healing ministry with his messianic role.[199] Tannehill emphasizes that a shift in the passage from joyous announcement to a potential rejection fits a pattern that can also be observed in the scene in Nazareth. "Jesus offended the people of Nazareth, and it remains true that he can only be accepted as the coming one by those who can face and accept his offensiveness."[200] The parable of the children in the marketplace is a commentary of Jesus on the accusations leveled against him for eating with toll collectors and sinners (5:29–32).[201] Tannehill notes that some of the marginal groups to whom Jesus ministers (7:22) also appear as fictional characters in some other parables (e.g., 14:21), a feature that helps to create thematic unity among separate scenes.[202]

John A. Darr is another commentator who examines the passage in his study of characterizations in Luke. Darr deals with character and characterization as they unfold in the author's rhetorical presentation as well as in the audience's interpretation of the narrative.[203] Through the characterization lens, Darr considers John's inquiry in 7:19 as the "correct question," since his ignorance is in accord with what thus far has happened in the narrative. The gaps that the audience experiences regarding the reaction of John to Jesus' statement are answered by the narrator, who portrays John as the paradigm of the "right" kind of Jew, open-minded and prepared to embrace the plan of God. The Baptist and his disciples and the toll collectors and sinners are characterized as those who have responded appropriately to that plan, while the Pharisees and scholars of the Law have not.[204]

---

198. Tannehill (ibid., 79) also pays attention to the order in which the list of destitute people is cast: "Furthermore, the poor and blind the two groups that relate to Isa 61:1, have positions of emphasis at the beginning and the end of the rhythmic series."

199. Ibid., 80.

200. Ibid., 80.

201. Ibid., 105–6.

202. Ibid., 108–10. This is also true for the role that 7:24–35 plays in the theme of the religious authorities' rejection of Jesus (176–77).

203. Darr, *Character Building*, 16–36.

204. Ibid., 75–78; 99–101.

Luke 7:18–35: A Historical Survey

In his investigation of the role of the Baptist in the theology and ethic of Luke, Peter Böhlemann also comments on the passage. Focusing on the Luke-Acts texts that allude to the relationship of the Baptist and Jesus as well as their respective followers, Böhlemann seeks to prove that the whole of the Lukan work is influenced by his dispute with groups sympathetic to the Baptist. According to Böhlemann, this argument shapes the theology and ethic of Luke.[205] Hence, he argues that the placement of 7:18–35 after the resuscitation of the son of the widow from Naim shows that Luke uses the mighty works of Jesus as proof of his power and superiority over the Baptist.[206] Emphasizing a more theological perspective than a historical one, Böhlemann highlights the motifs found in the passage. For instance, he notes that the references to the "greater" and "smaller" in 7:28 as well as to the children of wisdom in 7:35 are part of larger theological theme that Luke develops in his polemic with the followers of the Baptist.[207]

Another study that deals with the passage in its analysis of characterizations of people and/or groups of people in Luke-Acts is the work of S. John Roth. For Roth the point of departure is that there are in Luke 4:18 and 7:22 two programmatic statements that allow the readers to evaluate other texts related to the characters mentioned in these passages.[208] According to Roth, the people mentioned therein function as types that have to be interpreted within the context of the Lukan narrative and the LXX. Analyzing the passage under that perspective, Roth highlights the rhetorical features of the passage and points out how it makes an issue of the downtrodden and outcasts in their relationship to Jesus and John.[209] Roth argues that the passage clarifies the narrative logic of the Gospel. "The scene with John's disciples (7:18–23) recaps Jesus' ministry

---

205. Böhlemann, *Jesus und der Täufer*, 2.

206. Ibid., 59.

207. Ibid., 143–59. For instance, in reference to the motif of the "greater," after citing as examples 7:28, 9:48, and 22:26, Böhlemann concludes: "Die gennanten Stellen machen deutlich, daß Lukas sich sehr subtil mit dem Motiv der Größe des Täufers auseinanderstetzt" (145).

208. Roth, *Character Types*, 25–26.

209. Roth (ibid., 173–77) highlights several rhetorical devices used in the passage: the repetition of the "word-for-word" question of John, the use of the phrase σὺ εἶ (3:22, 4:41; 7:19), and the "freezing up" of the scene by the summary report introduced by the narrator in 7:21.

to this point and connects it to Jesus' reading in the synagogue."²¹⁰ The characterization of Jesus, John, the Pharisees, the scholars of the Law, the toll collectors, and the people occur around two subplots: (1) the doubt of John about Jesus; and (2) the antagonism by members of "this generation" against John and Jesus. Luke tries to reshape the audience's understanding of the relationship of the Messiah to sinners using a response to the inquiry of the Baptist that has great persuasive value to convince the audience that Jesus is God's unique eschatological agent of salvation.

Christoph Gregor Müller also analyzes the text in his work about the characterization of John the Baptist in the Gospel of Luke. Taking his cue from the stylistic features of Greek literature, Müller argues that Luke constructs an extended implicit comparison (*synkrisis*) between Jesus and the Baptist.²¹¹ He notes that the embassy of the Baptist renews the narrative about John and Jesus (see Luke 1:39–56).²¹² For Müller the passage that portrays John "as more than a prophet" connects the forerunner motif with the speech about his paramount importance.²¹³ Müller uses the passage to corroborate what has been said earlier in the narrative about the ascetic dressing and eating habits of the Baptist.²¹⁴ Based on these characteristics of the Baptist, Müller draws a parallel between John and Jesus, which he extends to their prophetic role.²¹⁵ In 7:29–30, Müller highlights the theme of the rejection of the Baptist's message by which he becomes a prototype of Jesus.²¹⁶ The parable of the playing children introduces into the narrative the wisdom theology and heightens the parallel between the Baptist and Jesus by suggesting that they are both "the children of wisdom" and the messengers of that wisdom for those who accept and reject it.²¹⁷ According to Müller, this passage plays

---

210. Ibid., 175.

211. Müller, *Charakterzeichnung*, 59–64.

212. Ibid., 217. Müller undertakes a brief tradition and redaction analysis and attributes essential elements of Luke 7:18–35 to Q (217–21). He also pays attention to how references within the text recall or highlight previous portions of the Gospel. For instance, Müller notes how the use of ἀγγέλων Ἰωάννου (7:24) forms an *inclusio* with ἀπήγγειλαν (7:18) and how through this *inclusio* Luke is adjoining sections 7:18–23 and 7:24–35 (222–26).

213. Ibid., 231–43.

214. Ibid., 232–33.

215. Ibid., 238–40.

216. Ibid., 242.

217. Ibid., 243–45.

an important role in the clarification of the identity of Jesus and the Baptist and their characterization as prophets in comparison with other prophetic figures such as Solomon and Jonah.[218]

A final author who examines the passage in his literary study of Luke is Patrick E. Spencer. He analyzes the four Galilean ministry speeches of Jesus in Luke (4:14–30; 6:17–49; 7:24–35; 8:4–18) and argues that within the context of Jesus' initial ministry these four speeches establish the foundation upon which readers will understand the meaning of the ensuing narrative.[219] As part of his study, Spencer analyzes the message in light of rhetorical categories.[220] He posits that the argument aims at persuading the implied and narrative audiences to evaluate the ethos of the Baptist and Jesus in a positive light.[221] The rhetoric places Jesus and his disciples above the Baptist and his followers. Spencer points out that through intertextual allusions the implied author compares Jesus and John with Elisha and Elijah to show how they embody the divine will in contradistinction to the "members of this generation."[222] For Spencer, this speech focuses on the characterization of the Baptist and Jesus and, by extension, on those groups of people who interact with them, namely, Pharisees, scholars of the Law, "all the people," and toll collectors. In explaining the role of these characters Spencer states: "As the narrative progresses, characters and character groups whose actions embrace those of Jesus and John the Baptist are viewed in a positive light by the implied reader, while those whose thoughts and actions coincide with those of the Pharisees and scholars of the Law are associated in a negative light."[223]

In sum, the historical reliability of the pericope remains a matter of discussion among specialized studies. Some of these authors presumed the early Christian community's modification of the Baptist's traditional material in order to present him as witness to the messiaship of Jesus.

218. Ibid., 246–48.

219. Spencer, *Rhetorical Texture*, 4–5.

220. To explain the rhetorical arrangement of the passage, Spencer (ibid., 101–13) divides its structure into an amplified chreia (7:17–23), quaestio (7:24–26), chreia (7:27), rationale (7:28), digression (7:29–30), statement by analogy (7:31–32), statement by example (7:33–34), and conclusion (7:35). He also highlights the use of irony, ecphrasis, synkrisis, and enthymemes throughout the rhetorical argumentation.

221. Ibid., 103.

222. Ibid., 146–53.

223. Ibid., 149.

Other authors uphold the fundamental historicity of the account and interpret it as testifying to Jesus' messianic manifestation. Some of these studies also highlight the literary connection and function of the passage in other parts of the narrative related to the Baptist and Jesus. They note the character role of the Baptist, the thematic unity that such characterizations create among scenes, and the literary parallel drawn between John and Jesus.

CONCLUSION

The preceding analysis provides a summary of some of the most influential interpretations of Luke 7:18–35 over the centuries. To conclude my overview, a number of summary observations are pertinent. First, the *Forschungsbericht* shows that from a very early period the first part of the passage, i.e., 7:18–23, has attracted the greatest attention. The reason for this persistent interest may be attributed to the fact that since the beginning Christian readers have been puzzled by the apparent contradiction between this passage and other texts in the Gospels (e.g., John 1:36). This attention has often resulted in the interpretative fragmentation of a block of material that appears to have been conceived as a cohesive unit by the tradition. Consequently, important parts of the text are routinely left out by interpreters who pick and choose for their respective studies the parts of the passage that most fittingly support their particular argument. Such interpretations tend to obscure the role that the entire unit may have been designed to play within the wider literary context of the Gospel.

Second, this overview also shows that while writers in early Christian and medieval periods favored the interpretation of the passage along paraenetic lines, historical considerations have overwhelmingly dominated contemporary analyses. Recent interpretations have focused on the plausibility of the account, its underlying *Sitz im Leben*, the redactional development of the pericope, and its social background. Many of these studies discuss the use of sources that may have been available to the author, the integrity of the unit, and whether the passage contains historically reliable information. Because the unit is one of the longest references to the Baptist in the Gospels, it has been a favorite for many contemporary historical reconstructions of the life and ministry of John. These historical considerations have generated the widespread opinion (with many nuances) that the text is influenced by a polemic between the Baptist and Christian factions. Such a proposal has directly influenced the question about the authenticity of the passage. However, the discussions about whether the pericope and/or some of its parts should be traced back to the historical Jesus or to early sectarian communities have not yielded a scholarly consensus.

Third, given the preponderance of historical studies in the analysis of the pericope, the passage has only recently been subjected to serious literary interpretation. The few studies that have undertaken such interpretations have done so with an emphasis on the characterization of John the Baptist and other personages in the passage.

Fourth, it is evident that the conclusions often drawn from the analysis of the pericope have not sufficiently taken into consideration the distinctions between the Matthean and the Lukan versions. Many remarks on the pericope show that commentators have frequently conflated both passages without paying adequate attention to the differences between the two. Consequently, the way in which each evangelist has used the traditional material has not always been properly accounted for. This has prevented some interpreters from acknowledging the distinctive nuances of each Gospel passage.

Although many commentators have interpreted Luke 7:18–35, none has yet undertaken a thorough analysis from a narrative-critical perspective within the larger literary context of Luke-Acts. While the similarities between the Matthean and Lukan versions are more or less clear, some peculiarities within the Lukan Gospel suggest that a narrative-critical analysis will shed new light into some of the disputed issues of the pericope. Three unique elements encourage the study of literary aspects such as setting, character, and plot in the Lukan version: (1) the purpose statement of the author expressed in the prologue; (2) the inclusion of the infancy narratives with its emphasis on the Baptist; and (3) the unity of Luke-Acts as a two-volume work. In what follows I will first examine the origin of the pericope and the differences between the Matthean and Lukan versions before undertaking a thorough narrative-critical analysis of the passage within the context of Luke-Acts.

2

The Origin, Redaction, and Literary Function of Luke 7:18–35

INTRODUCTION

JOHN THE BAPTIST'S QUESTION and Jesus' indictment of the religious leaders (Luke 7:18–35 // Matt 11:2–19) belong to what is known as the double tradition, i.e., the common material between Matthew and Luke not found in Mark. Although there are different ways of explaining this phenomenon, many contemporary scholars attribute it to a source commonly designated as Q. This explanation is part of the so-called two-source theory, the most widely held "solution" to the Synoptic problem.[1] In explaining the literary relationship between the Gospels of Mark, Matthew, and Luke, this theory holds that (1) Matthew and Luke depend on Mark (Markan Priority); (2) Matthew and Luke wrote independently of each other; and (3) both had access to a source no longer extant consisting mostly of traditional sayings of Jesus—the aforementioned Q.[2] A corollary of this theory posits that Matthew and Luke used their own special material (*Sondergut*),

---

1. The Synoptic problem, which has vexed scholars since before 1776, continues to be a matter of debate. Although the two-source theory enjoys widespread support, it does so less than a generation ago. Previously postulated theories (e.g., Griesbach's theory, Farrer's theory) continue to reemerge under new auspices. For an overview of the Synoptic problem, see Kümmel, *Introduction*, 38–80; Schnelle, *New Testament Writings*, 161–97. For the Lukan composition, see Fitzmyer, *Luke*, 1:63–97. Regarding the Proto-Luke hypothesis see Brodie, *Birthing*, 282–537.

2. Concerning the ongoing debate over Q and the latest attempt at reconstructing this hypothetical source, see Robinson et al., *Critical Edition*, xix–cvii; see also Kloppenborg, *Excavating Q*, 11–54; Tuckett, *Early Christianity*, 1–82; Meier, "Dividing Lines," 253–72; Goodacre, *Case against Q*, 81–104, 152–85; Goulder, "Juggernaut," 667–81; idem, "Self-Contradictions," 506–17.

written or oral, with which they supplemented their works. In the Gospels of Matthew and Luke this special material is designated as M and L respectively.[3] The comparative analysis that follows proceeds on the assumption of this modified two-source theory.[4]

THE ORIGIN OF LUKE 7:18–35: PRELIMINARY CONSIDERATIONS

The origin of the traditional material in Luke 7:18–35 (// Matt 11:2–19) is disputed and shrouded in uncertainty. Although many hypotheses have been proposed to explain the genesis of this passage, there is substantial disagreement about its historicity, source, literary integrity, and *Sitz im Leben*. For many, the material that makes up the pericope originated from independent sayings of Jesus that included a pronouncement story (7:18–23), a saying about John the Baptist (7:24–30), a parable (7:31–32), an explanation of the parable (7:33–34), and a wisdom saying (7:35). These independent pieces of tradition, all of which dealt with John the Baptist, would have been brought together at a later date amid the controversies between the early Christian community and the followers of John.[5] Some disagree partially or entirely with such proposals, including those that make claims about whether Matthew (11:2–19) or Luke (7:18–35) preserves the more original form of this traditional material.

Regardless of these disagreements, a broad consensus exists among supporters of the two-source theory that Matthew and Luke have drawn

---

3. Black and Beck, *Synoptic Problem*, 150–51.

4. In adopting this position I would subscribe to France's (*Matthew*, 20–21) cautionary remark about the two-source theory: "The simple x-copied-y approach to the Synoptic Problem which has characterized many of the proposed 'solutions' seems to me more appropriate to a modern scholar's study than to the real world of first-century church tradition. I incline to the view promoted by E. P. Sanders and developed by J. A. T. Robinson that neat theories of literary dependence (even complex ones like that of Boismard) are unlikely to do justice to the varied data of the Synoptic texts, and that we should think rather of a more fluid process of mutual influence between the various centers of Christian gospel writing as people traveled around the empire and visited and consulted with one another."

5. Dibelius, *Überlieferung*, 6–22; Ernst, *Johannes der Taüfer*, 55; Sabugal, *Embajada Mesiánica*, 117. According to Bultmann (*History*, 23–24) the essential element of this tradition would have been the phrase in Matt 11:5–6, which could have been transmitted independently and used against the followers of John by the disciples of Jesus regarding the messianic character of his mighty works. For Fitzmyer (*Luke*, 1:663) although this is not impossible, the pronouncement could date back to Jesus himself.

this material from the so-called Q source. Yet, despite this widespread consensus, considerable uncertainty exists regarding this hypothetical document and our ability to reconstruct it.[6] Given the hypothetical nature of Q, I will proceed carefully, taking into consideration some of the redactional and compositional tendencies of Matthew and Luke. However, the main goal of this comparison is not to determine the changes (additions and/or omissions) that each evangelist may have made to the original source, or to determine whether Matthew or Luke preserves the more pristine form of this traditional material. Some of these issues will be taken into consideration to illustrate the state of the discussion and for the sake of understanding how each evangelist may have shaped the meaning of the tradition. Rather, the main concern of my analysis is to determine the way in which a study of the differences between Matthew and Luke can illuminate the meaning of each pericope. Furthermore, this comparative study will elucidate how these differences play into each Gospel's theological perspectives.

A COMPARATIVE ANALYSIS OF MATT 11:2–19 AND LUKE 7:18–35

Matt 11:2–6 and Luke 7:18–23

To highlight the similarities and differences between Matthew and Luke, I will begin each section of this comparative analysis with a table that underscores the words that have an exact parallel in each Gospel.

The question of John the Baptist and Jesus' indictment of the religious leaders is found in Luke 7:18–35 and Matthew 11:2–19 with similar wording and in a common sequence. Both evangelists include, albeit with some variations, the three units that form the tradition. These consist of the question of the Baptist (Matt 11:2–6 // Luke 7:18–23), the testimony of Jesus concerning John (Matt 11:7–15 // Luke 7:24–30), and the parable of the children in the marketplace (Matt 11:16–19 // Luke 7:31–35).[7]

---

6. Although there have been various attempts at reconstructing Q, the results of these reconstructions remain tentative. As Hoffmann (*Studien*, 192) admits, despite the obvious similarities between 7:18–35 and Matt 11:2–19: "Da jedoch beide Evangelisten bei der Rahmung der Tradition die Ihnen vorgegebene Einleitung umgestalten, läßt sich der Text nicht mehr in allen Einzelheiten rekonstruieren."

7. Bultmann, *History*, 23; Lührmann, *Logienquelle*, 24–25. Dibelius (*Überlieferung*, 6) regarded 7:24–35 as a unit.

TABLE 1: Matthew 11:2–6 and Luke 7:18–23

| Matthew 11:2–6: Ὁ δὲ Ἰωάννης ἀκούσας ἐν τῷ δεσμωτηρίῳ τὰ ἔργα τοῦ Χριστοῦ πέμψας διὰ <u>τῶν μαθητῶν αὐτοῦ</u> (3) <u>εἶπεν αὐτῷ· σὺ εἶ ὁ ἐρχόμενος ἢ</u> ἕτερον <u>προσδοκῶμεν;</u> (4) <u>καὶ ἀποκριθεὶς ὁ Ἰησοῦς εἶπεν αὐτοῖς·</u> πορευθέντες ἀπαγγείλατε Ἰωάννῃ ἃ ἀκούετε <u>καὶ</u> βλέπετε· (5)<u>τυφλοὶ ἀναβλέπουσιν καὶ χωλοὶ περιπατοῦσιν, λεπροὶ καθαρίζονται καὶ κωφοὶ ἀκούουσιν, καὶ νεκροὶ ἐγείρονται καὶ πτωχοὶ εὐαγγελίζονται·</u> (6) <u>καὶ μακάριός ἐστιν ὃς ἐὰν μὴ σκανδαλισθῇ ἐν ἐμοί.</u> | Luke 7:18–23: Καὶ <u>ἀπήγγειλαν Ἰωάννῃ οἱ μαθηταὶ αὐτοῦ περὶ πάντων τούτων.</u> καὶ προσκαλεσάμενος δύο τινὰς <u>τῶν μαθητῶν αὐτοῦ ὁ Ἰωάννης</u> (19) ἔπεμψεν πρὸς τὸν κύριον λέγων· <u>σὺ εἶ ὁ ἐρχόμενος ἢ</u> ἄλλον <u>προσδοκῶμεν;</u> (20) παραγενόμενοι δὲ πρὸς αὐτὸν οἱ ἄνδρες εἶπαν· Ἰωάννης ὁ βαπτιστὴς ἀπέστειλεν ἡμᾶς πρὸς σὲ λέγων· σὺ εἶ ὁ ἐρχόμενος ἢ ἄλλον προσδοκῶμεν; (21) ἐν ἐκείνῃ τῇ ὥρᾳ ἐθεράπευσεν πολλοὺς ἀπὸ νόσων καὶ μαστίγων καὶ πνευμάτων πονηρῶν καὶ τυφλοῖς πολλοῖς ἐχαρίσατο βλέπειν. (22) <u>καὶ ἀποκριθεὶς εἶπεν αὐτοῖς·</u> πορευθέντες ἀπαγγείλατε Ἰωάννῃ ἃ εἴδετε <u>καὶ</u> ἠκούσατε· τυφλοὶ ἀναβλέπουσιν, χωλοὶ περιπατοῦσιν, λεπροὶ καθαρίζονται καὶ κωφοὶ ἀκούουσιν, νεκροὶ ἐγείρονται, πτωχοὶ εὐαγγελίζονται· (23) <u>καὶ μακάριός ἐστιν ὃς ἐὰν μὴ σκανδαλισθῇ ἐν ἐμοί.</u> |

In the first of these units (Matt 11:2–6 // Luke 7:18–23), the Baptist, evidently puzzled about the identity of Jesus, sends two of his disciples to inquire if he is "the one who is to come." Jesus replies by pointing to his healing and preaching ministry and with a beatitude. Although both passages are similar, the Lukan version contains a number of elements that are absent in the Matthean form. First, while Matthew mentions only that John in prison heard (ἀκούσας, 11:2) about "the works of Christ" (τὰ ἔργα τοῦ Χριστοῦ, 11:2), Luke points out that the disciples of the Baptist are the ones who bring him the news (ἀπήγγειλαν, 7:18) about all the things (περὶ πάντων τούτων, 7:18) that Jesus has done.[8] Second, Luke notes that John (repeating ὁ Ἰωάννης) summons two of his disciples (προσκαλεσάμενος δύο, 7:18) and sends them to the Lord (πρὸς τὸν κύριον, 7:19). Third, Luke mentions the arrival of John's mes-

---

8. Unlike Matthew (11:2), Luke does not mention John's imprisonment because he had already done so in 3:19–20.

sengers and repeats the question of the Baptist (7:20). Fourth, in 7:21 Luke relates that at that moment (ἐν ἐκείνῃ τῇ ὥρᾳ) Jesus healed a number of people of their infirmities. Because of these differences, the account in Luke is almost twice as long as that in Matthew and has more details.[9]

Although Matthew is certainly capable of abbreviating his sources and some modifications of the passage could be attributed to him, his version of the Baptist's question is usually regarded as more original than the version in Luke, who seems to have expanded the material to serve his theological interests.[10] Thus, the phrase τὰ ἔργα τοῦ Χριστοῦ probably represents Matthean redaction that reinterprets in a christological way the question of the Baptist: Jesus fulfills the prophetic promises through his teaching (Matt 5:1—7:29) and deeds (Matt 8:1—9:34) and so shows himself to be the expected Messiah.[11] But the use of προσκαλέω (Luke 15:26; 16:5; 18:16; Acts 2:39; 5:40; 6:2; 13:2, 7; 16:10; 23:17, 18, 23) and κύριος in verses 18-19 is considered typically Lukan. With the phrase περὶ πάντων τούτων (7:18), Luke connects the unit to the preceding material. The repetition of the Baptist's question in v. 20 is seen as part of Luke's stylistic tendency to repeat for dramatic effect (15:18, 21; 19:30-34). In addition, the verse shows signs of an editorial hand (e.g., παραγίνομαι, ἀνήρ, βαπτιστής).[12] Something similar can be said of verse 21, which fits Luke's style of providing summaries of healings (4:40; 5:15; 6:18) and includes a few expressions that seem to have come from his own hand (θεραπεύω ἀπό, χαρίζομαι).[13]

Except for the absence in Luke of ὁ Ἰησοῦς (Matt 11:4) and the mostly asyndetic form of the healings' list, Jesus' response to the dis-

9. Luke 7:18-23 has 103 words compared to 63 words in Matt 11:2-6. This word count includes every word form (including conjunctions and articles) and is based on the Greek text of Nestle-Aland *Novum Testamentum Graece*.

10. Dibelius, *Überlieferung*, 33 n. 1; Kümmel, *Jesu Antwort*, 25; Hoffmann, *Studien*, 192–93; Marshall, *Luke*, 289–92; Fitzmyer, *Luke*, 1:663–68; Sabugal, *Embajada*, 118–23; Ernst, *Johannes der Täufer*, 56–57; Backhaus, *Jüngerkreise*, 116; Robinson et al., *Critical Edition*, 118–26.

11. Hoffman, *Studien*, 191.

12. Some of the commentators who find Luke 7:20 redactional include Hoffmann, *Studien*, 192–93; Fitzmyer, *Luke*, 1:663; Nolland, *Luke*, 329. Others, however, consider the Lukan text more original: Marshall, *Luke*, 290; Schürmann, *Lukas*, 1:410 n. 18; Lührmann, *Logienquelle*, 26. Ernst (*Johannes der Täufer*, 57) notes the uncertainty in the discussion regarding the authenticity of the verse.

13. Marshall, *Luke*, 290–91.

ciples of John (Luke 7:22–23 // Matt 11:4–6) is almost identical in both Gospels. The only additional change is Luke's use of ὁράω instead of βλέπω and the reversal of the Matthean pair (i.e., ὁράω and ἀκούω instead of Matthew's ἀκούω and βλέπω). Whereas the sequence may have referred to Jesus' ministry in general in Matthew, in Luke the change corresponds to the deeds that the disciples of John have just witnessed and to the evangelist's interest in the works of Jesus.[14]

Changes like these may be nothing more than Lukan attempts to describe a better and more vivid portrayal of the episode—a case of *ekphrasis*.[15] These alterations are characteristics of an accomplished writer who knows how to make good use of his literary skills. However, through theses changes Luke has also achieved a number of narrative correspondences that have theological repercussions. Beyond the stylistic improvements that Luke's variations may represent, the real importance of the differences between him and Matthew lie in Luke's expansions, which are contrary to his general tendency to abbreviate entire scenes and even phrases from his sources.[16] Thus the repetition of the Baptist's question (7:19–20) underscores the issue of Jesus' identity, which, as we will see, forms a central concern of the Galilean ministry section (4:14—9:50). Moreover, the emphasis on the deeds performed by Jesus in verse 21 illustrates the program outlined in 4:18–19 and highlights Jesus' compassionate ministry.[17] This last feature points to an important Lukan motif: Jesus' special concern for the disadvantaged.[18] By focusing on the mighty works that Jesus performs the passage highlights a christological aspect that is related to the manner in which God brings salvation to the needy. Through this additional material (7:20–21) Luke addresses the concerns of John and his disciples by portraying Jesus as the healer of the sick—just as Jesus himself had anticipated (4:18–19).

---

14. Hoffmann, *Studien*, 193; Marshall, *Luke*, 291. Conzelmann (*Theology*, 192) notes that this difference may not be significant since both authors alter the order of this stock phrase in other parts of their respective Gospels (Matt 13:16; Acts 2:33; 4:20). However, several instances could indicate that for Luke "seeing" is more important than "hearing" (Luke 10:23; 19:37; Acts 2:7; 3:12; 4:12; 8:13; 13:12; 19:11; 22:14; 26:16). This may explain the significance that he attributes to Jesus' words and deeds.

15. Parsons, *Luke*, 17, 27.

16. Sanders, *Tendencies*, 82–87; Cadbury, "Lucan Style," 89.

17. Conzelmann, *Theology*, 191–92.

18. O'Toole, *Theology*, 109–48.

"This correspondence and repetition remind Luke's reader that Jesus is doing what he was anointed to do."[19]

Matt 11:7–15 and Luke 7:24–30

Table 2: Matthew 11:7–15 and Luke 7:24–30

| Matthew 11:7–15: Τούτων δὲ πορευομένων ἤρξατο ὁ Ἰησοῦς λέγειν τοῖς ὄχλοις περὶ Ἰωάννου· τί ἐξήλθατε εἰς τὴν ἔρημον θεάσασθαι; κάλαμον ὑπὸ ἀνέμου σαλευόμενον; (8) ἀλλὰ τί ἐξήλθατε ἰδεῖν; ἄνθρωπον ἐν μαλακοῖς ἠμφιεσμένον; ἰδοὺ οἱ τὰ μαλακὰ φοροῦντες ἐν τοῖς οἴκοις τῶν βασιλέων εἰσίν. (9) ἀλλὰ τί ἐξήλθατε ἰδεῖν; προφήτην; ναὶ λέγω ὑμῖν, καὶ περισσότερον προφήτου. (10) οὗτός ἐστιν περὶ οὗ γέγραπται· ἰδοὺ ἐγὼ ἀποστέλλω τὸν ἄγγελόν μου πρὸ προσώπου σου, ὃς κατασκευάσει τὴν ὁδόν σου ἔμπροσθέν σου. (11) Ἀμὴν λέγω ὑμῖν οὐκ ἐγήγερται ἐν γεννητοῖς γυναικῶν μείζων Ἰωάννου τοῦ βαπτιστοῦ· ὁ δὲ μικρότερος ἐν τῇ βασιλείᾳ τῶν οὐρανῶν μείζων αὐτοῦ ἐστιν. (12) ἀπὸ δὲ τῶν ἡμερῶν Ἰωάννου τοῦ βαπτιστοῦ ἕως ἄρτι ἡ βασιλεία τῶν οὐρανῶν βιάζεται καὶ βιασταὶ ἁρπάζουσιν αὐτήν. (13) πάντες γὰρ οἱ προφῆται καὶ ὁ νόμος ἕως Ἰωάννου ἐπροφήτευσαν· (14) καὶ εἰ θέλετε δέξασθαι αὐτός ἐστιν Ἡλίας ὁ μέλλων ἔρχεσθαι. (15) ὁ ἔχων ὦτα ἀκουέτω. | Luke 7:24–30: Ἀπελθόντων δὲ τῶν ἀγγέλων Ἰωάννου ἤρξατο λέγειν πρὸς τοὺς ὄχλους περὶ Ἰωάννου· τί ἐξήλθατε εἰς τὴν ἔρημον θεάσασθαι; κάλαμον ὑπὸ ἀνέμου σαλευόμενον; (25) ἀλλὰ τί ἐξήλθατε ἰδεῖν; ἄνθρωπον ἐν μαλακοῖς ἱματίοις ἠμφιεσμένον; ἰδοὺ οἱ ἐν ἱματισμῷ ἐνδόξῳ καὶ τρυφῇ ὑπάρχοντες ἐν τοῖς βασιλείοις εἰσίν. (26) ἀλλὰ τί ἐξήλθατε ἰδεῖν; προφήτην; ναὶ λέγω ὑμῖν, καὶ περισσότερον προφήτου. (27) οὗτός ἐστιν περὶ οὗ γέγραπται· ἰδοὺ ἀποστέλλω τὸν ἄγγελόν μου πρὸ προσώπου σου, ὃς κατασκευάσει τὴν ὁδόν σου ἔμπροσθέν σου. (28) λέγω ὑμῖν, μείζων ἐν γεννητοῖς γυναικῶν Ἰωάννου οὐδείς ἐστιν· ὁ δὲ μικρότερος ἐν τῇ βασιλείᾳ τοῦ θεοῦ μείζων αὐτοῦ ἐστιν. (29) Καὶ πᾶς ὁ λαὸς ἀκούσας καὶ οἱ τελῶναι ἐδικαίωσαν τὸν θεὸν βαπτισθέντες τὸ βάπτισμα Ἰωάννου· (30) οἱ δὲ Φαρισαῖοι καὶ οἱ νομικοὶ τὴν βουλὴν τοῦ θεοῦ ἠθέτησαν εἰς ἑαυτοὺς μὴ βαπτισθέντες ὑπ' αὐτοῦ. |

In the next subunit (Matt 11:7–11 // Luke 7:24–30) other examples show how Matthew and Luke have appropriated the tradition about John and Jesus. In this unit, both evangelists feature three rhetorical questions that Jesus asks the crowd, each of which emphasizes the lifestyle of the

---

19. Ibid., 127.

Baptist and Jesus' esteem for him. Once again, there are differences as well as striking similarities between the two passages.

While Matthew narrates without further detail the departure of John's emissaries (τούτων δὲ πορευομένων, 11:7), Luke specifies that it is after the "messengers of John depart" (ἀπελθόντων δὲ τῶν ἀγγέλων Ἰωάννου, 7:24) that Jesus begins to speak to the crowds. Luke, however, lacks Matthew's ὁ Ἰησοῦς and uses a preposition with the accusative plural (πρὸς τοὺς ὄχλους, 7:24) instead of Matthew's dative of interest (τοῖς ὄχλοις) to refer to the people. From the rhetorical questions of Jesus until the scriptural citation (Matt 11:7b–10 // Luke 7:24b–27), both passages have identical wording except for the reference to John's clothing and the absence of the emphatic ἐγώ, in Luke's quotation of Malachi. In reference to John's clothing, Luke uses the cognates ἱμάτιον and ἱματισμός to refer to the attire of those who live in palaces. He also varies Matthew's double combination of μαλακός plus participles (ἠμφιεσμένον, φοροῦντες) with another dative construction (ἐν ἱματισμῷ ἐνδόξῳ). Luke's form includes a note about the luxury (τρυφῇ ὑπάρχοντες) of the palaces, lacks Matthew's οἴκοις, and uses βασίλειος ("royal") in the dative instead of βασιλέων (king) in the genitive plural.

Each evangelist formulates Jesus' antithetic parallelism concerning the greatness of John (Matt 11:11 // Luke 7:28) in slightly different terms. Matthew includes the title τοῦ βαπτιστοῦ and underscores the position of John "among those born of women" with a solemn ἀμήν using the perfect οὐκ ἐγήγερται. These elements are absent from Luke, who with the same phraseology, although in a different word order, refers to the status of John by using the present οὐδείς ἐστιν instead of οὐκ ἐγήγερται. In the second part of the parallelism (Matt 11:11b // Luke 7:28b), the only difference is that Matthew uses τῶν οὐρανῶν in referring to the kingdom and Luke uses τοῦ θεοῦ.

Some of the differences between Matt 11:7–11 and Luke 7:24–28 involve minutiae that scarcely affect the meaning of the passage. There are minor variations in word order, changes in the cases of nouns, and differences in the transitional clause at the beginning of the unit in both passages (τούτων δὲ πορευομένων, Matt 11:7 // ἀπελθόντων δὲ τῶν ἀγγέλων Ἰωάννου, Luke 7:24).[20] Again, a few of these incidental differ-

---

20. Here, Luke is usually regarded as less original than Matthew (Fitzmyer, *Luke*, 1:673). Lührmann (*Logienquelle*, 25) considers this transitional phrase redactional in both evangelists.

ences could be attributed to the way in which Matthew and Luke have reworked some of their source material. But others suggest that in some small way Matthew and Luke may have been actively editing their source. For instance, the use of ἱμάτιον, ἱματισμός, ἔνδοξος, and ὑπάρχω are considered typically Lukan language.[21] Likewise τρυφή and βασίλειος, which accentuate a lavish lifestyle in contrast to the austerity of John the Baptist, could very well be attributed to Luke, who is interested in the theme of wealth and riches.[22] In fact, some redactional changes in the previous units suggest that Luke may have been accentuating this motif. According to Robert A. J. Gagnon, some of the redactional changes in 7:1–10 may have been intended as a reproach against the wealthy members of the community who used riches for power and prestige.[23] Finally, although the emphatic ἐγώ (Matt 11:10) may have been a Matthean addition, the lack of the solemn ἀμήν (Matt 11:11) is commonly attributed to a Lukan omission.[24]

The effect of these minor changes is twofold. On the one hand, the additions subtly underline an important aspect of Lukan theology: the proper use of material possessions. And on the other hand, the absence of certain expressions (e.g., τοῦ βαπτιστοῦ, ἐγώ, ἀμήν) tend to undercut the formality with which Jesus refers to John and the prominence of the Baptist.

The differences between Matthew and Luke in the verses that follow (Matt 11:12–15 and Luke 7:29–30) show more clearly the extent to which each evangelist has stamped his distinctive theological perspective in the redaction of his source. Whereas in the Gospel of Matthew the testimony of Jesus about John is followed by the words about the kingdom and the identification of the Baptist with Elijah (Matt 11:12–15),

---

21. Marshall, *Luke*, 294.

22. Nolland, "Money and Possessions" 178–93; Karris, "Poor and Rich," 112–25; Schmidt, *Hostility to Wealth*, 135–62; Fitzmyer, *Luke*, 1:247–51.

23. Gagnon, "Double Delegation," 142–43.

24. Although the first part of 7:27 (Matt 11:10) is a conflation of Mal 3:1 and Exod 23:20 (LXX), Luke's agreement with Mark 1:2 suggests for some that Matthew has added the emphatic ἐγώ (Marshall, *Luke*, 295; Bovon, *Luke 1*, 279). Others consider it a Lukan omission (Ernst, *Johannes der Täufer*, 61; Robinson et al., *Critical Edition*, 134–35). Nolland (*Luke*, 337) suggests that the absence of the emphatic ἐγώ makes the christological reference clearer. Some of those who see the ἀμήν as a Matthean addition include Hoffman, *Studien*, 194; Fitzmyer, *Luke*, 1:675; Nolland, *Luke*, 337. It is considered a Lukan omission by Marshall, *Luke*, 296; and Bovon, *Luke 1*, 279.

Luke follows his statement with a redactional variation that highlights the diversity of the Jews' responses to the ministry of John (7:29–30). Both passages are instrumental in the configuration of the traditional material's function within their literary context.

Matthew 11:12–15 identifies John and his role in proclaiming the kingdom of heaven.[25] Some of these verses (Matt 11:12–13) can be found in another context within the Lukan Gospel (16:16), but nowhere in Luke is there an exact equivalent to Matt 11:14 (cf. Luke 1:17). Despite its interpretative difficulties, Matt 11:12–15 underlines the struggle involved in the advent of the kingdom of heaven and highlights the prominent role of the Baptist in a period dominated by the Law and the Prophets.[26] In Matthew, the proclamation of the kingdom of heaven is central to Jesus' message.[27] At the same time, the theme of the kingdom of heaven is intimately related to two other concepts: the greater righteousness that the disciples of Jesus must observe (5:20) and Jesus' interpretation of the Law and the Prophets (5:17–19).[28] Through the verbal identification associated with the proclamation of the kingdom of heaven (i.e., μετανοεῖτε· ἤγγικεν γὰρ ἡ βασιλεία τῶν οὐρανῶν, 3:2; 4:17), Matthew heightens the relationship between the ministries

---

25. Hoffman (*Studien*, 191) considers Matt 11:12–15 an insertion. For Fitzmyer (*Luke*, 1:662–63), Matt 11:12–13 probably comes from Q, while vv. 14–15 are Matthean additions.

26. The disputed phrase βιάζεται καὶ βιασταὶ ἁρπάζουσιν αὐτήν complicates the interpretation of the passage. In its present context, these words could refer to the arrest of the Baptist (11:2) and the hostility faced by Jesus; see Nolland, *Matthew*, 457–59; Reid, "Violent Endings," 239–40; Moore, "ΒΙΑΖΩ, ΑΡΠΑΖΩ," 519–43; France, *Matthew*, 429–32; Davies and Allison, *Matthew*, 2:252–59.

27. Matthew employs the phrase "kingdom of heaven" (32 times) more often than the "kingdom of God," (5 times). Matthew also has a more extensive presentation of the kingdom (50 times) than either Mark (14 times) or Luke (39 times). (The Gospel of John refers to kingdom only 5 times.) Luke prefers "kingdom of God" to the "kingdom of heaven," which he never uses (see Caragounis, "Kingdom," 425–29; McKnight, "Matthew," 537). The phrase "kingdom of heaven" is probably a Semitic circumlocution for "kingdom of God," which would have been in use in the Matthean community to avoid using the holy name (Luz, *Matthew 1–7*, 167). However, Foster ("Kingdom of Heaven," 499) has argued that: "KH [Kingdom of Heaven] was part of Matthew's overall rhetorical and sociological strategy to reassure his readers that they were the true people of God and to undermine the criticism of the leaders of formative Judaism by impugning their character and their relationship to God."

28. Matera, *Theology*, 28–36.

of John and Jesus.²⁹ Thus, in 11:2–19 Matthew reiterates not only the connection between John and Jesus but also their relationship to the concepts of righteousness, the kingdom of heaven, and the Law and the Prophets.³⁰ By doing so, Matthew expands on the importance of John in relation to these notions of salvation history (3:2; 21:32) and links the passage to other parts of the Gospel that deal with these concepts. In 11:2–19, Matthew presents John as an important transitional prophet who precedes the inauguration of the kingdom of heaven.³¹ Within this context the role of John reaches its climax because he is identified in his function and significance as the link between Israel and the kingdom of God. "As Elijah-who-has-returned John is, as it were, the personified continuity between the kingdom of God and the prophets of Israel who prophesied about Jesus."³²

Furthermore, in these verses the question of John about "the one who is to come" (ὁ ἐρχόμενος, 11:3) at the beginning of the pericope receives a different interpretation. In Matt 11:14, Jesus refers to the Baptist as Elijah, "the one who is to come" (ὁ μέλλων ἔρχεσθαι). By identifying John in this way, Jesus reverses the question of the Baptist and casts him in the role of Elijah *redivivus*.³³ Although this sense is also implicit in Luke's use of the Malachi prophecy in 7:27, in Matthew's Gospel this claim is explicit and becomes a key element of the passage.³⁴ Through this reversal of roles, John appears here, more clearly than in Luke, as the precursor of the Lord. John is Elijah *redivivus*, "something greater than a prophet." This emphasis on John's role in the development of salvation history makes his character a dominant figure, next to Jesus, within

---

29. Ibid., 28.

30. In 11:2–19, the idea of righteousness is implicit in the ascetic portrayal of the Baptist.

31. McKnight, "Matthew," 537.

32. Luz, *Matthew 8–20*, 142.

33. Fitzmyer, *Theologian*, 97–99; 109; Robinson, "Elijah, John, and Jesus," 266–67. Although Faierstein ("Elijah Must Come First," 75–86) has claimed that, contrary to contemporary scholarly opinion, the concept of Elijah as forerunner of the Messiah was not widely known or accepted in the first century AD, Allison, ("Elijah Must Come First," 256–58) has contended that the expectation may have been indeed current in first-century Judaism.

34. According to Wink (*John the Baptist*, 43–45), Luke has divested John of the role of Elijah *redivivus* and instead has felt free to compare Jesus to Elijah. It is possible, however, that Luke would have felt no need to repeat the statement about Elijah because he had already suggested it in 1:17 (ἐν πνεύματι καὶ δυνάμει Ἠλίου).

The Origin, Redaction, and Literary Function of Luke 7:18–35

the pericope. More than in Luke's account, this episode highlights *the Baptist's role* within Matthew's presentation of the kingdom of heaven.[35] As Nolland points out: "For Matthew, John is a transitional figure who in important ways stands shoulder to shoulder with Jesus in working for God in bringing in the coming of the kingdom: both John and Jesus are preachers of the kingdom, and a brutal fate awaits both at the hands of the governing authorities."[36] Matthew attributes more importance than Luke to the relationship of John the Baptist to the kingdom of heaven and to the role that he plays as an Elijah-like figure who acts as the precursor of Jesus. Through these verses Matthew prepares the narrative for the announcement of judgment in 11:16–24.[37] Furthermore, by placing the verses that deal with the relationship of John to the kingdom of heaven in this context, Matthew sets the stage for Jesus' key explanation of the kingdom in the parable discourse of chapter 13.

As noted above, Matthew's statements in 11:12–15 are absent from Luke 7:18–35. The Lukan parallel to Matt 11:12–15 is found in a different context (Luke 16:16). The discussion about whether the original location of these verses was in the Matthean or Lukan sequence is a matter of debate.[38] Although a full discussion of the authenticity of their original context would take us beyond the scope of the present analysis, I will make some observations to show how differently Luke has used this material.

In Luke, the statement about the Law, the Prophets, and John (Matt 11:12–15 // Luke 16:16) appears in the section that recounts Jesus' journey to Jerusalem (9:51—19:46). Within this section of the Lukan Gospel, which consists of sayings and deeds of Jesus, the remark about the Baptist is one of four short sayings dealing with the themes of wealth and the Law (16:14–18). In these verses, Jesus reproaches the avarice and hypocrisy of the Pharisees (16:14–15), upholds the relevance of the Law (16:16–17), and warns against divorce and adultery (16:18). In comparison to Matt 11:12–15, the Lukan statement about the Baptist appears with essentially the same idea, but more condensed and in a different

---

35. Luz, *Matthew 1–7*, 41.
36. Nolland, *Matthew*, 457.
37. Luz, *Matthew 8–20*, 142.
38. For a full discussion of these parallel passages, see Hoffmann, *Studien*, 50–79; Ernst, *Johannes der Täufer*, 63–72; for a brief but helpful survey of contemporary scholarly opinions, see also Kloppenborg, *Q Parallels*, 56.

order. The following table shows the differences and similarities between Matt 11:12–15 and Luke 16:16:

TABLE 3: Matthew 11:12–15 and Luke 16:16

Matthew 11:12–15: ἀπὸ δὲ τῶν ἡμερῶν Ἰωάννου τοῦ βαπτιστοῦ ἕως ἄρτι ἡ βασιλεία τῶν οὐρανῶν βιάζεται καὶ βιασταὶ ἁρπάζουσιν αὐτήν. (13) πάντες γὰρ οἱ προφῆται καὶ ὁ νόμος ἕως Ἰωάννου ἐπροφήτευσαν· (14) καὶ εἰ θέλετε δέξασθαι αὐτός ἐστιν Ἠλίας ὁ μέλλων ἔρχεσθαι. (15) ὁ ἔχων ὦτα ἀκουέτω.	Luke 16:16: Ὁ νόμος καὶ οἱ προφῆται μέχρι Ἰωάννου· ἀπὸ τότε ἡ βασιλεία τοῦ θεοῦ εὐαγγελίζεται καί πᾶς εἰς αὐτὴν βιάζεται.

Since the connection of thought in this part of the travel account is far from obvious, many scholars posit that Luke, in following his source, has introduced 16:16–18 into an alien context.[39] By placing the statement about the Baptist within this setting, Luke puts more emphasis on the ongoing importance of the Law than on John himself. Thus, in contrast to Matthew 11:12–15, Luke 16:16 has a significantly different meaning and function. The focus is not so much on John as on the role of the Law itself. As Marshall points out: "Luke's purpose is to underline the fact that the Pharisees—and the disciples—still stand under the law."[40]

Instead of placing the statement of 16:16 after Jesus' remarks regarding the importance of John (7:24–28), Luke follows it with a commentary about the acceptance of the baptism of John by the people and toll collectors and the rejection of God's plan by the religious leaders (7:29–30).[41] In these verses, Luke underscores that the ministry of the

---

39. Marshall, *Luke*, 624–25; 626–27.

40. Ibid., 626.

41. It is debated whether these verses belong to Q or are part of Luke's *Sondergut* (L) (Kloppenborg, *Q Parallels*, 58, n. on 7:29–30). While some hesitate to attribute these verses to Q because they find no specific counterpart in Matthew (Fitzmyer, *Luke*, 1:670–71), others consider it similar to Matt 21:31b–32 (Bultmann, *History*, 23). For Meier (*Marginal Jew*, 167–70) they are part of a "strayed tradition." If the verses belong to Q, Luke has modified them, because traces of his redactional tendencies are present. For instance, in 7:29 Luke points out that "everyone" (πᾶς) was baptized, a sign of a Lukan tendency used in previous parts of the Gospel (e.g., 3:7, 10) (Conzelmann, *Theology*, 21; Cadbury, *Luke-Acts*, 216). In addition, the relationship of 7:29–30 to 7:24–28 is problematic. While some see the verses as part of Jesus' ongoing speech (Schürmann, *Lukasevangelium*, 422), most regard them as a narrative aside (Sheeley, *Narrative Asides*, 114–15).

Baptist has been vindicated by "all the people," who accepted the baptism of John. By virtue of the extended parallel that Luke has established thus far in the narrative between John and Jesus (Luke 1:5—2:52)—a parallel that will be affirmed in the parable of the children in the marketplace (7:31-35)—this vindication extends also to Jesus. By contrast, the Pharisees and the scholars of the Law have frustrated God's plan by not accepting the baptism of John. These remarks serve as an indictment against the religious leaders for having rejected John's (and so Jesus') offer of salvation.

With 7:29-30 Luke summarizes the plot of the previous narrative that relates that many people have responded positively to the message of Jesus while the religious leaders have opposed his ministry. Moreover, Luke uses these verses as a bridge to the following parable of the children in the marketplace (7:31-35), which functions as a further indictment against the "people of this generation."[42] Luke's inclusion of this material adds a distinct nuance to the previous statements about John the Baptist (7:18-28). Whereas in Matthew the concept of the "kingdom of heaven" prevails in the verses following Jesus' praise of the Baptist, in Luke the "plan of God" has a more important function.[43] Here Luke's key phrase "the plan of God" appears for the first time. More importantly, the phrase appears within the context of the opposition presented by the Pharisees and the scholars of the Law. This initial and explicit acknowledgement of the opposition to the plan of God shapes the thrust of the narrative in the subsequent chapters, in which Jesus faces increasing rejection from the religious leaders.

In these verses another important aspect is underscored: the freedom to respond to the will of God. As Squire notes: "[T]he freedom of the human will is asserted in the very same phrase as the plan of God is introduced, and thus it is absolutely clear that Luke is not utilizing a notion of an inexorable and inevitable Fate."[44] Although the kingdom is an essential element of the salvific plan of God, Luke does not emphasize the intimate connection between these concepts in 7:29-30.

---

42. Lührmann, *Logienquelle*, 28.

43. The "plan of God" plays an important role in the Gospel of Luke. See Matera, *Theology*, 56–57; Fitzmyer, *Luke*, 1:179–81; O'Toole, *Theology*, 26–28; Squires, *Plan of God*, 180–81.

44. Squires, *Plan of God*, 180.

Through these statements (7:29–30), Luke shifts the focus of the passage from the Baptist to the Jews' response to the plan of God as it is manifested through the ministry of John. Although John remains an important character in the unit, his role becomes secondary to the theme of the people's reaction to the plan of God.[45] From the perspective of the ensuing narrative, the response of the people prepares the atmosphere for the mounting opposition that Jesus will face in subsequent chapters. As Fitzmyer notes: "Their reaction provides the background to judge that of the Pharisees and the lawyers. Thus, Luke begins to pit the authorities in Israel over against the masses of the people and those who are not so highly regarded."[46] Luke makes the function of the Baptist subsidiary and the passage begins to shape the growing conflict that will unfold in the rest of the story. With this material Luke reconfigures the tradition and puts greater emphasis on the response of the people to God's divine purpose of salvation. The role of the Baptist begins to fade even as it retains a measure of importance. While Matt 11:12–15 explicitly makes John Elijah *redivivus*, "the one who is to come," Luke's supplementary material makes the reception of the Baptist's and Jesus' ministries the primary focus of the developing narrative. Both Matt 11:12–15 and Luke 7:29–30 "prepare and intensify" the accusation against the "people of this generation," but in Matthew the function of the Baptist is more crucial than in Luke.[47]

---

45. According to Conzelmann (*Theology*, 25–26), Luke creates a tension by trying to adapt the tradition about the Baptist as the precursor of the kingdom of God to his own limited portrayal of the Baptist as a preacher of repentance. He notes that this Lukan concern is also present in Acts 1:5; 10:37; 11:16; 13:23–25; 18:24—19:7. However, Conzelmann's denial of the Baptist's role as precursor and his claim that in 7:28–30 John becomes the "greatest prophet" have been corrected with greater precision by Fitzmyer (*Theologian*, 108–9): John *is* portrayed as the precursor of the Lord.

46. Fitzmyer, *Luke*, 1:673.

47. Luz (*Matthew 8–20*, 129) highlights John's crucial role when he says, "Israel rejects its own Elijah just as it does Jesus."

Matt 11:16-19 and Luke 7:31-35

TABLE 4: Matthew 11:16-19 and Luke 7:31-35

Matthew 11:16-19: Τίνι δὲ ὁμοιώσω τὴν γενεὰν ταύτην; ὁμοία ἐστὶν παιδίοις καθημένοις ἐν ταῖς ἀγοραῖς ἃ προσφωνοῦντα τοῖς ἑτέροις (17) λέγουσιν· ηὐλήσαμεν ὑμῖν καὶ οὐκ ὠρχήσασθε, ἐθρηνήσαμεν καὶ οὐκ ἐκόψασθε. (18) ἦλθεν γὰρ Ἰωάννης μήτε ἐσθίων μήτε πίνων, καὶ λέγουσιν· δαιμόνιον ἔχει. (19) ἦλθεν ὁ υἱὸς τοῦ ἀνθρώπου ἐσθίων καὶ πίνων, καὶ λέγουσιν· ἰδοὺ ἄνθρωπος φάγος καὶ οἰνοπότης, τελωνῶν φίλος καὶ ἁμαρτωλῶν. καὶ ἐδικαιώθη ἡ σοφία ἀπὸ τῶν ἔργων αὐτῆς.	Luke 7:31-35: Τίνι οὖν ὁμοιώσω τοὺς ἀνθρώπους τῆς γενεᾶς ταύτης καὶ τίνι εἰσὶν ὅμοιοι; (32) ὅμοιοί εἰσιν παιδίοις τοῖς ἐν ἀγορᾷ καθημένοις καὶ προσφωνοῦσιν ἀλλήλοις ἃ λέγει, ηὐλήσαμεν ὑμῖν καὶ οὐκ ὠρχήσασθε, ἐθρηνήσαμεν καὶ οὐκ ἐκλαύσατε. (33) ἐλήλυθεν γὰρ Ἰωάννης ὁ βαπτιστὴς μὴ ἐσθίων ἄρτον μήτε πίνων οἶνον, καὶ λέγετε, δαιμόνιον ἔχει. (34) ἐλήλυθεν ὁ υἱὸς τοῦ ἀνθρώπου ἐσθίων καὶ πίνων, καὶ λέγετε, ἰδοὺ ἄνθρωπος φάγος καὶ οἰνοπότης, φίλος τελωνῶν καὶ ἁμαρτωλῶν. (35) καὶ ἐδικαιώθη ἡ σοφία ἀπὸ πάντων τῶν τέκνων αὐτῆς.

In the parable of the children in the marketplace (Matt 11:16-19 // Luke 7:31-35), the fourth and final subunit of this pericope, there are further differences between the two passages. In this subunit, Jesus compares "the people of this generation" with hard-to-please children who are satisfied neither by the actions of John nor by those of Jesus. Despite the criticism of their adversaries, Jesus proclaims their mutual vindication by "the children of wisdom." As in the two previous units, while the similarities between both passages are substantial, there are a number of differences.[48]

Both evangelists begin their introductory phrase (Matt 11:16 // Luke 7:31) with the interrogative pronoun τίνι, but whereas Matthew follows it with the coordinating conjunction δέ Luke uses οὖν. While Matthew uses only τὴν γενεὰν ταύτην as the object of ὁμοιόω Luke employs τοὺς ἀνθρώπους τῆς γενεᾶς ταύτης. Luke also adds the coordinating clause καὶ τίνι εἰσὶν ὅμοιοι. While Matthew uses the plural ἐν ταῖς ἀγοραῖς (11:16b) to allude to marketplaces, Luke employs the singular (ἐν ἀγορᾷ, 7:32a). In this portion of the verse the word order also varies as each evangelist formulates his statements with differ-

---

48. One such difference is the number of words: 65 in Matt 11:16-19 and 76 in Luke 7:31-35.

ent participial forms as required by the syntax (προσφωνοῦντα, Matt 11:16; προσφωνοῦσιν, Luke 7:32).

In the same verse (Matt 11:16 // Luke 7:32), Luke uses the article τοῖς to refer to the children sitting in the marketplace, while Matthew uses ἅ to refer to παιδίοις. Whereas Luke introduces the children's complaints with the relative clause ἃ λέγει Matthew does so through λέγουσιν.[49] Moreover, Luke expresses the children's reciprocal exchange with ἀλλήλοις while Matthew uses τοῖς ἑτέροις. The grievance of the children is identical except for Matthew's use of ἐκόψασθε, whereas Luke uses ἐκλαύσατε.[50] Jesus' justification for making the analogy (Matt 11:18-19a // Luke 7:33-34) has the same meaning for both evangelists, but a few differences in wording are obvious. First, Luke uses the perfect ἐλήλυθεν in both verses instead of Matthew's aorist ἦλθεν. Second, the Lukan version has three additional nouns ὁ βαπτιστής, ἄρτος, and οἶνος. Third, the double use of the second-person plural (λέγετε) in Luke (instead of Matthew's λέγουσιν) transforms Jesus' statement into a direct address. Fourth, Luke uses μή once instead of Matthew's double μήτε. Fifth, each evangelist has the phrase φίλος τελωνῶν in a different order. Sixth, Luke has πάντων τῶν τέκνων in the final verse whereas Matthew uses τῶν ἔργων.

Some of these differences, such as word order, verb tense, or variations in small particles, can be attributed to the way in which each evangelist has adapted the source material. These may be no more than stylistic improvements without a deliberate editorial purpose.[51] However, some of these details give each passage a distinct nuance and may reflect the manner in which each evangelist has handled the tradition.[52] While the double introductory question (τίνι οὖν ὁμοιώσω... καὶ τίνι εἰσὶν

---

49. Marshall (*Luke*, 300) considers τοῖς a Lukan addition.

50. According to Marshall (ibid., 300) "[M]ore probably Luke has avoided a Palestinian expression referring to the passionate beating of the breast in favour of one more typical of Hellenistic custom."

51. This could be the case, for instance, with Luke's use of ἐλήλυθεν instead of ἦλθεν. Bultmann (*History*, 155, 165) has taken the change as the product of a post-Easter community. It is hard to decide whether the aorist or the perfect is the original form (Nolland, *Luke*, 345); ἐλήλυθεν is secondary for Hoffman, *Studien*, 197; Ernst, *Johannes der Täufer*, 72-73; Robinson et al., *Critical Edition*, 144-47; Marshall, *Luke*, 301.

52. Although some of these differences are indeed minor, they are not, as Lührmann (*Logienquelle*, 29) notes, inconsequential.

ὅμοιοι, 7:31) is usually considered original,[53] the phrase προσφωνοῦσιν ἀλλήλοις ἃ λέγει (7:32) is regarded as secondary.[54] Some commentators view John's title ὁ βαπτιστής and the two objects ἄρτον and οἶνον as Lukan expansions.[55] The title and the objects add greater clarity and precision to the narration. Moreover, Luke's use of the second person (λέγετε) instead of Matthew's third person (λέγουσιν) makes the Lord's summary of the opponents' accusations a direct address, which presumes that those who levy the charges against the Baptist and Jesus are among the audience.[56]

Luke's use of the singular ἐν ἀγορᾷ instead of the plural ἐν ταῖς ἀγοραῖς allows Jesus' remarks to be interpreted as referring to a specific location.[57] The use of τοὺς ἀνθρώπους (7:31) and τοῖς (7:32; i.e., children, namely "the ones who"), which gives Jesus' criticism of his adversaries a personal dimension, are probably Luke's improvements.[58] It is possible that Matthew's use of ἔργον rather than τέκνον was a deliberate attempt to harmonize the concluding verse with ἔργον in Matt 11:2.[59] If so, Luke has maintained the more natural form of the closing phrase (7:35), which, as a final vindication of John and Jesus, emphasizes the behavior of the children (τέκνα) of wisdom over against that of the capricious children (παιδία) of the marketplace.

---

53. Bultmann, *History*, 172; Hoffmann, *Studien*, 196; Fitzmyer, *Luke*, 1:678.

54. Bovon, *Luke 1*, 280; Fitzmyer, *Luke*, 1:678; Backhaus, *Jüngerkreise*, 69; Robinson et al., *Critical Edition*, 142–43; Nolland, *Luke*, 343. However, for Hoffmann (*Studien*, 197) the *lectio difficilior* (i.e., προσφωνοῦσιν ἀλλήλοις ἃ λέγει) in Luke is to be preferred as the original reading.

55. Hoffmann, *Studien*, 196; Marshall, *Luke*, 301; Fitzmyer, *Luke*, 1:678; Klein, *Lukasevangelium*, 287 n. 6.

56. Some consider λέγετε Lukan (Fitzmyer, *Luke*, 1:678; Nolland, *Luke*, 345); others regard it as original (Schürmann, *Lukasevangelium*, 426 n. 132; Robinson et al., *Critical Edition*, 144–47; Ernst, *Johannes der Täufer*, 73).

57. Probably a Lukan improvement (Marshall, *Luke*, 300; Fitzmyer, *Luke*, 1:678; Robinson et al., *Critical Edition*, 142–43). ἐν ἀγορᾷ is authentic for Hoffmann, *Studien*, 196–97; Schürmann, *Lukasevangelium*, 423 n. 114; Ernst, *Johannes der Täufer*, 72.

58. Marshall (*Luke*, 300) also points out that τοὺς ἀνθρώπους stresses the "serious situation of *men* who behave no better than *children*." The personal dimension of τοὺς ἀνθρώπους is highlighted by O'Toole (*Theology*, 167–68, 172); see also Schürmann, *Lukasevangelium*, 423 n. 112; Hoffmann, *Studien*, 196 n. 28.

59. Fitzmyer, *Luke*, 1:681; Schürmann, *Lukasevangelium*, 428; Hoffmann, *Studien*, 197–98.

Although the meaning of the Matthean and the Lukan versions of this unit is essentially the same, the differences in Luke contribute to a more vivid, personal, and engaging account. Whereas in the preceding verses Matthew emphasizes the role of the Baptist (11:12–15) and Luke underscores the response of the Jews (7:29–30), here both evangelists focus on the reaction of the adversaries of John and Jesus, both of whom stand together against the "people of this generation."[60] But Luke's use of the second person plural makes it a direct address and a better indicator of how it is meant to supplement the preceding indictment against the Pharisees and the scholars of the Law (29–30). Jesus is no longer just talking about what others have said regarding John and himself, he is addressing those who have raised similar accusations. The shift of focus from the Baptist to the response of the Jews highlighted in 7:29–30 remains the chief concern of the narrative here. The transition of the Baptist to a supportive role continues, and he no longer dominates the plot of the scene.

Conclusion

This comparison between the Matt 11:2–19 and the Luke 7:18–35 has shown that there are remarkable similarities between both passages. Not surprisingly, many scholars have seen a common source behind these mutual agreements.[61] Yet despite these verbal similarities there are important differences. As the different opinion of scholars shows, it is not always easy to account for these differences. They may have been the result of intentional editorial activity or the unintentional freedom with which each evangelist redacted the traditional material. Some of them are irrelevant for the interpretation of the passage and may be more important for the history of the transmission of the traditional material than for the meaning of the pericope. But others have certain functional and/or theological significance. My analysis suggests this possibility. Although the aim of the comparison between Matthew and Luke is not to determine which of the two has omitted or added this or that word or

---

60. Lührmann, *Logienquelle*, 29.

61. An exact parallel occurs in the final remark of Jesus to the messengers of the Baptist (Matt 11:6 // Luke 7:23) and in the first two questions of Jesus to the crowd up to the description of the Baptist's attire (Matt 11:7b–8b // Luke 7:24b–25b). An almost exact parallel (except for the absence of the emphatic ἐγώ in Luke) appears in the Scripture quotation (Matt 11:10 // Luke 7:27).

The Origin, Redaction, and Literary Function of Luke 7:18–35

phrase, it is worth noting that a significant number of scholars consider much of the extra material in Luke to be the result of his redactional activity.

The analysis has shown that the Lukan passage is significantly longer than Matthew's—there are 305 words in the Lukan version compared to 265 words in Matthew. This expansion of Lukan material has a number of theological repercussions. First, the repetition of the Baptist's question (7:19–20) and the enhanced narration of the mighty works performed by Jesus (7:21) highlight the issues of his identity and the nature of his mission. Second, the differences between Matt 11:7–11 and Luke 7:24–28 underline Luke's concern about material wealth and lessen the solemnity of Jesus' declaration about the Baptist. Third, the material in Matt 11:12–15 and Luke 7:29–30 is quite different and modifies the meaning and focus of each pericope. In Matthew the reinterpretation of the Baptist as an Elijah-like figure heightens the role of John in the manifestation of the kingdom of heaven.[62] In Luke the remarks of Jesus about the mixed response of the Jews to God's gracious offer of salvation through John functions as an indictment against the religious leaders as representatives of those who reject the will of God. Fourth, Luke's version of the parable of the children in the marketplace (7:31–35) becomes a direct address intended to supplement the previous verses (7:29–30).

To summarize, while the figure of John the Baptist plays a prominent role in both passages, his function is more dominant in Matthew than in Luke, particularly in the central statements (11:12–15) regarding the relationship of John to the kingdom of heaven. This feature is absent in Luke, who instead emphasizes the identity of Jesus (7:20), his special concern for the needy (7:21), and his reproach of the religious leaders for their rejection of God's plan of salvation manifested in the parallel ministries of John and Jesus (7:29–35).

THE LITERARY CONTEXT OF LUKE 7:18–35

According to the Gospel of Luke, the question of John the Baptist and the indictment against the religious leaders (7:18–35) appears in the section on Jesus' Galilean ministry (4:14—9:50).[63] This section is preceded by

---

62. Luz, *Matthew 8–20*, 142.

63. While most authors agree that the prologue (1:1–4) along with the infancy narratives (1:5—2:52) constitute distinct literary sections within the Lukan Gospel, some view the ministry of John the Baptist (3:1–20) and the prefatory appearance of Jesus

(1) a prologue (1:1–4) and an infancy narratives that parallels the births of John and Jesus (1:5—2:52), and (2) an account of the Baptist's ministry (3:1–20) and of Jesus' initial public appearance (3:21—4:13). The next narrative section, Jesus' ministry in Galilee (4:14—9:50), is followed by his journey to Jerusalem (9:51—19:46),[64] a report of Jesus' ministry in that city (19:47—21:38), a passion narrative (22:1—23:56), and a post-resurrection account (23:56—24:53).

Since, as Michael Hartmann has recently reminded us in his study about the death of John the Baptist, "kein Text ist eine Insel," the following section analyzes the immediate and proximate context of 7:18-35 in order to help one understand its meaning within the Gospel's literary structure.[65]

The Immediate Context of Luke 7:18-35: Jesus' Ministry of Healing and Compassion (7:1—8:3)

The question of John and Jesus' indictment of the religious leaders in Luke 7:18-35 plays an important role within the central plot of the Galilean ministry section. The passage highlights not only the response that Jesus receives from different people but also the narrative's ongoing concern for defining his identity. While more will be said below about these two aspects of the passage, it is relevant here to emphasize the ways in which Luke adds some of his source material to the pericope to facilitate the flow and coherence of the narrative.[66]

With the remarkable faith response of a Gentile in the healing of the centurion's servant story (Luke 7:1-10; Matt 8:5-13; cf. John 4:46–

(3:21—4:30) either as an introduction or as part of his Galilean ministry (e.g., Klein, *Lukasevangelium*, 51; Holladay, *Introduction*, 163). This seems possible, given Luke's own assessment of the appearance of the Baptist as the beginning of the story of Jesus (cf. Acts 1:22; 10:37) and the correspondence of the evangelist's account with the Markan sequence (Mark 1:2 // Luke 3:4). However, a division between 3:1—4:13 and the following material is indicated by the summary statement of 4:14-15 and Luke's programmatic presentation of Jesus' visit to Nazareth (4:16-30); see Fitzmyer, *Luke*, 1:134-42, 450; Brown, *Introduction*, 226; Kümmel, *Introduction*, 125-28; Schnelle, *New Testament Writings*, 347-49; Nolland, *Luke*, xli–ii; Green, *Luke*, 25-29.

64. Although there is widespread consensus that Jesus' journey to Jerusalem begins at 9:51, the end of the travel account is debated. Based on the changes of time and place, it seems better to regard the conclusion of Jesus' journey at 19:46; see Matera, "Journey," 57-77.

65. Hartmann, *Tod Johannes des Täufers*, 35-39.

66. Bacon, "John the Baptist," 35.

53), Luke moves the narrative into a series of episodes that portray the reaction of different characters to the ministry of Jesus. In the raising of the widow's son (7:11–17), Jesus is called a "great prophet" (προφήτης μέγας, 7:16) and Luke reports the favorable response that he receives from the people of Nain. In 7:18–35, the Baptist seems puzzled by Jesus' ministry (σὺ εἶ ὁ ἐρχόμενος;) while, in contrast to the two preceding scenes where Jesus is sought and accepted (7:1–10, 11–17), the Jewish religious leaders are chastised for having rejected the messages of John and Jesus (7:29–35). Afterwards, a forgiven sinful woman (Luke 7:36–50; Mark 14:3–9; Matt 26:6–13) reacts with gratitude to Jesus in contrast to the inability of the Pharisees to recognize the meaning of his actions (οὗτος εἰ ἦν προφήτης . . .).[67] Luke concludes this sequence of episodes with a summary about Jesus' preaching activity throughout Galilee, and underscoring his association with the Twelve and a group of women (8:1–3).

Luke has appended to 7:18–35 two examples of the works of Jesus, the healing of the centurion's servant (7:1–10) and the raising of the widow's son (7:11–17).[68] These units have, among other things, a christological function: they raise the issue of the identity of Jesus.[69] With this arrangement, Luke paves the way for Jesus' response to the disciples of John: "Go and tell John . . . the dead are raised, the poor have the good news proclaimed to them" (7:22). By inserting the story of the raising of the widow's son (7:11–17) into this part of the narrative, Luke has anticipated more clearly than Matthew Jesus' response to the emissaries of the Baptist (νεκροὶ ἐγείρονται, Luke 7:22).[70] Luke creates a more coher-

---

67. The story is probably a conflation received by Luke from tradition; see Fitzmyer, *Luke*, 1:684.

68. Save for a few transpositions, additions, and omissions, Luke has kept the order of events of his Markan source more closely than Matthew, who has dismantled the sequence of his sources for the sake of arranging his Gospel around five sermons (chs. 5–7, 10, 13, 18, 23–25) preceded by their corresponding narrative material. In the interest of this arrangement, Matthew has not only reduced "Mark's order for the Galilean ministry to chaos," but has also made a liberal use of his Q source; Bacon, "John the Baptist," 28; Kümmel, *Introduction*, 105–19; Nolland, *Matthew*, 10–11; Robinson et al., *Critical Edition*, lxxxix.

69. Gagnon, "Double Delegation," 131 n. 25.

70 Whereas Luke's account of the raising of the widow's son (7:11–17) immediately precedes Jesus' reference to the resuscitation of the dead (7:22), Matthew's nearest resuscitation story appears in Matt 9:18–26, almost two chapters before Jesus' νεκροὶ ἐγείρονται statement in Matt 11:5.

ent sequence by providing a psychological or rhetorical justification for Jesus' answer.[71] Likewise, Jesus' assessment of Israel's mixed response to the message of the Baptist (7:29–30) and his summary of the accusations raised against him and John (7:31–35) set the stage for the rejection of the Pharisees in the scene of the forgiven sinful woman (7:36–50).

Just as Luke alternates the words (6:20–49; 7:18–35) and deeds (7:1–10, 11–17, 36–50) of Jesus in the section (6:20—8:3), so he contrasts the good responses of some people with the rejections of others, especially of religious leaders.[72] The interpretative significance of this arrangement is seen in the ironic juxtaposition of the different ways in which Jesus' message is received. By contrasting the good example of those who seek and welcome Jesus (7:3, 11, 16, 37–38) with the bad example of those who reject him (7:34, 39, 44–46, 49), Luke skillfully exposes the moral failure of the Pharisees and scholars of the Law. In the nucleus of this sequence (7:18–35), the irony is further highlighted by the parallel between the ministries of John and Jesus. Unlike the people and toll collectors, who have believed in God by accepting the messages of John and Jesus (7:29–35), the Pharisees and the scholars of the Law have rejected them (7:30–34).[73] Thus the contrast of the positive reactions with the negative ones dramatically illustrates the failure of the Jewish religious leaders to recognize the identity of the one whom the outcasts and downtrodden members of society so wisely acknowledged (7:35).

The significance of this arrangement is perceived better when we compare it to its corresponding section in Matthew. Within its immediate context, the narrative logic of the Lukan passage as well as its literary function is smoother and less abrupt than its Matthean counterpart (11:2–19). The connection of the Matthean passage with the immediately

---

71. This is an example of what Parsons (*Luke*, 44–47) calls "rhetorically persuasive order." Here the order of events (καθεξῆς, cf. 1:3) has less to do with chronology than with persuasive presentation. As Parsons notes: "Luke's motive in writing includes an attempt to present these events that have been fulfilled and about which the audience has already been instructed in such a rhetorically compelling order that the authorial audience finds the narrative's truthfulness confirmed" (46); see also Fitzmyer, *Luke*, 1:560, 655.

72. As Bovon (*Luke 1*, 277) notes, Luke has arranged his sources (Mark, Q, and his special material) to alternate between words (6:20–49; 7:18–35; 8:4–18) and deeds (7:1–17, 36–50).

73. This claim supports a similar assertion later on in the narrative (cf. 20:3–7); see Tannehill, *Luke-Acts*, 1:191.

The Origin, Redaction, and Literary Function of Luke 7:18-35

preceding material is not so clear, and the relationship with what follows is sometimes viewed as a collection of "loosely connected pieces."[74] As we will see, the importance of the Matthean passage is grasped more easily within its broader literary context than within its immediate one.

While there are functional similarities between Matt 11:2-19 and Luke 7:18-35, the break of the Matthean version with its immediately preceding material, emphasized by the summary statement in 11:1, is critical.[75] Matthew prefaces 11:2-19 with Jesus' instructions to the Twelve (10:1-42) and follows it with a series of sayings of Jesus that include the woes over the unrepentant cities of Galilee (11:20-24), a call to rejoice (11:25-27), and an invitation to come to him (11:28-30). On the one hand, Luke and Matthew are similar in that the narrative section in which Matt 11:2-19 appears has something to do with the presentation of Jesus and the different set of responses that his ministry elicits.[76] The pericope underscores who Jesus is and how the people of Israel will accept or reject him—a question that in Matthew finds its answer in Peter's confession (16:16).[77] But on the other hand this function fits more appropriately what follows the pericope than what immediately precedes it since this passage introduces the different responses of the people of Israel to Jesus: indifference (11:20-24), conspiracies (12:14), incomprehension (13:13), rejection (13:57), and acceptance (14:33).[78] In this sense, the thematic relationship of the Matthean passage with what follows is closer than with what precedes.[79] Through the repetition of key words, Matthew adds to this context a sense of final urgency which presses a decision for or against Jesus. It prepares for the coming crisis

---

74. Schmid, *Matthäus*, 188. Luz (*Matthew 8-20*, 129) adds: "There are difficulties involved in determining the internal structure of Matthew 11." France (*Matthew*, 417) notes that the "tight organization which has characterized" chapters 5-7 and 8-9 becomes at this point in the narrative "less easy to discern."

75. Carter, *Matthew*, 246.

76. France, *Matthew*, 417-18; Matera, "Plot of Matthew," 251-52.

77. Matera, "Plot of Matthew," 248-49. Fitzmyer (*Luke*, 1:771) points out that Peter's confession does not have the relevance here that it has in Mark and Matthew.

78. Matera, "Plot of Matthew," 244.

79. For instance, γενεά appears in 11:16 and four times in ch. 12. Jesus' judgment upon "this generation" is echoed by the term κρίσις (11:22, 24; 12:18, 20, 36, 41, 42); Luz, *Matthew 1-7*, 37 n. 14. Luz also highlights the use of ὁ υἱὸς τοῦ ἀνθρώπου as catchwords—a Matthean technique—for this section (ibid., 39; idem, *Matthew 8-20*, 129); regarding Matthew's technique of echoing language to establish thematic continuity, see also Nolland, *Matthew*, 27.

more than Luke's account because in Matthew Jesus' judgment upon the unrepentant people of Israel follows immediately. "The 'works of Christ' intensify the judgment on an Israel that is not brought to repentance by these powerful deeds (vv. 20–24)."[80]

The following table illustrates the thematic and the stylistic differences between Matthew and Luke in the passage's immediate context:

FIGURE 1: The Immediate Context of Matthew 11:2–19 and Luke 7:18–35

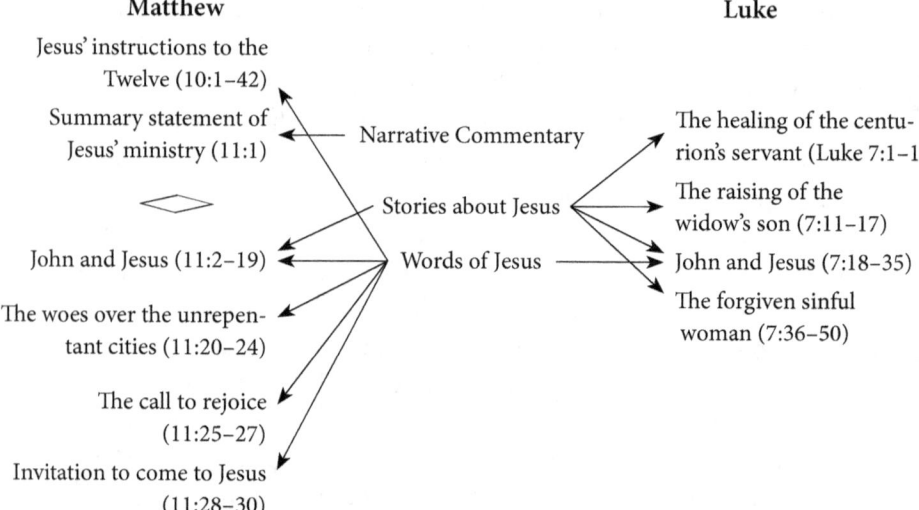

In the preceding table, the diagonal figure (◇) signals the thematic shift that takes place in Matthew, which, in comparison to the greater narrative unity of Luke, marks a change in the thrust of the story. Moreover, the arrows indicate the different narrative styles that each evangelist has chosen to introduce the account about John and Jesus. While Matthew inserts the passage into a section dominated by the words of Jesus, Luke weaves the episode among a set of stories about Jesus. In Matthew the organization of the disciples' mission (10:1–42) forms a threshold in the development of Jesus' successful ministry, next to which 11:2–19 signals a change of atmosphere. From this moment in the Matthean narrative Jesus begins to face mounting opposition.[81] The passage creates a the-

---

80. Luz, *Matthew 8–20*, 129. Nonetheless, there is always room for repentance. "However, the invitation to the entire nation is still open. Chapters 12–16 will portray how the people respond to it" (ibid.).

81. Beare, *Matthew*, 254–55; Hoffmann, *Studien*, 191.

matic shift that separates the preceding material from what follows. The mostly positive responses that Jesus had thus far received begin to fade as his discourse turns to the unrepentant cities of Galilee (11:20–24) and his mission encounters increasing resistance. Whereas in the Lukan context Jesus is allowed to continue a while longer with his preaching and healing ministry (7:36—8:3), in Matthew that ministry turns more quickly into confrontational episodes. Thus, in its transitional role, Matt 11:2–19 functions as the conclusion of a phase in the ministry of Jesus and the beginning of a new one.[82] This shift in the narrative from the ministry of Jesus and the mission of his disciples to a discourse mostly characterized by words of judgment and episodes of conflict emphasizes the transitional role of Matt 11:2–19, in contrast to the greater thematic integrity of the Lukan passage within its immediate literary context.

The Proximate Literary Context of Luke 7:18–35: The Galilean Ministry (4:14—9:50)

The meaning of 7:18–35 is best understood within its proximate literary context—the section that recounts Jesus' Galilean ministry. From the outset, this section has found its tension and movement in the gradual revelation of the identity of Jesus through his words and deeds and in the reaction of the people to his ministry.[83] After Luke's redactional summary illustrates the works of Jesus throughout Galilee (4:14–15), the evangelist recounts Jesus' visit to his hometown of Nazareth, where he is both welcomed and rejected (4:16–30).[84] In light of the Isaian passage (4:18–19), Jesus defines his ministry as one of compassion for the poor and downtrodden—an episode that foreshadows the nature of his mission and the divergent reactions that it will garner.[85]

---

82. Luz, *Matthew 8–20*, 129.

83. Aletti, *Luc*, 87–109; Green, *Luke*, 204, 236, 281–82; Fitzmyer, "Luke, Chapter 9," 139–52.

84. Whereas in Mark 1:16 and Matthew 4:13 the beginning of Jesus' public appearance takes place in Capernaum (i.e., παρὰ τὴν θάλασσαν τῆς Γαλιλαίας), Luke follows his initial introduction recounting Jesus' visit to Nazareth (Luke 4:16–30; Matt 13:53–58). Jesus' visit to Nazareth is most likely inspired by Mark 6:1–6a but developed further by Luke (Fitzmyer, *Luke*, 1:526–30).

85 Busse, *Nazareth-Manifest*, 51. The pattern by which Jesus makes a gracious offer of salvation that is refused and then offered to others foreshadows a similar one in Acts (Matera, *Theology*, 56).

Immediately after Jesus' inaugural speech, Luke features four scenes in which he presents Jesus' works in Capernaum. These events include the exorcism of a possessed man in the synagogue (4:31–37), Jesus' healing of Simon's mother-in-law (4:38–39 // Matt 8:14–15), a summary of healings and exorcisms (4:40–41 // Matt 8:16–17), and a brief account of the people's interest in the proclamation of Jesus (4:42–44).[86] These episodes reveal the power, authority, and compassion of Jesus and begin to define the character of his mission.[87] They exemplify what had been anticipated by Jesus' speech in Nazareth: he has been sent to bring glad tidings to the poor and to heal the afflicted (4:18–19). They also mirror the approval (θάμβος, 4:36) with which the ministry of Jesus had originally been received in his hometown (ἐθαύμαζον ἐπὶ τοῖς λόγοις, 4:22; see also 4:40, 42).[88]

Luke follows his early presentations of Jesus' ministry in Capernaum with the calling of the first disciples (5:1–11). Here, despite Peter's initial reservation, the people are amazed (θάμβος, 5:9) by Jesus' works, and Peter along with his companions leave everything and follow him (ἀφέντες πάντα ἠκολούθησαν αὐτῷ).[89] With the account of the cleansing of the leper (5:12–16 // Matt 8:1–4), Luke concludes his first presentation of Jesus and the sympathetic responses that his ministry receives.[90]

Luke then narrates a series of stories that recount the beginning of the encounters between Jesus and Jewish religious leaders.[91] The healing of a paralytic triggers the first of these encounters (5:17–26 // Matt 9:1–8), which is followed by a reproach of Jesus for sharing a meal with toll collectors and sinners, an episode anteceded by the calling of Levi

---

86. In these episodes, Luke follows his Marcan source with few modifications; cf. Mark 1:21–28; 29–31; 32–34; 35–39.

87. Fitzmyer, *Luke*, 1:543.

88. With minor exceptions (e.g., 4:28; 8:37; 23:13) Luke usually depicts the crowd (ὄχλος, πλῆθος) as sympathetic to Jesus (O'Toole, *Theology*, 19).

89. For the sake of better narrative order (i.e., Peter's reaction makes more sense after the presentation of Jesus' growing popularity in the preceding units), Luke withholds this episode, which he has modified from his Marcan source (Mark 1:16–20), until now (Parsons, *Luke*, 24).

90. With this passage, Luke resumes Jesus' healing ministry in Galilee in conformity with Mark's order of events (Mark 1:40–45).

91. Aside from some modifications, Luke follows here the sequence of Mark (2:1–12, 13–17, 18–22; 2:23—3:6).

(5:27-32 // Matt 9:9-13). In the next scene, Jesus replies to questions of why his disciples eat and drink, unlike the followers of the Baptist and the Pharisees, who fast and pray (5:33-39 // Matt 9:14-17). This set of encounters ends with two reports in which Jesus is questioned for violating the Sabbath by allowing his disciples to pluck grains from a field and by healing a man with a withered hand (6:1-5; 6-11 // Matt 12:1-8; 9-14).

The mounting tension with the Jewish religious leaders illustrates what had been foreshadowed by his appearance in Nazareth: his ministry would face opposition, incomprehension, and eventually rejection. Jesus' association with the outcasts of society and his unconventional lack of observance of religious practices depict the compassionate character of his mission and the growing antagonism against him.

Luke alternates these encounters by reporting the choosing of the Twelve (6:12-16 // Matt 10:1-4) and the emergence of Jesus' popularity (6:17-19).[92] The "Sermon on the Plain" (6:20-49; see Matt 5:1—7:27), which sums up Jesus' instructions to those who are to become his followers, balances Luke's accounts of the works of Jesus with a speech that clarifies the nature of his ministry. This leads into the already discussed immediate context of 7:18-35, which includes accounts about the healing of the centurion's servant (7:1-10), the raising of the widow's son (7:11-17), the forgiven sinful woman (7:36-50), and a summary of Jesus' ministry in Galilee (8:1-3).

As the story progresses, Luke underscores the elements of identity and response to Jesus' ministry by continuing to alternate reports about his words and deeds.[93] In the rather long and variegated section (twenty episodes) that follows (8:3—9:50) and climaxes Jesus' Galilean ministry, a number of parables and sayings reveal his teaching and characterize his ministry. These are supplemented with a series of episodes that illustrate how his message is being received. Both elements (words and deeds)

---

92. Up to this point Luke has followed the Marcan sequence with only minor changes (Mark 1:21—3:19 = Luke 4:31—6:19). Here, however, Luke alters the order of his Marcan source by placing the choosing of the Twelve (Luke 6:12-16; Mark 3:7-12; Matt 10:1-4) before the spreading fame of Jesus' healing power (Luke 6:17-19; 3:13-19; Matt 4:24-25), thus creating a better setting for the Sermon on the Plain (Luke 6:20-49). This is the beginning of Luke's "small interpolation" (6:20—8:3) in which the evangelist inserts material from Q, L, and some editorial work from his own hand.

93. Achtemeier ("Miracles of Jesus," 156-61) points out that the balancing of Jesus' miraculous activity with his teaching helps to validate his identity.

advance the narrative through various sayings (8:4–15, 16–18; 9:1–6, 22, 23–27, 43b–45), pronouncement stories (8:19–21; 9:46–48, 49–50), episodes of extraordinary natural events (8:22–25; 9:10–17), accounts of exorcisms (8:26–39), a resuscitation story (8:40–42a; 49–56), episodes of healings (8:42b–48; 9:37–43a), and stories about Jesus (9:7–9, 18–21, 28–36).[94]

Thus, within the broader literary context of Jesus' Galilean ministry, the evangelist identifies Jesus through a number of episodes that relate his words and his deeds, while he records the reactions of different characters in the story.[95] These words and deeds are intimately related and form a narrative pattern that helps to clarify who Jesus is.[96] The question of John the Baptist and the indictment of Jesus (7:18–35) recapitulates the previous plot of the story by summarizing the ministry of Jesus thus far: "the lame walk" (5:17–26), "the lepers are cleansed" (5:12–16), "the dead are raised" (7:11–17), and "the good news is preached to the poor" (4:18–21; 6:20–23). The passage is also linked to the ongoing narrative by its sustained interest in the identity of Jesus (7:18–23), the reaction

---

94. After Luke's small interpolation (6:20—8:3), the evangelist takes up again the Markan order in 8:4. From this point until the end of the Galilean ministry (Luke 9:50), Luke follows Mark's sequence closely (Mark 4:1—9:40). However, there are a number of stylistic modifications, omissions, and transpositions. Luke omits from his Markan source a couple of parables dealing with the kingdom of God (Mark 4:26–34), the report about the death of the Baptist (Mark 6:17–29), and the remarks concerning the return of Elijah (Mark 9:11–13). Luke compensates for the omission of the parables (Mark 4:26–34) by transposing the account about the visit of Jesus' relatives (Mark 3:31–35). The omission about the death of John the Baptist (Mark 6:17–29) is partially explained by his previous reference to John's imprisonment (Luke 3:19–20) and by Herod's remarks in 9:7–9. Meanwhile, the omission about the return of Elijah (Mark 9:11–13; cf. Luke 1:17, 76) could have been caused by a desire not to distract the narrative from its christological focus (Fitzmyer, *Luke*, 1:756–68, 805–6). Beside these omissions, Luke skips over Mark 6:45—8:26 (the "great omission") perhaps to avoid the duplication with Mark 4:35—6:44, which has similar material. Luke also glosses over Mark 6:1–6a because he had already transposed it to 4:16–30.

95. Even with its additions (Q, L), omissions, and transposition Luke has not changed the essential character of his Markan source but edited it so as to achieve a different theological aim (Kümmel, *Introduction*, 137–42). Luke's basic concern in 4:14—9:50 is similar to Mark 1:14—9:41: who is Jesus? (see Moloney, *Mark*, 28). This is not to say, however, that Luke's plot is the same as Mark's. Luke achieves a different portrayal of Jesus by carefully balancing reports about his teaching and healing activity (Green, *Luke*, 205).

96. As Green (*Luke*, 204) points out, in the message of Jesus his teaching/preaching ministry is inseparable from his mighty works; see also Talbert, *Literary Patterns*, 105–6; Percy, *Botschaft Jesu*, 189–91; Schnackenburg, *God's Rule*, 117–29.

of the people (7:24–30), and the growing conflict with the religious leaders (7:31–35). Here, for the first time in the narrative, Luke explicitly ascertains by Jesus' own words how his ministry has been received (7:31–35).[97]

The narrative's ongoing concern for the identity of Jesus and the place that the Baptist's question occupies within this framework can be observed in the following graphic:

FIGURE 2: Jesus' Galilean Ministry (4:14—9:50)

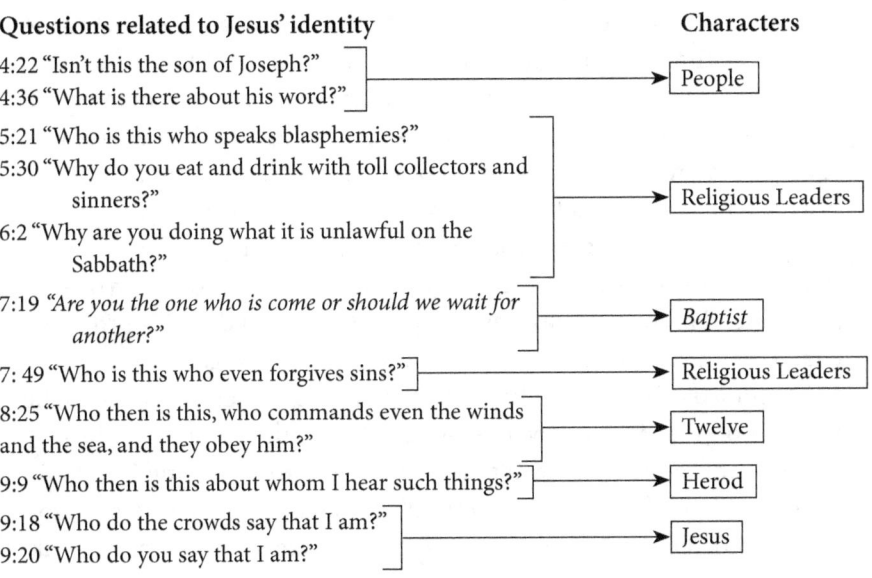

Through the literary device of questions, Luke highlights the issue about the identity of Jesus. Although anonymous people and religious leaders raise the questions, Luke gradually heightens the drama of the narrative by identifying the characters that raise such concerns. Within this arrangement, the Baptist is the first named character who questions the identity of Jesus. He will be followed by a group of Pharisees, whom Simon represents, the Twelve, and Herod. Finally, Jesus himself will pose the question.

---

97. This underscores Luke's concern for illustrating the way in which different groups of people react to the ministry of Jesus. As Aletti (*Luc*, 103) points out: "À Part Lc 4, 23–27 et 9, 22. 44, ce passage est le seul de la section où Jésus lui-même évoque explicitement la reconnaissance et le rejet dont il sera l'objet." See also Matera, *Theology*, 74, 77; O'Toole, *Theology*, 191–224; Tannehill, *Luke-Acts*, 1:103–39.

As the narrative unfolds, this set of inquiries finds a partial response in the words and deeds of Jesus and in the way different characters of the story react to him.[98] While Jesus is identified as (or confused with) a "prophet" (7:17; 9:8, 19), "Lord" (6:46), "John the Baptist" or "Elijah" (9:7-8, 19), and the "Chosen Son" of God (9:35), and even demons recognized him as the "Messiah of God" (9:20), the "Holy One of God" (4:35), the "Son of God" (4:41; 8:28), Jesus refers to himself only as the "Son of Man" (5:24; 6:5, 22; 7:34; 9:22, 26, 44). It is within this framework that 7:18–35 provides two contrasting answers that contribute to shape the thread of the narrative. Jesus responds to the question of the Baptist by portraying himself as the one who heals, raises the dead, and proclaims the good news (7:22). The answer alludes to his programmatic speech in the synagogue of Nazareth (4:18–19) and sums up Luke's preceding portrayal of Jesus as the savior of the disadvantaged.[99] In this sense, it reiterates one of Luke's most important motifs: Jesus' concern for the needy.[100]

In ironic contrast to the favorable responses that Jesus has received, the religious leaders can only manage to call Jesus "a glutton and a drunkard, a friend of toll collectors and sinners" (7:34) and deny his prophetic character (7:39). Through the reactions of those who accept and oppose Jesus' ministry, Luke exemplifies what is the appropriate response to the message of Jesus.[101] Moreover, Jesus' response to the Baptist and the repetition of his opponent's insults set the stage for the growing interest in his identity in the following chapters.[102] In the final units of this section (8:4—9:50), the question about Jesus' identity reaches its climax not only through the questions of Herod and Jesus, but also through the answer of Peter (9:20) and Jesus' own clarifications (9:22, 43b–45). All these christological statements and diverse reactions to the ministry of Jesus serve to establish his power, authority, and compassion and function as a prelude to the Jerusalem journey account (9:51—19:46). Through the concerns raised by different characters and by the answers provided by

---

98. Green, *Luke*, 204.

99. According to Talbert (*Literary Patterns*, 39–43), the correspondence between these passages results from a structural parallelism between panels 4:16—7:17 and 7:18—8:56. For a critique of Talbert's proposal, see McComiskey, *Literary Structure*, 126–35.

100. O'Toole, *Theology*, 109–48.

101. Green, *Luke*, 228.

102. Fitzmyer, "Luke, Chapter 9," 139–52.

The Origin, Redaction, and Literary Function of Luke 7:18–35   73

some of them, Luke creates a portrait of Jesus that supports the ensuing narrative as he prepares for his decisive journey to Jerusalem. In Fitzmyer's words: "Both the question [Herod's 9:9] and the subsequent answers sketch a christological portrait of Jesus upon which the Travel Account builds."[103] This dynamic has been building gradually throughout the preceding Galilean ministry section, and the underlying concern for the identity of Jesus plays into Luke's stated aim of providing a reliable account of the events that had taken place "among us" (1:1–4).[104]

In addition to the concerns about the identity of Jesus, Luke 7:18–35 has further correspondences and thematic links to the wider literary context. The passage supplements the parallel between John and Jesus that began with their birth accounts in the infancy narratives (1:5—2:52).[105] By drawing an analogy between the ministries of John and Jesus the passage confirms the close association of both characters and their roles as special agents of God's salvific purposes: John as the precursor of the Lord, and Jesus as the Messiah, the son of God. Furthermore, in naming the Baptist, who, besides a brief allusion in 5:33, had not been mentioned since the report of his public ministry (3:1–18) and arrest (3:19–20), the passage highlights the relevance of John's ministry within the Gospel. As the final reference to the Baptist, 7:18–35 sets the stage for Herod's passing remarks about the death of John (9:7). In referring to the relationship between John and his disciples, the passage supports the future request of Jesus' disciples to teach them how to pray (11:1). Jesus' affirmation of the Baptist's ministry in this passage also foreshadows his remarks about John's role with regard to the ongoing significance of Law and the Prophets and the kingdom's appearance (16:16). Furthermore, Jesus' reproach of the religious leaders' rejection of John (7:29–35) prefigures Jesus' confrontation with the religious leaders in the temple regarding his authority and their unresponsiveness to John's baptism (20:1–8).

The question of John and Jesus' indictment of the religious leaders (7:18–35) supports the conflict motif in this section and contributes to

---

103. Ibid., 144.

104. Aletti (*Luc*, 108) concludes: "La section prolonge et vérifie l'épisode de Nazareth: la reconnaissance de Jésus comme Prophète, Envoyé et Messie devait se faire et s'est faite, par des groupes différents, sa renommée est allée au-delà même des frontières et personne n'est indifférent à son endroit."

105. Luke's extended comparison of John and Jesus is widely acknowledged (e.g., Müller, *Charakterzeichnung*, 59–64).

its development in subsequent parts of the narrative.[106] By witnessing to the opposition that the religious leaders have thus far exercised against John and Jesus, it confirms what had been predicted about Jesus earlier in the narrative (2:34–35). In this way, it summarizes in concrete terms (7:29–35) the hostility against John and Jesus previously recorded in the Gospel (3:19–20; 4:28–29; 5:21, 30, 33; 6:2, 7, 11). Furthermore, by emphasizing the rejection that will materialize in the form of conspiracies and antagonisms later in the narrative, the passage foreshadows Jesus' final demise.

The passage also moves the narrative of the Gospel forward through the theme of eating and drinking (7:33–34). By dismissing the accusations concerning the ascetic lifestyle of John and the alleged lax practices of Jesus at table (7:33–34; cf. 1:15; 6:1–5), the passage not only helps to vindicate their behavior but also connects the narrative to other meal scenes within its proximate literary context (5:27—6:5; 7:36–50; 9:10–17) and beyond.[107] Through this thematic correspondence, the passage reinforces Jesus' message of repentance and forgiveness in the previous episode in which the Pharisees and scribes harassed him for sharing the table with toll collectors and sinners and contrasted his eating and drinking habits with the Baptist's (5:27–39). Finally, the pericope prepares the narrative for the following episode in which Jesus shares a meal in the house of Simon the Pharisee (7:36–50).

By recalling the signs that the disciples of John "see and hear" (7:22), the passage serves as a thematic bridge regarding the importance of hearing the word of God, a motif that frames this scene (6:47–49; 8:4–15).[108] While the final parable of the Sermon on the Plain (6:47–49) contrasts those who hear and practice the word of God with those who hear but do not practice, the parable of the sowed seed (8:4–15) emphasizes the different ways in which people receive the message of God.

The pericope even foreshadows Luke's presentation of the Christian community's growth in the Acts of the Apostles. The influence of the Baptist reflected in 7:18–35 anticipates the references to the importance of John during Jesus' ministry noted in Acts 1:21–22 and the testimony of Peter to Cornelius in Acts 10:37. The significance of John as well as the

---

106. Tannehill, *Luke-Acts*, 1:191; Kingsbury, *Conflict in Luke*, 30–31; Grangaard, *Conflict and Authority*, 21–34.

107. Heil, *Meal Scenes*, 41–43.

108. Bacon, "John the Baptist," 35.

caveat regarding his relationship to the kingdom (7:28) foreshadows the relative importance of his ministry in a number of passages of Acts (1:5; 11:16; 13:24–25; 18:25; 19:4–5). Finally, Jesus' reproach of the religious leaders (7:29–35) anticipates many of the conflicts and rejections that Peter, John, Stephen, and Paul will face in Acts.[109]

Although within its immediate context this pericope shows greater literary symmetry and fluidity in Luke than in Matthew, the differences between both passages are less significant when one compares their function within each Gospel's organic structure. From a pragmatic perspective, each evangelist has employed this tradition similarly, even if there are variations in the literary correspondences of each pericope with the rest of the material. Although the structure of Matthew remains a matter of discussion, the overall narrative of the Gospel agrees with the general contours of the Markan (and Lukan) sequence.[110] Matthew, like Luke, begins his Gospel with a set of stories related to the birth of Jesus (1:1—2:23) and follows them with a report about the ministry of John and the appearance of Jesus (3:1—4:11), an account of the inauguration of Jesus' public ministry (4:12–25), and a series of episodes that relate his words (5:1—7:29; 9:35—11:1) and deeds (8:1—9:34).[111] To this complex also belongs chapter 10, where the disciples are urged to participate in the preaching and healing ministry of Jesus. The pericope (Matt 11:2–19) is then framed by a number of stories that recount Jesus' preaching and healing ministry in Galilee (11:20—16:12).[112] The similarity in order

---

109. Matera, *Theology*, 56.

110. Different types of structures have been proposed for Matthew. A longstanding view is that Matthew has arranged his material within five sermons (chs. 5–7, 10, 13, 18, 23–25; the so-called "five books of the commandments"), each one of them preceded by its corresponding narrative introduction (Bacon, "John the Baptist," 28). Some have suggested a chiastic structure for the Gospel and others a tripartite division based on Jesus' public ministry after the overall narrative pattern of Mark: Jesus in Galilee, on his travels through Galilee and Judea, and in Jerusalem. For a summary of the discussion regarding the structure of Matthew, see Neirynck, "Rédaction Matthéenne," 72–73; Luz, *Matthew 1–7*, 35–44; Matera, "Plot of Matthew," 251–52; Carter, "Kernels," 463–64, esp. nn. 1–5; France, *Matthew*, 2–5. Regarding the ongoing debate over the structure of Matthew, France has noted recently: "It is not surprising, therefore, that this gospel, like most other NT books, has been analyzed in several different and sometimes contradictory ways" (2).

111. The close link between the Sermon on the Mount and "mighty deeds" in chs. 8–9 is suggested by the almost identical formulations of Matt 4:23 and 9:35 (Schnelle, *New Testament Writings*, 226–27).

112. The rest of the Gospel is comprised by a set of episodes in which Jesus instructs his followers about the kingdom and prepares them for the upcoming confrontations

with the Markan (and Lukan) sequence explains some of the functional parallels between Matthew and Luke.

As a result of this structural affinity, in Matthew the passage also connects the narrative to John's initial proclamation of the "coming one" (3:11; cf. 21:9) and to his ministry in previous parts of the Gospel (ch. 3; 4:12).[113] Like Luke, the Matthean passage (11:5) reviews the words (5:1—7:29) and deeds (8:1—9:38) of Jesus, as well as the association of his closest followers to his ministry of preaching and healing (10:1-42) that has preceded in the narrative.[114] Moreover, both in Matthew and Luke the passage forms a nucleus that introduces the Parable of the Sower (Matt 13:1-23 // Luke 8:4-15), which is intended to justify the reproach against those who "having ears do not hear" and who rejected God's offer of salvation.[115] Thus, the passage plays a transitional role within the broader literary context of the Gospel by looking back to the ministry of Jesus in chapters 4-10 and forward to the growing conflicts that Jesus and his disciples will have to face.[116] This last feature, however, is heightened in Matthew because the episodes in the proximate context of the passage (11:20-24; 12:1-8, 9-14, 22-29, 30-37, 38-42) highlight more immediately than in Luke the hostility that Jesus and his followers encounter in the rest of the narrative.[117]

(16:13—20:34), stories about the conflicts of Jesus with religious leaders in Jerusalem (21:1—25:46), a passion narrative (26:1—28:15), and the account of the great commission (28:16-20).

113. Unlike Luke, the passage does not review Jesus' programmatic discourse in Nazareth (Luke 4:16-30) because in Matthew the location and the abbreviated form of this account has a different narrative function: it highlights the rejection of Jesus (Matt 13:54-58); see Kingsbury, "Jesus in Matthew's Story," 12; Nolland, *Matthew*, 450.

114. Matera, "Plot of Matthew," 248. The structural and thematic unity of the chapters that precede the pericope (the Sermon on the Mount [5-7] and the two mighty works chs. [8-9]) is preserved by the inclusions in 4:23 and 9:35, which summarize Jesus ministry of words and deeds; see France, *Matthew*, 417; Nolland, *Matthew*, 24, 49; Luz, *Matthew 1-7*, 42. Moreover, the passage has other thematic links with the previous narrative. For instance, in 9:27-31 two blind men are healed; in 9:2-8 the lame walk; in 8:1-4 a leper is cleansed; in 9:18-26 a dead person is raised; there are references to Jesus' feasting in 9:10-13 and John's ascetic habits in 9:14 (Luz, *Matthew 1-7*, 42). The passage also looks back to the τὰ ἔργα (chaps. 8–9; 11:2, 19) of Jesus, which are presented as a vindication of his ministry (Nolland, *Matthew*, 449).

115. Bacon, "John the Baptist," 35.

116. Nolland, *Matthew*, 449.

117. Luz, *Matthew 1-7*, 39; idem, *Matthew 8-20*, 143. The "violence saying" becomes the central logion of the section (Matera, "Plot of Matthew," 248).

The Origin, Redaction, and Literary Function of Luke 7:18–35

Despite these similarities, structurally and thematically the Matthean passage plays a more crucial role within the Gospel's overall organization than the Lukan pericope. Within the broader literary structure of the Gospel, Matt 11:2–19 forms a watermark as part of Jesus' final words to Israel.[118] "We may say, therefore, that Matthew 11 is the concluding discourse of the Messiah Jesus to his people Israel after his initial activity. It is as if Jesus were drawing the consequences of chaps. 8–10. If they do not lead to repentance, John, the last prophetic witness, and the deeds of the Christ become the accusing witness."[119] Hence, in Matthew the question of the Baptist constitutes the crux of this section, which deals with the crisis that ensues in Jesus' ministry and climaxes in the parable discourse in chap. 13.[120] There Jesus' disciples, who understand his teaching (13:51), stand in sharp contrast to his adversaries, who neither see, nor hear, nor understand (13:13).[121] By its emphasis on the kingdom of heaven, Matt 11:2–19 leads logically into that chapter and is more expressive of Matthew's concern about Jesus' ethical proclamation of the kingdom of heaven than is Luke.[122]

Conclusion

The contextual analysis of Luke 7:18–35 shows the literary skill with which the evangelist has incorporated into his Gospel the traditional material dealing with John the Baptist and Jesus. The comparison with Matt 11:2–19 also highlights the distinctive application that each evangelist has made of this tradition in his respective narratives. The most important points may be summarized as follows. First, Luke has shown his literary skill by inserting the raising of the widow's son account (7:11–17) before Jesus' reply to the question of the Baptist, thus weaving the passage more coherently within its immediate context than Matthew.[123] Second, Luke has demonstrated similar literary skill by plac-

---

118. Luz, *Matthew 8–20*, 129.
119. Ibid., 129.
120. Matera, "Plot of Matthew," 248.
121. Ibid., 248.
122. The phrase appears twice in 11:2–19 (vv. 11, 12) and eight times in ch. 13 (vv. 11, 24, 31, 33, 44, 45, 47, 52); Luz, *Matthew 1–7*, 44; France, *Matthew*, 417.
123. Keefer (*New Testament as Literature*, 38) notes: "Luke's insistence on an *orderly account* manifests itself later, when Jesus first heals a slave of a Roman soldier (7:1–10) and then raises the dead son of a widow (7:11–17)."

ing 7:18–35 in juxtaposition within a set of episodes that illustrate the favorable and unfavorable responses to Jesus' ministry, which underscored the failure of the religious leaders to respond appropriately to God's plan of salvation. Third, by integrating the pericope within this literary pattern Luke has suggested the way in which it ought to be interpreted: in relation to the section's ongoing concern with the identity of Jesus and the diverse set of responses that his ministry evokes.[124] Fourth, the pragmatic function of the passage within its broader literary context is similar in both Matthew and Luke, although the transitional significance of the Matthean version is greater.

Building on the findings of historical, form-critical, and redaction-critical research, contemporary scholars have routinely interpreted Luke 7:18–35 (// Matt 11:2–19) in light of the early church's polemic against the disciples of John the Baptist.[125] Thus, the prevailing interpretation of the passage is that some of Luke's redactional changes either (1) reflect the polemical concerns of Luke or (2) seek to set limits on the esteem of John without necessarily being apologetic.[126] The previous contextual and comparative analysis may suggest yet a third possibility.

At the beginning of his Gospel, Luke stated that his aim was to provide a reliable account of the events that had taken place "among us" (1:1–4). Some of the redactional changes that have been pointed out can be attributed to the efforts of an accomplished writer who wishes to provide such a reliable account. In this passage, these changes would have been guided less by a desire to be polemical or set limits on John than by christological considerations and thematic interests such as the care for the needy and the proper use of wealth. The literary patterns of which this pericope forms an integral part demonstrate the care with which Luke has integrated 7:18–35 into his other sources and supports

---

124. As Johnson (*Luke*, 124) points out: "The rule of thumb for interpreting Luke-Acts—that *where* something is said is as significant as *what* is said—is appropriately applied here." The point has been recently emphasized by Anderson, "Enigmatic Parable Tradition," 743–44.

125. Winks (*John the Baptist*, 23–26) provides a brief but helpful summary.

126. In refuting the anti-Baptist interpretation of this and other passages in Luke-Acts, Winks sums up his position as follows: "We see only the same tendency [in Luke] as in Matthew, to fix limits on the evaluation of John which would safeguard the distinctiveness of Christ (ibid., 84)." "We may conclude, therefore, that while Luke is familiar with Baptist history and practice, he does not regard the disciples of John as contemporary rivals of the Christian church and is thus not directly engaged in polemic or apologetic with them" (86). See also Backhaus, *Jüngerkreise*, 136–37.

this possibility. Therefore, the differences between Matthew and Luke need not be interpreted as apologetic or revisionist but as part of Luke's literary goal of providing an orderly account in order to clarify the identity of Jesus and designate the appropriate response to his message. The following narrative-critical analysis of the text will seek to shed more light on this possibility. This analysis will pay particular attention to the narrative conventions as well as the stylistic features that may have influenced Luke's shaping of the tradition. I will seek to highlight from a literary perspective the different techniques that Luke has employed in the development of character, plot, setting, and other narrative features. The manifold varieties of these narrative means—some of which Luke may have inherited and others added himself—may account for the differences with the Matthean version and explain the particular meaning of the passage within Luke-Acts.

3

A Narrative-Critical Interpretation of 7:18–28

PRELIMINARY REMARKS

As noted in the preceding chapter, Luke's literary concern is an element that should not be overlooked in the course of interpreting his work. One scholar has noted recently that when early commentators described Luke's writing as "elegant," "learned," and "clear" they were acknowledging his rhetorical training.[1] Indeed, Luke's literary skills played

---

1. Parsons, *Luke*, 17. Although the formula κατὰ Λουκᾶν appears in 𝔓⁷⁵, the oldest Lukan manuscript extant, nowhere in the Gospel or in the Acts of the Apostles does the author reveal his name. The identification of Luke with the Gospel and Acts dates back to a long-standing church tradition (e.g., the Muratorian Canon). His name appears three times in the NT (Philemon 24; Col 4:14, and 2 Tim 4:11). In the NT, Luke is called a "fellow worker" of Paul, and the tradition has identified him as a physician. Some authors locate his native land in Syria of Antioch, and the debate continues as to whether he should be considered a Gentile Christian or a Jewish Christian (Fitzmyer, *Luke*, 1:35–53; Parsons, *Luke*, 1–8). While the identity and the provenance of Luke remain a matter of uncertainty, commentators have often acknowledged the writing skills of the author of Luke-Acts. Since in antiquity Jerome called Luke "the most skilled writer of Greek" in the NT (*Ep. Dam.* 20.4. 4), many commentators have taken note of his talent. Today almost every exegete would agree with Cadbury's observation "that the writings of Luke are rather more elegant in diction than most of the other writings in the New Testament" (Cadbury, *Literary Method*, 5). This assessment is corroborated by the recognition that Luke has been received as a "consummate literary artist," an author with a mind for "the aesthetic," a writer with "sensitiveness to style" far beyond some literary men of antiquity, "an accomplished writer," and an author with a "rich imagination" (see the summaries in Talbert, *Literary Patterns*, 1; Parsons, *Luke*, 15–16). The use of literary conventions, vocabulary, structure, and variation of style—which changes according to the situation and the event that he is describing—warrant this evaluation (Talbert, *Literary Patterns*, 1–5; Cadbury, *Luke-Acts*, 127–39; 194–238). As Fitzmyer (*Luke*, 1:35) sums up: "[H]e is obviously a rather well-educated person, a writer of no little merit, acquainted with both OT literary traditions (especially as they are known from the Greek Bible) and Hellenistic literary techniques."

a key role in making his work one of the most outstanding achievements of the NT.[2] Yet, as Cadbury once pointed out, determining precisely how competing forces controlled the transmission of the material received by Luke may be beyond our means: "Motive is not so much a creative as a molding force. But the extensive part it played in the selection and presentation of what in the first instance was instructed by history to the vicissitudes of an oral transmission would perhaps surprise us if we knew all the facts, both because of its scope and because of its various and unsuspected forms."[3] The process of ascertaining authorial motive is a rather difficult task because the procedure of selecting, emphasizing, transforming, omitting, or adding specific material is "rarely attributable to a single individual with a conscious aim."[4] Despite this difficulty, we can be sure that these elements played a decisive role in Luke's shaping of the material contained in 7:18–35.

Luke shares the tradition of the question of John the Baptist and Jesus' indictment of the religious leaders with Matthew (Matt 11:2–19 // Luke 7:18–35), but some literary features of Luke's version stand apart. In shaping the material that he received, Luke made his work more akin to formal literature than the other evangelists.[5] The traditional material provided Luke with another standard of writing, which he partially edited to transform "the things fulfilled among" the Christians into a work of literary quality.[6] This is particularly true in 7:18–35 where Luke's literary traits are evident.

Taking into account Luke's literary skills, the following exegesis analyzes 7:18–35 from a narrative-critical perspective. This analysis takes into consideration literary aspects such as characterization, point of view, setting, and plot.[7] As part of the exegesis, I will highlight those elements

---

2. Kurz (*Biblical Narrative*, 11) describes Luke as "a master of both Hellenistic and biblical styles of Greek." As Keefer (*New Testament as Literature*, 41) points out regarding Acts, "As an author who makes his compositional role explicit, Luke is indebted to the literary genres of his milieu." See also Aune, *Literary Environment*, 116–57; Danker, *Luke's Gospel*, 2.

3. Cadbury, *Luke-Acts*, 48.

4. Ibid., 34; see also 33–38.

5. Ibid., 137.

6. Ibid., 138; Fitzmyer, *Luke*, 1:107.

7. Alter, *Biblical Narrative*, 12–13; see also Powell, *Narrative Criticism*, 23–83; Resseguie, *Narrative Criticism*, 87–240. Working with a different literary corpus (Hebrew Bible), Alter (ibid., 21; 47–49) emphasizes the importance of understanding the literary conventions in order to achieve not a more imaginative interpretation but

of the passage that have repercussions for the whole of Luke-Acts. This will help the reader understand how different aspects of this pericope such as the characterization of John and the relationship between the Baptist and Jesus play into the rest of the Lukan narrative. I will also point out how some of Luke's contemporary literary conventions may have influence his editorial activity.[8]

Regarding Luke's contemporary literary conventions, scholars have for some time emphasized the profitability of paying attention to the rhetorical exercises that for centuries had been developing across the Greco-Roman landscape, some of which at least survive in the *progymnasmata* tradition.[9] Parson notes that some of these works represent "the kind of rhetorical exercises practiced in the first century, many of which had been practiced as early as the first or second centuries, B.C.E." with which Luke may have been familiar.[10] In my analysis of 7:18–35 the exercises of the *progymnasmata* tradition will provide a convenient source against which to gauge Luke's editorial activity in 7:18–35.

---

a more precise one. Although Alter's remarks are primarily concerned with the Hebrew Bible, some of his observations can be applied to Luke, not only because of his presumed knowledge of the LXX and Semitic background, but also because of the fluidity of means that necessarily exists between literary traditions. As Alter (*World of Biblical Literature*, 10) argues: "... [I]t must be stressed that writers in different ages and traditions, after all, have a finite spectrum of formal possibilities available to them, so there will necessarily be many continuities and striking analogies in literary expression from ancient to modern, from China to Peru." The importance of interpreting the Gospel of Luke and the Acts of the Apostles as two volumes of a single work has been emphasized by many authors; see Matera, *Theology*, 52–59.

8. My comments on Luke's use of literary conventions will be based primarily on the *progymnasmata* of Aelius Theon of Alexandria (ca. 50–100 CE), whose textbook is the only one preserved that is roughly contemporaneous with Luke (Parsons, *Luke*, 19). The translation used here is by Kennedy, *Progymnasmata*, 1–72.

9. Robbins, "Rhetorical Composition"; Parsons, *Luke*, 15–32; Müller, *Charakterzeichnung*, 51–52. According to Morgan (*Literate Education*, 1–49) in Greco-Roman society literate education was widespread through "vast geographical distances" and "a wide social spectrum" and included a curriculum that in many respects had a cogent curriculum, which came to be known as *enkyklios paideia* and "began with learning to read and write and progressed through the reading of Greek and Latin authors, grammar, literary criticism, arithmetic, geometry and algebra to music, rhetoric, philosophy and astronomy" (33).

10. The suggestion that Luke may have been familiar with some of the exercises or techniques present in the *progymnasmata* tradition and in the rhetorical handbooks does not imply any type of literary dependence (Parsons, *Luke*, 19); Satterthwaite, "Classical Rhetoric," 1. 337–79. Cadbury (*Luke-Acts*, 139) notes, "The specific influences of these [Luke's contemporary literary] standards may therefore be appropriately reckoned among the formative factors of Luke's work."

A Narrative-Critical Interpretation of 7:18–28

Given the length of the pericope, I will divide the text and treat the section in two separate chapters. This chapter focuses on 7:18–28 and chapter 4 on 7:29–35.[11] Before beginning the exegesis of 7:18–28, I provide here an annotated translation of the text followed by an outline.

ANNOTATED TRANSLATION OF LUKE 7:18–35[12]

Καὶ ἀπήγγειλαν Ἰωάννῃ οἱ μαθηταὶ αὐτοῦ περὶ πάντων τούτων. καὶ προσκαλεσάμενος δύο τινὰς τῶν μαθητῶν αὐτοῦ ὁ Ἰωάννης (19) ἔπεμψεν πρὸς τὸν κύριον[13] λέγων· σὺ εἶ ὁ ἐρχόμενος ἢ ἄλλον[14] προσδοκῶμεν; (20) παραγενόμενοι δὲ πρὸς αὐτὸν οἱ ἄνδρες εἶπαν· Ἰωάννης ὁ βαπτιστὴς ἀπέστειλεν ἡμᾶς πρὸς σὲ λέγων· σὺ εἶ ὁ ἐρχόμενος ἢ ἄλλον[15] προσδοκῶμεν;	And the disciples of John told him about all these things. And John summoned two of his disciples and (19) sent them to the Lord, inquiring, "Are you the one who is to come or should we wait for another?" (20) When the men came to him, they said, "John the Baptist sent us to you, inquiring, 'Are you the one who is to come or should we wait for another?'"

11. The division of 7:18–28 and 7:29–35 into two separate sections is dictated by practical reasons—for the sake of keeping the chapters within proportionate lengths.

12. The text-critical notes, translation, and interpretation of the passage are based on the Greek text of Nestle-Aland's *Novum Testamentum Graece*. Luke 7:18–35 is a relatively set text with only minor variants. These variants include a number of omissions, replacements, additions, and transpositions, most of which are attempts to smooth out the syntax. Others try to improve the narrative by adding explanatory glosses (e.g., 7:18, 22, 26). Some of these changes are poorly attested by the external evidence or are not theologically significant for establishing the meaning of the text. Those of a more relevant character are discussed below.

13. Codices ℵ, A, W, Θ, Ψ, manuscripts *f*¹, 𝔐, *it*, vg^cl, sy, and bo read Ἰησοῦν. Other witnesses (B, L, Ξ, *f*¹³, 33, a few other Greek witnesses, a, ff², vg^st, sa, and bo^mss) have κύριον. Both readings are well supported by the external evidence. However, since Luke has previously used κύριος (7:13) in a context devoted to define the identity of Jesus and because the title accords with Luke's style, κύριον is the preferred reading (see Metzger, *Textual Commentary*, 119).

14. Codices ℵ, B, L, W, Ξ, Ψ, manuscripts 33, 579, 892, 1241, 1424, 2542, and other Greek texts read ἕτερον, while A, D, Θ, *f*¹·¹³, and 𝔐 reads ἄλλον. Based on external evidence, some authors find it difficult to decide which one is more probably the original reading (e.g., Plummer, *St. Luke*, 202). The use of ἕτερον may have been an effort to harmonize with Matt 11:3. Based on the Lukan preferences within this context (ἄλλον [7:20], and the use of the reciprocal pronoun ἀλλήλοις [7:32]), ἄλλον is the preferred reading (Bovon, *Luke 1*, 278 n. 4).

15. Codices ℵ, D, L, W, Ξ, Ψ, manuscripts *f*¹, 33, 579, 892, 1241, and a few others Greek texts read ἕτερον. The reading ἄλλον is supported by 𝔓⁷⁵, A, B, Θ, *f*¹³, and 𝔐. Based on the superior external evidence, ἄλλον is retained here.

(21) ἐν ἐκείνῃ¹⁶ τῇ ὥρᾳ ἐθεράπευσεν πολλοὺς ἀπὸ νόσων καὶ μαστίγων καὶ πνευμάτων πονηρῶν καὶ τυφλοῖς πολλοῖς ἐχαρίσατο βλέπειν. (22) καὶ ἀποκριθεὶς εἶπεν αὐτοῖς· πορευθέντες ἀπαγγείλατε Ἰωάννῃ ἃ εἴδετε καὶ ἠκούσατε¹⁷ τυφλοὶ ἀναβλέπουσιν, χωλοὶ περιπατοῦσιν, λεπροὶ καθαρίζονται καὶ κωφοὶ ἀκούουσιν, νεκροὶ ἐγείρονται, πτωχοὶ εὐαγγελίζονται· (23) καὶ μακάριός ἐστιν ὃς ἐὰν μὴ σκανδαλισθῇ ἐν ἐμοί. (24) Ἀπελθόντων δὲ τῶν ἀγγέλων Ἰωάννου ἤρξατο λέγειν πρὸς τοὺς ὄχλους περὶ Ἰωάννου· τί ἐξήλθατε εἰς τὴν ἔρημον θεάσασθαι; κάλαμον ὑπὸ ἀνέμου σαλευόμενον; (25) ἀλλὰ τί ἐξήλθατε ἰδεῖν; ἄνθρωπον ἐν μαλακοῖς ἱματίοις ἠμφιεσμένον; ἰδοὺ οἱ ἐν ἱματισμῷ ἐνδόξῳ καὶ τρυφῇ ὑπάρχοντες ἐν τοῖς βασιλείοις εἰσίν. (26) ἀλλὰ τί ἐξήλθατε ἰδεῖν; προφήτην; ναὶ λέγω ὑμῖν, καὶ περισσότερον προφήτου. (27) οὗτός ἐστιν περὶ οὗ γέγραπται· ἰδοὺ ἀποστέλλω τὸν ἄγγελόν μου πρὸ προσώπου σου, ὃς κατασκευάσει τὴν ὁδόν σου ἔμπροσθέν σου.

(21) At that hour he healed many from their diseases and afflictions and evil spirits and granted sight to many who were blind. (22) And he replied to them, Go tell John what you have seen and heard: the blind recover their sight, the lame walk, lepers are cleansed and the deaf hear, the dead are raised, the poor have the good news proclaimed to them. (23) And blessed the one who is not scandalized by me. (24) When the messengers of John departed he began to say to the crowds concerning John, "What did you go out into the desert to see? A reed shaken by the wind? (25) But what did you go out to see? A man dressed with soft clothing? Behold, those with glorious clothing and living in splendor are in royal palaces! (26) But what did you go out to see? A prophet? Yes, I tell you, even more than a prophet. (27) This is the one about whom it is written, 'Behold, I send my messenger ahead of you, who will prepare your way before you.'

16. Several manuscripts read αὐτῇ δὲ (A, D, Θ, Ξ, Ψ, 33, 𝔐, lat) instead of ἐκείνῃ (𝔓⁷⁵, ℵ, B, L, W, ƒ¹·¹³, 579, 892, 1241, and a few others). Although statistically the phrase ἐν αὐτῇ τῇ ὥρᾳ is preferred by Luke (Craghan, "Redactional Study," 361–63), ἐκείνῃ is supported by superior external evidence. Hence, ἐκείνῃ is the preferred reading.

17. A few manuscripts begin the summary of mighty works with the conjunction ὅτι (A, D, 33, 𝔐, lat, and sy^h). The conjunction is probably a scribal effort to introduce a quote. The omission of the conjunction is better attested (𝔓⁷⁵ᵛⁱᵈ, ℵ, B, L, W, Θ, Ξ, Ψ, ƒ¹·¹³, 579, 700, 892, 1241, 1424, 2542, a few other Greek manuscripts, it, sa^ms, and bo) and therefore is omitted here.

(28) λέγω¹⁸ ὑμῖν, μείζων ἐν γεννητοῖς γυναικῶν Ἰωάννου¹⁹ οὐδείς ἐστιν· ὁ δὲ μικρότερος ἐν τῇ βασιλείᾳ τοῦ θεοῦ μείζων αὐτοῦ ἐστιν. (29) Καὶ πᾶς ὁ λαὸς ἀκούσας καὶ οἱ τελῶναι ἐδικαίωσαν τὸν θεὸν βαπτισθέντες τὸ βάπτισμα Ἰωάννου. (30) οἱ δὲ Φαρισαῖοι καὶ οἱ νομικοὶ τὴν βουλὴν τοῦ θεοῦ ἠθέτησαν εἰς ἑαυτοὺς μὴ βαπτισθέντες ὑπ' αὐτοῦ. (31) Τίνι οὖν ὁμοιώσω τοὺς ἀνθρώπους τῆς γενεᾶς ταύτης καὶ τίνι εἰσὶν ὅμοιοι.	(28) I tell you, among those born of women there is no one greater than John; but the least in the kingdom of God is greater than he." (29) And all the people who listened, including toll collectors, and who were baptized with the baptism of John acknowledged the righteousness of God. (30) But the Pharisees and the scholars of the law rejected the plan of God for themselves because they were not baptized by him. (31) "To what, then, shall I compare the people of this generation and what are they like?

18. Several witnesses begin Jesus' statement either with ἀμήν (ℵ, L, Ξ, 579, 892, 2542, and a few other Greek witnesses), λέγω γάρ (A, Θ, ƒ¹, 𝔐, f, q, vg, and sy^h), λέγω δέ (D, W, ƒ¹³, a few other Greek witnesses, it and vg^mss) or just λέγω (B, Ψ, 33, 700, 1241, a few other Greek witnesses, sy^s.p, and co). The conjunctions are probably scribal attempts to explain the relation of the statement (epexegetical [γάρ] or adversative [δέ]) to the preceding quotation. The use of ἀμήν could be original or an effort to harmonize with Matt 11:11 (Marshall, *Luke*, 296). Although ἀμήν is one of the few Aramaisms that Luke usually retains, his style within this particular context and the slightly superior external attestation of the omission makes the simple use of λέγω the preferred reading.

19. John's identification is attested differently: (1) Ἰωάννου τοῦ βαπτιστοῦ (K, 33, 565, other Greek manuscripts, it, syh^mg, sa^ms), (2) προφήτης Ἰωάννου τοῦ βαπτιστοῦ (A, [D], Θ, ƒ¹³, 𝔐, lat, sy^p.h, and bo^pt), (3) προφήτης Ἰωάννου (Ψ, 700, [892 and 1241 with minor differences], a few other Greek manuscripts, and sy^s), and (4) Ἰωάννου (𝔓⁷⁵, ℵ, B, L, W, Ξ, ƒ¹, 579, a few other Greek manuscripts, sa^mss, and bo^pt). Variants (1) and (3) are not strongly supported by the external evidence and are probably assimilations to Matt 11:11. Although variant (2) is supported by good witnesses, it is probably a copyist's effort to exclude Christ from the comparison (Metzger, *Textual Commentary*, 119). The shortest reading (4), which has superior external support, is preferred (Plummer, *St. Luke*, 205).

(32) ὅμοιοί εἰσιν παιδίοις τοῖς ἐν ἀγορᾷ καθημένοις καὶ προσφωνοῦσιν ἀλλήλοις ἃ λέγει,[20] ηὐλήσαμεν ὑμῖν καὶ οὐκ ὠρχήσασθε,[21] ἐθρηνήσαμεν καὶ οὐκ ἐκλαύσατε. (33) ἐλήλυθεν γὰρ Ἰωάννης ὁ βαπτιστὴς μὴ ἐσθίων ἄρτον μήτε πίνων οἶνον, καὶ λέγετε, δαιμόνιον ἔχει (34) ἐλήλυθεν ὁ υἱὸς τοῦ ἀνθρώπου ἐσθίων καὶ πίνων, καὶ λέγετε, ἰδοὺ ἄνθρωπος φάγος καὶ οἰνοπότης, φίλος τελωνῶν καὶ ἁμαρτωλῶν. (35) καὶ ἐδικαιώθη ἡ σοφία ἀπὸ πάντων τῶν τέκνων αὐτῆς.[22]	(32) They are like children, who are sitting in the marketplace, and who call to one another and say: 'We played the flute for you but you did not dance, we mourned but you did not cry.' (33) For John the Baptist came neither eating food nor drinking wine and you say, 'He has a demon.' (34) The son of man has come eating and drinking and you say, 'Behold a man who is a glutton and a drunkard, a friend of toll collectors and sinners.' (35) But wisdom is justified by all her children."

OUTLINE OF LUKE 7:18-35

Previous exegetical methods have emphasized the composite character of the tradition found in Luke 7:18-35. While these methods have helped us to understand the compositional history of the passage, from a narrative-critical perspective Luke 7:18-35 forms a single literary unit that the author has woven into his story of Jesus.[23] Externally, the

20. The witnesses differ on the introductory phrase to the children's complaints: καὶ λέγουσιν (A, Θ, Ψ, 33, 𝔐, aur, f, vg, sy^h), λέγοντες (D, L, f^{13}, and 2542), λέγοντα (ℵ², W, Ξ, and a few other Greek manuscripts), ἃ λέγει (ℵ*, B, f^1, and 700'), and the word and/or phrase is not found in sy^s. Although these readings are well represented by the manuscript tradition, they also attest to the difficulties created by the *lectio difficilior*: ἃ λέγει (Bovon, *Luke 1*, 282 n. 68). Since the ἃ λέγει has slightly better support from the external evidence, the phrase is retained here.

21. Several codices read here ὑμῖν (A, Ψ, f^1, 33, 𝔐, it and sy). The pronoun is best seen as an addition to balance ἐθρηνήσαμεν with the previous clause (i.e., ηὐλήσαμεν ὑμῖν, see Metzger, *Textual Commentary*, 120). The shorter reading, which is better attested (ℵ, B, D, L, W, Θ, Ξ, f^{13}, 892, 1241, a few other Greek manuscripts, lat and co) is preferred.

22. The manuscript tradition differs in the final phrase: (1) τῶν τέκνων αὐτῆς πάντων (A, Ξ, 33, and 𝔐), (2) τῶν τέκνων αὐτῆς (D, L, Θ, Ψ, f^1, 700, 1241, 2542, and some other Greek manuscripts), (3) πάντων τῶν ἔργων αὐτῆς (ℵ²) and (4) πάντων τῶν τέκνων αὐτῆς (B, W, f^{13}, 579, and 892). Variants (2) and (3) are probably scribal attempts to simplify the interpretation of the phrase or to conform to Matt 11:19. The use of πάντων in (1) and (4) fits Lukan style. Probably in (1) the adjective πάντων was restored in the wrong place once it had been omitted. Thus, the order of variant (4) is the preferred reading (Plummer, *St. Luke*, 209; Metzger, *Textual Commentary*, 120).

23. In the exegesis I am concerned not only with the passage in its final form but

delimitation of the passage is determined by the source used by Luke, which is also found in Matthew 11:2–19 with similar wording and in a common sequence. Internally, the change of settings and the characters in the two episodes that frame the passage (7:11–17; 7:36–50) determine its outer boundaries. The coherence of 7:18–35 is seen in the continuous references to John and Jesus, the two main characters in the passage. Although in Luke the pericope establishes its own contours, the source's common material consists of the question of the Baptist (Matt 11:2–6 // Luke 7:18–23), the testimony of Jesus concerning John (Matt 11:7–15 // Luke 7:24–30), and the parable of the children in the marketplace (Matt 11:16–19 // Luke 7:31–35).[24]

Luke has shaped this common tradition into an essential part of his narrative and, in doing so, he has transformed it into one of the most intriguing and important scenes of his gospel. Robert Alter has defined this sort of literary phenomenon in the following terms:

> A proper narrative event occurs when the narrative tempo slows down enough for us to discriminate a particular scene; to have the illusion of the scene's 'presence' as it unfolds; to be able to imagine the interaction of personages or sometimes personages and groups, together with the freight of motivations, ulterior aims, character traits, political, social, or religious constraints, moral and theological meanings, borne by their speech, gestures, and acts.[25]

Regardless of the transmission history of the passage, the story about John and Jesus in this episode forms an integral part of the narrative through which Luke articulates the concerns, motivations, and reactions of its characters and defines the plot of the Gospel.

The passage, which Luke links with a prepositional phrase (περὶ πάντων τούτων) that relates the episode to the previous narrative, opens with the disciples of John telling him about the activity of Jesus (7:18). Following John's directive to inquire about the identity of Jesus, two of the Baptist's disciples find Jesus and deliver John's question (σὺ εἶ ὁ ἐρχόμενος ἢ ἄλλον προσδοκῶμεν; 7:19–20). Jesus then per-

---

also "as a functional member of the total narrative"; see Tannehill, *Luke-Acts*, 1:3; Green, *Luke*, 11–20.

24. Bultmann, *History*, 23; Lührmann, *Redaktion*, 24–25. Dibelius (*Überlieferung*, 6) regarded 7:24–35 as a unit.

25. Alter, *Biblical Narrative*, 63.

forms a number of healings and asks John's messengers to tell him what they have seen and heard (εἴδετε καὶ ἠκούσατε, 7:21–22).²⁶ Jesus concludes his reply to John with a poignant remark that defines the boundary of the first subunit (7:23).²⁷

The departure of the two disciples of John (ἀπελθόντων δὲ τῶν ἀγγέλων Ἰωάννου, 7:24; see 7:18) and the speech of Jesus (the implicit subject of ἤρξατο, 7:24) connect the following material (7:24–28) to the preceding scene in logical sequence.²⁸ The passage continues with Jesus' interrogation of the crowds through three consecutive rhetorical questions that aim at ascertaining the identity of John (7:24–26). After the final question, Jesus identifies John not only as more than a prophet (7:26) and a prophesied forerunner (7:27) but also as the greatest of those born of women, who nonetheless is subordinated to the least in the kingdom of God (7:28).

Luke then intercalates a narrative commentary in which he emphasizes that the people and toll collectors have glorified God by accepting the baptism of John, while the Pharisees and the scholars of the Law, by rejecting it, have rejected the plan of God (7:29–30).²⁹

The theme of how the people have reacted to God's message continues in Jesus' rhetorical question: "To what, then, shall I compare the people of this generation?" (7:31). Jesus' assessment of the different ways in which they have responded to God's initiative leads him to compare the present generation to bickering children sitting in a market (7:32).

---

26. Nolland (*Luke*, 327) notes that the twofold presentation of the question of John (7:19–20) is balanced by the bipartite form in which Jesus replies to his inquiry, first giving them something to see (7:21) and then giving them something to hear (7:22–23).

27. Except for the parenthetical commentary in 7:29–30, this manner of expression will characterize the conclusion of every subunit; see Du Plessis, "Contextual Aid," 120.

28. Green (*Luke*, 294–95) notes that the "organization of the subunit is determined by the movement of John's disciples, who report to John, are summoned by John, are sent by John, come to Jesus, and are sent by Jesus."

29. There is some disagreement about whether 7:29–30 should be interpreted as part of the preceding (7:24–28) or the following material (7:31–35) (Fitzmyer, *Luke*, 1:670; Nolland, *Luke*, 335). Vv. 29–30 play a transitional role in the flow of the narrative. Given the significance of the statement for the meaning of the passage (7:18–35), vv. 29–30 should be regarded as a narrative comment that constitutes a distinct literary subunit. This narrative summary fulfills three distinct functions: (1) it relates the actions essential to the unfolding of the plot; (2) it communicates data supplementary to the plot; and (3) it confirms what the characters have expressed in direct discourse; see Alter, *Biblical Narrative*, 76–77.

He compares the attitude of the children to those who, despite the efforts made to please them, have rejected John's ministry and his own (7:33–34). The episode ends with another poignant saying that contrasts the behavior of the sullen children with the children of wisdom (7:35).

The unity of the first subunit of the passage is secured by the dialogue between its three main characters—John (7:18, 20, 22), the disciples of the Baptist (7:18, 19, 20, 22), and Jesus (7:19, 20, 21, 22, 23). This dialogue also establishes its thematic coherence, which gravitates toward the identity of the "one who is to come." A summary of healings in 7:21 balances Jesus' answer to the disciples of John, which rhythmically outlines a series of benefits on behalf of the needy (7:22) that enhance the style of the verse and highlight the importance of the statement.[30] The final remark, formulated as a beatitude (7:23), marks the end of the subunit.

A report about the departure of the disciples of John (7:24) and a different narrative style (third person) signal the beginning of the second subunit (7:24–28). In it, Jesus addresses the crowd with a series of questions focused on the identity of the Baptist. Three consecutive rhetorical questions (7:24b, 25, 26) marked by identical beginnings (τί ἐξήλθατε) and complemented with three different alternatives supply the outline in the central structure of the subunit. A Scripture citation (7:27) that supplements the three rhetorical questions and an antithetical parallelism that qualifies the significance of John (7:28) complete the final organization of the subunit.

A variation in theme and a change of the narrative style mark the beginning of the third subunit (7:29–30). In this subunit, the narrator introduces an explanatory gloss in the form of another antithetical parallelism that contrasts two types of responses to the ministry of John. Two pairs of character types (ὁ λαός / οἱ τελῶναι // οἱ Φαρισαῖοι / οἱ νομικοί) balance the structure of the verses designed to illuminate the meaning of previous narrative events.

The fourth and final subunit (7:31–35) is signaled by a return to direct speech and a change in characters and thematic emphasis. In an extended comparison, Jesus equates the people of "this generation" to

---

30. Roth, *Character Types*, 174. Regarding the balance of the sentence, Tannehill (*Luke-Acts*, 1:79) points out: "These words have been shaped with a precise sense of form. . . . There is a series of two word sentences with noun subjects first, always masculine plural, followed by a present tense verb."

children sitting in the marketplace. In this subunit, Jesus' initial question (7:31) alternates with two more antithetical parallelisms (7:32, 33-34), which report in indirect speech the charges raised against John and Jesus.[31] A final reference to the children of wisdom (7:35), who are parallel to the children sitting in the marketplace (7:32), closes the passage and forms an *inclusio* that frames the final subunit.[32]

In terms of narrative tempo, the scene develops as a continuous unfolding event that, except for the healing account reported in 7:21, keeps a close proportion between narrated time and narrating time. Concerning the setting, the scene unfolds with minimal indication of location or movement away from the purported locale. Thus the entire scene (7:18–35) consists of four interrelated subunits: the question of John the Baptist (7:18–23), Jesus' encomium of John (7:24–28), Luke's narrative comment regarding the diverse responses to the ministry of John (7:29–30), and the parable of the children in the marketplace (7:31–35). All four subunits are demarcated by discrete thematic emphases, changes of explicit and/or implicit characters (the Baptist, the messengers of John, Jesus, the crowds, the Pharisees and toll collectors), as well as by the swift shifts in narrative styles (narration, indirect and direct discourse).[33] The outline of the scene is as follows:

First Subunit: The Question of John the Baptist (7:18–23)

A. The ministry of Jesus and the report of John's disciples (7:18a)

B. The delegation of the Baptist (7:18b–19)

C. The disciples of John and their message (7:20)

D. The healing power of Jesus (7:21)

E. Jesus commissions the disciples of John (7:22)

F. Blessedness and scandal: Reactions to the ministry of Jesus (7:23)

---

31. Nolland (*Luke*, 341) refers to the form of vv. 32–34 as a "double binary structure" determined by the contrasting parallelism between John and Jesus.

32. The final verse (7:35) also forms a balancing antithesis over against vv. 31–32; Nolland, *Luke*, 341.

33. Bovon (*Luke 1*, 281) notes the transitions, except for the one in 7:31; see also Green, *Luke*, 294.

A Narrative-Critical Interpretation of 7:18–28

Second Subunit: Jesus' Encomium of John the Baptist (7:24–28)

A. The first rhetorical question: The moral fiber of John (7:24)

B. The second rhetorical question: The austerity of John (7:25)

C. The third rhetorical question: John the prophet (7:26)

D. John the forerunner of the Lord (7:27)

E. The greatness of John and the kingdom of God (7:28)

Third Subunit: The People and the Religious Leaders: Different Responses to the Plan of God (7:29–30)

A. The baptism of John and the glorification of God (7:29)

B. The frustration of the plan of God (7:30)

Fourth Subunit: The Parable of the Children in the Marketplace (7:31–35)

A. Jesus and the present generation (7:31)

B. The children playing in the marketplace (7:32)

C. The false accusations against John and Jesus (7:33–34)

D. Wisdom prevails (7:35)

EXEGESIS OF LUKE 7:18–28

First Subunit: The Question of John the Baptist (7:18–23)

The Ministry of Jesus and the Report of John's Disciples (7:18a)

The first subunit of the passage begins with the report that the disciples of the Baptist bring him news about the activity of Jesus (περὶ πάντων τούτων, 7:18a). Luke does not mention the location of John, who presumably remains in prison (3:20), and throughout the rest of the passage the description of the episode's setting will be kept at a minimum.[34]

---

34. Unlike Matt 11:2, Luke does not mention that John is in prison, probably because he had already noted this in 3:20. When Theon (*Progymnasmata*, 84) discusses "conciseness" as one of the virtues of a narration (διήγησις), he states: "Furthermore, things that can be supplied [by the reader] should be altogether eliminated by one who wants to compose concisely . . ." Regarding the location of the episode, the last place mentioned in the narrative is Nain (7:11), but the summary report at the end of the previous unit (7:17) broadens the geographical focus by noting that the word about Jesus

Equally vague are the references to the disciples of John (οἱ μαθηταί), which exclude any information about their identity and provenance.[35] Before this episode, the disciples of John have been mentioned only once (5:33), when they were portrayed as ascetic and prayerful followers of the Baptist, who, unlike the followers of Jesus, fasted and prayed regularly.[36] This portrayal of John's disciples explains the later request of the followers of Jesus to teach them to pray "the way John taught his disciples" (11:1). The disciples of John will appear again in Acts as a group in need of further instruction (Acts 13:23–25; 18:24—19:7).[37]

The same brief reference to the fasting and praying habits of the Baptist's disciples (5:33) also contains the first mention of John (Ἰωάννης) since the report of his arrest in 3:20. Nevertheless, John's credentials have been well established and no other character, aside from Jesus, has occupied such a prominent place in the plot of the narrative.[38]

After the prologue, in which the author announces his purpose of providing "an orderly account" of the events that have taken place "among us" (1:1–4), Luke turns his attention to John and begins to position him as a central figure of his message about Jesus. In the infancy narratives, Luke intimates that it was through the birth of John that God's actions began to unfold. Luke relates how the prayers of Zechariah were answered in the annunciation of John's birth (1:13). Through the words of the angel, Luke begins to cultivate the significance of John for future events by emphasizing the joy with which he would be received, the greatness of his destiny, the austerity that would characterize his life, the impact that his call to repentance would have on the people of Israel,

---

spread "throughout all of Judea and the neighboring territory." Therefore, the comings and goings of John's disciples are not tied to a specific location.

35. The fact that Luke later says that John called "two of his disciples" could imply here that more than two disciples brought him the news about Jesus.

36. This lack of information emphasizes the secondary nature of the disciples' role in the narrative. They will reenter the Lukan narrative in Acts 19:1–7, but again they remain nameless.

37. Many authors consider that Acts 13:23–25 and 18:24—19:7 reflect Luke's apologetic intent against sectarian followers of John (Dibelius, *Überlieferung*, 88, 95–97; Haenchen, *Acts of the Apostles*, 556–57).

38. John the Baptist is named 24 times in the Gospel of Luke (1:13, 60, 63; 3:2, 15, 16, 20; 5:33; 7:18, 20, 22, 24, 28, 29, 33; 9:7, 9, 19; 11:1; 16:16; 20:4, 6) and 9 times in Acts (1:5, 22; 10:37; 11:16; 13:24, 25; 18:25; 19:3, 4). Regarding John's characterization in Luke 1–2, see Darr, *Character Building*, 60–69; Ernst, *Johannes der Täufer*, 81–88; Müller, *Charakterzeichnung*, 91–151.

A Narrative-Critical Interpretation of 7:18-28

and God's sanctioning of his future mission (1:14-17). John's birth is depicted as a sign of God's favor (1:25, 36-37) and the importance of his role is emphasized while he is still in his mother's womb (1:41, 44; see also 1:67, 80).

Luke sets up John's prominence by describing how his birth was accompanied by wonders. He was born of a sterile woman (στεῖρα, 1:7, 36) who, together with Zechariah, was advanced in age (ἀμφότεροι προβεβηκότες, 1:7, 18). John's name is given by the angel (1:13) and the events that take place during the circumcision confirm the providential character of his birth (1:59-64). He is called a "prophet of the Most High" (προφήτης ὑψίστου, 1:76), the one who would prepare the way of the Lord by instructing the people about salvation through the forgiveness of sins (1:76-77). In a brief aside, the author confirms the significance of John by emphasizing that "the hand of the Lord was with him" (1:66).

Later, Luke identifies John as a chosen agent of God (3:2-3). Quoting the book of Isaiah, Luke presents John as "the voice that cries in the desert" (3:4) and as the spokesman of God whom the people recognized and respected (3:7-15). John's role as the forerunner of the Lord is emphasized and qualified in reference to someone more powerful than he (ἔρχεται δὲ ὁ ἰσχυρότερός μου, 3:16) and to whom the Baptist is subordinated. Now in 7:18, although John has remained out of sight since his imprisonment, Luke brings him back to hear from his disciples the things that Jesus has been doing (περὶ πάντων τούτων). This phrase (περὶ πάντων τούτων) is meant to summarize not only the events just reported (i.e., 7:1-10, 11-17) but the whole of Jesus' public ministry.[39] After such an ample presentation of John in the opening chapters, the author feels no need to refer to him with any fuller designation than John (Ἰωάννης).

The Delegation of the Baptist (7:18b-19)

As the narrative continues, John summons two of his followers and sends them to ask Jesus: "Are you the one who is to come or should we wait for another?" (σὺ εἶ ὁ ἐρχόμενος ἢ ἄλλον προσδοκῶμεν;). While Luke does not mention the number of disciples that brought the news about Jesus to John, here we learn that John calls and sends two (δύο) of his

---

39. Klein (*Lukasevangelium*, 281) notes: "Sie [the disciples of John] sagen ihm alles, was die Leser des Evangeliums wissen, also was Jesus bisher tat." See also Marshall, *Luke*, 289; Fitzmyer, *Luke*, 1:665.

followers.⁴⁰ They are commissioned to relate to the Lord (τὸν κύριον)—a christological title that in Luke's narrative emphasizes the special status of Jesus—a question about his identity.⁴¹

As noted in chapter 1, the question of John the Baptist poses one of the great dilemmas in the interpretation of the NT, and this episode has received numerous and various explanations. The puzzling question of the Baptist has been interpreted diversely as referring to: (1) John's difficulty in accepting that the "one who is to come" had to face death; (2) a pedagogical device to lead his disciples into a deeper understanding of who Jesus is; (3) a conflict between John's expectation of a fiery judge and Jesus' compassionate ministry; and (4) real ignorance, hesitation, astonishment, and impatience.⁴² Among these interpretations the prevailing view is that John's question is motivated by a "substantial and striking" difference between John's expectation of a "coming one" destined to bring fire and judgment and the character of Jesus' ministry. This interpretation emphasizes the apparent incongruence between John's own temperament (3:7–9) and the portrayal of "the stronger one" (3:16–17) with Jesus' compassionate ministry (4:16—7:17). Green's assessment is typical: "For John (and, no doubt, for others), the nature of Jesus' activity seems to disqualify any claim he might have to this status."⁴³ However, while this interpretation recognizes the importance of John's

---

40. Matthew 11:2 does not specify how John heard about the activity of Jesus. Luke's mention of the two disciples recalls the familiar OT legislation concerning two witnesses (Deut 17:6; 19:15) and the early Christian community practice (e.g., Peter/John and Barnabas/Paul in Acts 4:13, 19–20; 13:2–3); Jeremias, "Paarweise Sendung," 136–43; Craghan, "Redactional Study," 361–63.

41. Jesus has been referred to as the "Lord" several times before this episode (2:11, 26; 5:8, 12; 6:5, 46; 7:13). In Luke-Acts, κύριος is used with the same ambiguity than in other NT writings, where the term is applied either to God or Jesus; see Bovon, *Theologian*, 214–18.

42. For a summary of interpretations, see Dupont, "Jean-Baptiste," 806–13; Sabugal, *Embajada*, 6–27.

43. Green, *Luke*, 295–96. This and similar interpretations rely heavily on Luke's previous portrayal of John's expectations of an eschatological figure in 3:16–17. However, as some authors have pointed out (e.g., Hollenbach, "John the Baptist," 893) many interpreters tend to understand these verses too much in terms of judgment and wrath with little consideration to any positive aspect of a baptism involving God's Spirit and fire. If an incongruence between the Baptist's expectations of the "coming one" and Jesus' ministry were to be sought as the sole reason for John's question, it seems that a more important element would be Jesus' rather liberal practices regarding fasting, prayer, and table fellowship (5:33, 7:33–34).

A Narrative-Critical Interpretation of 7:18–28

views about "the coming one" regarding the meaning of the question, it neglects other elements embedded in the Lukan narrative. Hence, from a narrative-critical perspective John's question merits a more nuanced interpretation.

Unlike Matthew, whose presentation of the Baptist begins with his public ministry (Matt 3:1), the meaning of John's question in Luke is rooted in the infancy narratives' implicit assumption of an expected prophetic figure.[44] This figure is first alluded to in the annunciation of John's birth to Zechariah (1:17). As the infancy narratives unfold, Luke methodically makes known through the words of representative characters that the expectation of a prophetic Messiah is widespread among the people of Israel.

During the annunciation to Mary scene, the angel reveals that her future child will fulfill the OT prophecies of Davidic succession (1:30–33). Later, when she visits Elizabeth, the latter rejoices at the appearance of the "mother of my Lord" (1:43). At the circumcision of John, Zechariah proclaims the fulfillment of the messianic prophecies in reference to the birth of Jesus (1:69, 76). After Jesus' birth, the angel of the Lord reveals to the shepherds that a Messiah has been born (2:9–14), and the shepherds in turn repeat the message they have heard to the parents of Jesus (2:17). During the presentation in the temple, Simeon proclaims the fulfillment of the salvation and the judgment of the people in the birth of Jesus (2:29–32, 34–35). Afterwards, Anna praises God and speaks about the child "to all those who looked forward to the deliverance of Jerusalem" (2:38), an allusion to the fulfillment of prophetic promises.

Through references to key terms such as the "Lord," "savior," and "Messiah," as well as by the use of phrases that allude to the fulfillment of prophetic promises, Luke skillfully articulates the hopes of the people of Israel for a Messiah and identifies this figure with Jesus. By so doing Luke lays the foundation for the plot of the ensuing narrative in which

---

44. Besides the fact that several authors have emphasized that during the Second Temple period there were a number of messianic hopes and expectations among the Jews in Palestine, the variety of christological titles in the Lukan narrative allows Jesus to be characterized either as a messianic, royal, priestly, eschatological, or prophetic figure. When Luke wrote his Gospel, the messianic hopes would have been formulated with a variety of titles that in their origin would not have had a messianic connotation, but which were interpreted so eventually. Following the precedents of some extrabiblical Jewish writings, Luke predicates some of these titles of Jesus; see Fitzmyer, *One Who Is to Come*, 82–145. Regarding the Jewish expectation of a coming Messiah in stage I of the gospel tradition, see Fitzmyer, *Luke*, 1:197–200, 471–72.

the desire for, and the identification of, a prophetic figure becomes the controlling motif of an important section (4:13—9:50).

Luke's identification of Jesus with a messianic figure occurs not only through the elevated language with which the different characters speak about him but also through the extraordinary circumstances that surround his birth. Moreover, the narrator expresses his point of view that Jesus is the awaited Messiah through a subtle narrative aside (2:26). Hence, in the infancy narratives it is clear that Jesus is, from the narrators' point of view, the royal descendant of David, the savior, the son of God, and the Messiah.[45]

However, although Jesus is the expected Messiah from the narrator's point of view, from the perspective of the characters in the ensuing narrative this identification has yet to occur.[46] Therefore, as the story unfolds people begin to wonder whether John or Jesus will fulfill the messianic expectations. As John preaches to the crowds, the people debate among themselves whether he might be the Messiah (μήποτε αὐτὸς εἴη ὁ Χριστός, 3:15). John acknowledges the expectations of the people but implicitly denies he is the Messiah, alluding to a coming figure who is "stronger" than himself (ἔρχεται δὲ ὁ ἰσχυρότερός μου, 3:16). The Baptist describes "the stronger one" with a number of harvest-related images that characterize this figure as exercising a superior ministry (3:16–17).[47]

Although human characters are uncertain about who Jesus is, supernatural beings recognize his identity. After Jesus' baptism, a voice from heaven reveals that he is the "beloved son" (σὺ εἶ ὁ υἱός μου ὁ ἀγαπητός, 3:22; see 9:35). Twice the devil challenges Jesus to prove that he is the son of God (εἰ υἱὸς εἶ τοῦ θεοῦ, 4:3, 9), and other evil spirits know that he is the holy one of God (οἶδά σε τίς εἶ, ὁ ἅγιος τοῦ θεοῦ, 4:34; see also 4:41; 8:28). In contrast, when Jesus inaugurates his public

---

45. Matera, *Christology*, 54.

46. Brawley, *Luke-Acts*, 6–27; Aletti, *Luc*, 87–109.

47. John's proclamation of the "stronger one" has received many interpretations. For a convenient discussion, see Webb (*John the Baptizer*, 261–306), who concludes that there is "little explicit evidence" by which to determine what kind of eschatological agent John was expecting. Although Luke's characterization of John's expectation of the "stronger one" certainly includes elements of judgment and wrath, Fitzmyer's (*Luke*, 1:473–74) observation is worth noting: "If John's own water-baptism were intended to produce 'repentance,' it might at least be thought that a baptism involving God's Spirit and fire would be expected to accomplish something positive too."

ministry in Nazareth, those who supposedly know him best are disconcerted by his words and actions (οὐχὶ υἱός ἐστιν Ἰωσήφ οὗτος; 4:22), while the rest of the people can only speculate about the identity of Jesus (τίς ὁ λόγος οὗτος ὅτι ἐν ἐξουσίᾳ καὶ δυνάμει ἐπιτάσσει..., 4:36). The expectation heightens as the conflicts with religious authorities increase, and they debate who Jesus may be and why he behaves the way he does (τίς ἐστιν οὗτος, 5:21; see also 5:30; 6:2). Throughout the episodes in which the identity of Jesus becomes the controlling motif, some characters manifest their approval while others reject him. It is within this framework of acceptance, rejection, and uncertainty that John sends two of his disciples to ask Jesus whether he is "the one who is to come."

Thus, Luke has inserted the question of the Baptist within the narrative's implicit assumption of a promised prophetic figure and the plot's ongoing concern for the identity of Jesus. Within this context, the question expresses the uncertainty of John, the most important character in the story after Jesus, about whether he is the expected eschatological agent of God. The Baptist's question dramatizes like that of no one else the predicament in which many other characters find themselves: how to respond to the ministry of Jesus. John's question emerges, hence, as an initial probe about who Jesus is. Within the thrust of the story, this question seems motivated more by the ignorance of John regarding Jesus' identity than by an absolute difference between the Baptist's expectation of a "coming one" and Jesus' ministry. Several redactional and compositional elements in the preceding narrative support this interpretation.

First, in the infancy narratives Luke has cautiously distanced John from Jesus since their childhood by placing John in the desert (1:80) and Jesus in Nazareth (2:39, 51). Despite the fact that Luke records rather extensively, and in parallel panels, the births of John and Jesus, the two figures never cross paths except for the meeting of Elizabeth and Mary (1:44). The geographical separation in Luke between John and Jesus extends until the Baptist's manifestation to the people of Israel, without any indication that a relationship ever developed between them.

Second, while according to Matt 3:14–15 John converses with Jesus and expresses his subordination to and respect for him, in Luke there is no description that John ever explicitly met Jesus or identified him as a superior figure.[48] Consequently, the direct association of "the stronger one" with Jesus is less evident in Luke.

---

48. Luke never reports a personal, physical meeting between John and Jesus; any personal knowledge of each other is at least ambiguous. Darr (*Character Building*, 73)

Third, Luke has further alienated John from Jesus by placing the account of the Baptist's imprisonment (3:19–20) before the inauguration of Jesus' public ministry.

Fourth, Luke edits the baptismal scene (3:21–22) so that, in contrast to Mark 1:9 and Matt 3:13, Jesus is no longer explicitly baptized by John (ὑπὸ Ἰωάννου).[49] Luke's redaction does not necessarily imply than John and Jesus never met during the baptismal scene, but it does make that event inconsequential.[50]

Fifth, unlike Matthew, where the portrayal of the eschatological prophet expected by John (a fiery reformer) contrasts without qualification with the compassionate ministry of Jesus, Luke's redactional and stylistic modifications in the parallel material (Matt 3:1–17 // Luke 3:1–18) yield a more nuanced characterization of John's expectations. Three points merit consideration in this regard:

(a) Luke alone among the evangelists extends the quote from Isaiah (Luke 3:4–6; Isa 40:3–5 [LXX]) to include the reference about the "salvation of God." Nolland explains the effect of this addition: "In view of the actual ministry of Jesus, v. 6 helps to balance or moderate the rather stern and threatening tone of vv. 7–17: the fulfillment of the purposes of God is supremely in salvation and not in judgment."[51]

(b) Luke's additional material on John's ethical preaching (3:10–14)—with its emphasis on concern for one's neighbor—makes the Baptist's

---

adds: "Contrary to what we read in John 1:23, 29–38, Luke's Baptist neither identifies the Christ nor points to himself as a sign of the arrival of divine salvation."

49. Dibelius, *Überlieferung*, 60. Conzelmann (*Theology*, 21) notes that by placing the baptism account *after* the imprisonment of John and by omitting Jesus' baptism *by* John, Luke has completely separated John from Jesus. Moreover, Wink (*John the Baptist*, 83 n. 1) contends (erroneously) that in 3:21 βαπτισθέντος is middle and means that Jesus baptized himself.

50. Darr, who considers the baptismal scene "highly enigmatic" and opaque (*Character Building*, 68, 74), points out: "The lack of interaction between the two protagonists in this critical juncture creates an unmistakable tension for readers who have been waiting for John and Jesus to meet." Luke's editing functions somewhat similarly to what Alter (*Biblical Narrative*, 44) describes as the "artful procedure of variously suppressing motive (in this case action) in order to elicit moral inferences and suggest certain ambiguities." The ambiguity about the meeting between John and Jesus is never explicitly cleared, even though Luke's account (Luke-Acts) of John is the most extensive in the entire NT.

51. Nolland, *Luke*, 143–44.

identification of Jesus with the expected prophetic figure less problematic.[52] Although John's ethical exhortation does not directly refer to the Messiah, its connection to his eschatological preaching colors the radical character of the expected prophetic figure and yields a different emphasis: concern for the needy.[53] Hence, John's eschatological preaching is not only concerned with the judgment of the prophetic figure but also with the conditions that are to be associated with the manifestation of God's agent.

(c) In Luke's characterization, John associates the arrival of the eschatological age with good works on behalf of the disadvantaged. To illustrate the conditions that must prevail then, Luke employs a number of agricultural metaphors, which Jesus uses later in his public ministry (6:43-44; see also 8:8; 13:6-9; 20:10).[54] This association suggests that for Luke there is continuity rather than opposition between the message and the ministry of John and Jesus.[55]

Kazmierski's remarks regarding John's characterization exclusively as an apocalyptic preacher of judgment are worth noting:

> This model [apocalyptic preacher of judgment] is often said to represent the authentic John sometimes to the exclusion of all other possibilities. He is the ultimate ascetic preacher of hell and damnation who opposes the powerful and indeed any who

---

52. Regarding the debate as to whether this special material comes from Q or L, see Meier, *Marginal Jew*, 2:40-42; Ernst, *Johannes der Täufer*, 93-98; 312-13. Müller, (*Charakterzeichnung*, 156) posits "daß Lukas diese Verse gebildet hat"; see also Bovon, *Luke 1*, 123; Bultmann, *History*, 145.

53. Johnson (*Luke*, 124) notes: "Salvation and judgment are equally emphasized in this passage"; see also Taylor, *Immerser*, 113-49; Fitzmyer, *Luke*, 1:465.

54. John speaks about the trees that produce good fruit (3:8-9) and refers to an eschatological figure who will gather the wheat and will burn the chaff (3:17). Later, in his public ministry, Jesus also speaks about the trees that produce good and bad fruit; see Tannehill, *Luke-Acts*, 1:145. Moreover, some commentators find in Luke's summary in 3:18 (ἕτερα παρακαλῶν εὐηγγελίζετο τὸν λαόν) an allusion to John's proclamation of other aspects of the good news of the kingdom (Webb, *John the Baptizer*, 63 n. 47; Taylor, *Immerser*, 149-54). Müller (*Charakterzeichnung*, 178) concludes: "Auch Johannes ist in der Charakterzeichnung des Lukas ein Freudenbote (vgl. Jes 61,1f), der das Heil Gottes ansagt."; see also Ernst, *Johannes der Täufer*, 89; Becker, *Johannes der Taüfer*, 12-15; 66-70.

55. Against Conzelmann's interpretation of the Baptist in Luke, Tannehill (*Luke-Acts*, 1:47-53) highlights the continuity regarding the mission and the message between John and Jesus.

might consider themselves among the pious in Israel, a kind of Savanarola of the first century. But, as we have pointed out, there are serious difficulties with this view. While it is altogether likely that there was a negative side to John's proclamation, we have argued that it must not dominate our understanding of the Baptist and his ministry. It is at most the flip side of the announcement of the good news of salvation that he proclaimed in the strains of the prophecies of the Second Isaiah.[56]

Kazmierski's observations caution us against adopting an overly negative view regarding Luke's presentation of John's proclamation.

Therefore, the reason for John's question in the Gospel of Luke is neither a revision of a previous identification of Jesus with the Messiah nor a doubt provoked by an absolute contrast between an expected fiery reformer and Jesus' compassionate ministry. Rather the question is best interpreted as an initial attempt, occasioned by John's ignorance, to identify Jesus with God's eschatological agent. Dibelius offers a good synthesis of the meaning of John's question in Luke's narrative: the Baptist's question is ambiguous, and this suggests that John had not yet developed a definite relationship with Jesus.[57] In Luke, John's question is prompted by the reports he now receives about Jesus' activity (περὶ πάντων τούτων, 7:18).[58] With more reason than those characters who have previously "known" Jesus but have not really discovered his identity (4:22), John, who has not been privy either to the life or to the ministry of Jesus, now questions whether he is the awaited (προσδοκῶμεν, cf. 3:15) prophet.[59] Hence, the question of John is an appeal for a confirmation of Jesus' identity, not because Jesus had not met the Baptist's expectations, but because, on the basis of the reports he has received

---

56. Kazmierski, *John the Baptist*, 116; see also 32–41.

57. Dibelius, *Überlieferung*, 38. For a list of commentators who have interpreted John's question along this line, see Sabugal, *Embajada*, 11. In Darr's (*Character Building*, 76) words: "John's ignorance of Jesus fully accords with what has happened in the story thus far. Since a recognition scene has not occurred and John was not privy (so far as we were told) to the Spirit's descent upon Jesus, the Baptist cannot be faulted for his lack of knowledge about Jesus."

58. Achtemeier, "Miracles of Jesus," 158.

59. According to Tannehill (*Luke-Acts*, 1:80): "John, who to this point has made no confession of Jesus as the fulfillment of his prophecy, is now raising that possibility." In a sense, Luke portrays John every bit as anxious and as ignorant about the identity of the expected eschatological figure as the rest of the people.

A Narrative-Critical Interpretation of 7:18–28

from his disciples, John realizes for the first time that Jesus may be God's eschatological agent.

The question about the identity of Jesus will echo throughout the rest of the narrative as different characters in the story confront him and address this issue.[60] Just as Jesus interrogates his disciples about who they and the people say he is (9:18; 20; also 8:25), so too the religious leaders (7:49; 22:67; 22:70), the crowds (23:37), his adversaries (23:39), and the Roman authorities (9:9; 23:3) will question whether Jesus is (σὺ εἶ) God's agent, either to taunt or harass him. In the Acts of the Apostles the identity question will resurface when Paul encounters the risen Lord (9:5; also 22:8; 26:15). Finally, when Paul meets the disciples of Ephesus who have only received the baptism of John, Paul will recall that John proclaimed a baptism of repentance in preparation for the "one who was to come" (τὸν ἐρχόμενον, 19:4) after him.

The Disciples of John and Their Message (7:20)

After Luke relates John's commissioning of his disciples, Luke describes their encounter with Jesus. Although John's disciples move from one location to another (παραγενόμενοι δὲ πρὸς αὐτὸν), the actual location (like the locale at the beginning of the pericope) remains unidentified. The disciples of John, to whom Luke now refers as "the men" (οἱ ἄνδρες)—in this instance without further specification of their number—accurately convey John's question. They repeat verbatim what John has asked: "Are you the one who is to come or should we wait for another?"[61] The disciples emphasize that it was John the Baptist (Ἰωάννης ὁ βαπτιστής) who sent them to pose the question.[62]

By repeating John's question, Luke elongates the time of the narrative and improves the logic of the scene without adding elements that would potentially distract from the focus of the episode.[63] The repetition of the question emphasizes the central point of the passage—who Jesus is—and highlights its importance for the plot of the narrative.[64]

---

60. Brawley, *Luke-Acts*, 133–54.

61. The repetition of the question is typically Lukan (cf. Luke 19:31, 34). Luke's repetition of John's question is an artful literary convention (Alter, *Biblical Narrative*, 88–113).

62. This is the first time that Luke uses John's formal title; see also 7:33; 9:19.

63. Spencer, *Rhetorical Texture*, 102.

64. Roth, *Character Types*, 173; Green, *Luke*, 295.

The Healing Power of Jesus (7:21)

Whereas in Matt 11:4 Jesus' answer to the envoys of John follows their question immediately, in the Gospel of Luke the response is preceded with a summary of healings.[65] The response of Jesus to John's inquiry is threefold. First, Luke describes a series of healings (7:21). Second, Jesus alludes to a quotation from the prophet Isaiah (7:22). Third, Jesus concludes his answer with a final beatitude (7:23).

In the first part of the response, Luke notes that "at that hour" (ἐν ἐκείνῃ τῇ ὥρᾳ) Jesus performs a number of healings (ἐθεράπευσεν).[66] The phrase ἐν ἐκείνῃ τῇ ὥρᾳ emphasizes the importance of the moment. "This is a propitious moment, for the fundamental question of Jesus' identity has been raised by John—that is, by a person who has himself been recognized within the narrative as one miraculously conceived and divinely endowed for prophetic ministry and who had proclaimed the good news and been imprisoned on account of his message of repentance."[67] The beneficiaries of Jesus' actions include those with diseases (νόσων) and afflictions (μαστίγων),[68] people under the influence of evil spirits (πνευμάτων πονηρῶν), and the blind (τυφλοῖς).[69]

Luke's summary of healings reinforces the portrayal of Jesus' ministry in the previous narrative.[70] In 4:40–41 Luke notes that all those who had people weakened by a variety of diseases (ἀσθενοῦντας νόσοις ποικίλαις) brought them to Jesus, who healed (ἐθεράπευεν)

---

65. The material in Luke 7:21 is absent from Matt 11:2–6. Verse 21 is a characteristic Lukan summary statement of the ministry of Jesus (4:40–41; 6:18–19).

66. The phrase ἐν ἐκείνῃ τῇ ὥρᾳ emphasizes the instantaneous reaction to the question of John's disciples and heightens the significance of the moment; see Craghan ("Redactional Study," 358–61) who, however, considers ἐν αὐτῇ τῇ ὥρᾳ the original reading. Theon (*Progymnasmata* 78) points out that one of the elements of a good narrative is the time at which a particular event takes place.

67. Green, *Luke*, 296.

68. Μάστιξ is used literally to refer to a scourging or metaphorically to refer to a plague or a bodily illness. In Acts 22:24 it refers to Roman torture and in Heb 11:36 to the scourge received in the synagogue (Schneider, "μάστιξ," 518–19).

69. In the past, the discussion about this verse has revolved around whether the list of mighty works should be interpreted literally or metaphorically (Plummer, *St. Luke*, 203; Sabugal, *Embajada*, 174–75 nn. 197–98).

70. Some commentators have suggested that the references to the resuscitation of the dead and the cleansing of lepers are part of an elaborate Lukan scheme to depict John and Jesus after the Elijah/Elisha cycle (Brodie, *Birthing*, 317–24; Wink, *John the Baptist*, 43–45).

them and cast out many demons (δαιμόνια). In 5:15–16 Luke describes how the crowd gathered to hear Jesus and be healed (θεραπεύεσθαι) by him from their weaknesses (ἀσθενειῶν). Luke depicts Jesus as curing (ἰαθῆναι, ἰᾶτο) the diseases of many and healing (ἐθεραπεύοντο) those who were troubled by impure spirits (πνευμάτων ἀκαθάρτων, 6:18–19).[71]

Besides these summaries of healings, Luke relates a number of particular episodes in which Jesus cures people from their illnesses. In the synagogue of Capernaum, Jesus cures a man possessed by a demon (4:33–35) and later heals Simon's mother-in-law (4:38–39). Jesus cures a man with a skin disease (5:13), a paralytic (5:17–25), and a man with a withered hand (6:10). He also heals the servant of the centurion (7:1–10) and resuscitates the widow's son (7:11–17). Only the giving of sight has not been featured in the previous narrative (cf. 18:35–43).[72]

The review of Jesus' healings serves four functions in this episode. First, by listing an additional number of mighty works, Luke strengthens the persuasive force of Jesus' forthcoming reply to John.[73] Second, the summary of healings improves the literary logic of the passage. By describing Jesus' healing activity before his response to the messengers of John, Luke illustrates concretely what is referred to by Jesus' reply, "Go and tell John what you have seen and heard." Third, the summary of healings recalls Jesus' programmatic speech in the synagogue of Nazareth (4:16–30). Luke's summary thus supports ongoing concern of the sections (4:16—9:50) for defining Jesus' identity and portraying him as God's agent of salvation.[74] As a fourth and final function, the gesture of Jesus highlights a literary aspect of Luke's version of the episode.

---

71. Jesus' healing ministry continues throughout the rest of the Gospel (8:2, 27–33, 43, 47; 9:1, 2, 6, 11, 42; 10:9; 13:14; 14:3–4; 17:15; 22:51). Jesus' followers imitate his healing ministry in the Acts of the Apostles (4:14; 5:16; 8:7; 9:34; 10:38; 17:25; 19:12; 22:24; 28:8–9, 27).

72. Some commentators find a special meaning in the reference to the healing of the blind. The use of χαρίζομαι, a verb associated with benefaction, combined with κύριος in v. 19 may be trying to highlight the identity of Jesus and foreshadowing the role of John's disciples to illuminate the Baptist (Green, *Luke*, 296–97). Moreover, the restoration of sight in Luke is often associated with the reception of the kingdom (Culpepper, "Metaphor of Sight," 434–43).

73. Theon (*Progymnasmata* 79) recommended that "if the subject is naturally believable one should sometimes use conciseness [and] sometimes also brevity, but mostly in confirmations and things that make the matter under discussion persuasive."

74. Roth, *Character Types*, 26, 215–21.

The description of Jesus' healings slows down the tempo of the narrative and creates a momentary expectation that heightens the drama of the scene.⁷⁵ The episode loses its sense of time as Jesus initiates a spontaneous healing session among a group of people who up to this moment have remained in the background as silent witnesses to his exchange with the disciples of John.

While a mechanical response—a simple "yes"—would have logically answered the question of John, Luke's description of the scene adds vividness to the episode. For, by evoking deeds that are related to the dawn of an eschatological age, Luke begins to shape Jesus' response to John in a way unparalleled by Matthew's account.⁷⁶ The anonymous beneficiaries of Jesus' mighty works help to define Jesus as the "one who is to come." As Roth points out, "The fact that Jesus saves these character types as only God or God's agent in the LXX can do confirms his status as God or God's agent."⁷⁷

Jesus Commissions the Disciples of John (7:22)

As Luke concludes his description of Jesus' impromptu healing session, the narrator has Jesus address the messengers of John in direct speech (καὶ ἀποκριθεὶς εἶπεν αὐτοῖς). Jesus instructs the disciples of John that, after they have gone back (πορευθέντες) to the Baptist, they should tell (ἀπαγγείλατε) him about the things that they have seen (εἴδετε) and heard (ἠκούσατε).⁷⁸ The expression regarding the things that they have "seen and heard" refers to the healings Jesus has just performed (7:21). Jesus commands John's disciples to report not only what they have witnessed ("seen") but also "heard," even though in 7:21 Luke does not mention any speeches or conversations. Jesus' request could refer either to the people's comments after he performed the mighty deeds (cf. 7:16–17) or to what he said that was not mentioned by Luke.⁷⁹ Given the

---

75. Ibid., 173–74.

76. Dupont, "Jean-Baptiste," 945; Sabugal, *Embajada*, 191.

77. Roth, *Character Types*, 215.

78. Tannehill (*Luke-Acts*, 1:79–80) notes that the Lukan sequence εἴδετε καὶ ἠκού- σατε (different from ἀκούετε καὶ βλέπετε in Matthew 11:4) reflects the order of the following Isaian quote in which the last element—the preaching of good news to the poor—is *heard*. Moreover, Culpepper ("Seeing the Kingdom," 434) points out, "In the Gospel of Luke references to seeing and hearing often evoke reflection on the perception of the kingdom of God."

79. Jesus' healing activity is commonly associated with his preaching (5:15).

proximity of the statement about the "proclamation [εὐαγγελίζονται] of the good news to the poor" (7:22), what the messengers of John have "heard" refers probably to the latter (see also 8:1).[80]

After instructing the disciples of John to return to him, Jesus spells out the content of the message that they should bring: "the blind recover their sight, the lame walk, lepers are cleansed, and the deaf hear, the dead are raised and the poor have the good news proclaimed to them."[81] In the preceding narrative (4:31—7:17) Luke has shown Jesus' concern for the downtrodden and, except for the healing of the deaf (cf. 11:14), the actions recorded in 7:22 recapitulate his Galilean ministry.[82] Jesus has cured paralytics (χωλοὶ περιπατοῦσιν, 5:17-26) and lepers (λεπροὶ καθαρίζονται, 5:12-14). He has raised the dead (νεκροὶ ἐγείρονται, 7:11-17) and proclaimed the good news to the poor (πτωχοὶ εὐαγγελίζονται, 5:1, 15; 6:18; 6:20—7:1).[83] In 7:21, Luke also notes that Jesus gave sight to the blind (τυφλοὶ ἀναβλέπουσιν).[84] Like the healings

---

80. Εὐαγγελίζω, κηρύσσω, and διδάσκω are three key terms that Luke uses to describe the preaching activity of Jesus. The disciples of Jesus also share in this ministry (9:1-6), and in Acts the followers of Jesus will carry on with his preaching activity (5:42; 8:5, 25; 10:42; 11:20; 14:7; 17:18; 19:13); see Tannehill, *Luke-Acts*, 1:78 n. 4.

81. Jesus' list of healings echoes Isaianic signs of salvation (Isa 29:18-19; 35:5-6; 42:18; 43:8; 61:1; Schürmann, *Lukasevangelium*, 410-11). Jeremias (*Promise*, 46) notes that in the quote of Isaiah the idea of "vengeance" has been omitted. Dupont ("Jean-Baptiste," 951) makes a similar claim by emphasizing that the book of Isaiah has no shortage of oracles that insist on the arrival of the threatening end of time, when the wicked would suffer punishment for their sins, but Jesus keeps only the oracles of consolation, those that preach that God will take pity on his people and will send a merciful Savior. But the interpretation that Jesus (or Luke) premeditatedly omitted the references to a vengeance has been refuted (Flender, *Luke*, 152-53; Poirier, "Elijianic Figure," 362).

82. The healing of a deaf man in Mark 7:31-37 is part of Luke's "great omission" (Mark 6:45—8:26).

83. In Luke, "the poor" (πτωχοί) is an elastic term that comprises more than just those who have material needs. They are also those who suffer or who by their perceived violation of moral standards live on the fringes of society (prostitutes, lepers, and toll collectors); Fitzmyer, *Luke*, 1:250-51; Johnson, *Possessions in Luke-Acts*, 132-44; Green, *Luke*, 297. Luke's characterization of the "poor" is closely associated with the mass of people (ὄχλος, λαός) that often seek Jesus (4:40-42; 5:15) to be healed from their infirmities. Although as Roth (*Character Types*, 215-21) has noted that in Luke "the poor" have a specific rhetorical function, in 7:18-35 (specifically in 7:24, 29) they form together with the mass of people an undifferentiated secondary character group that has its own rhetorical purpose (see Tannehill, *Luke-Acts*, 1:103-39, 143-66). This character group (the mass of people) is also closely associated with the ministry of the Baptist (3:7, 10); see Strathmann, "λαός"; Meyer, "ὄχλος," 586-90.

84. Blindness is the only specific illness that Luke notes in the healing summary

recorded in 7:21, Jesus' message to the disciples of John recalls his appearance in the synagogue of Nazareth (4:16–30), where the words of the prophet Isaiah (61:1) become part of his programmatic speech.[85] Jesus' response to the messengers of John, which alludes to the passage from Isaiah, is not only reminiscent of his speech at the synagogue but also an implicit reiteration of its prophetic role as a herald of consolation to Israel.[86] As in Nazareth, Jesus now defines his identity in terms of Isaianic prophetic categories, urging John to recognize that what Isaiah was for his people, Jesus is for the present generation.[87] With this response, Jesus reiterates his implicit prophetic claim and answers John with a coded response that he is able to decipher.[88] Jesus' reply to the messengers of John adds christological focus, helps to clarify the plot of the narrative, and provides an interpretative clue with which to understand the meaning of Jesus' ministry and identity.

Blessedness and Scandal: Reactions to the Ministry of Jesus (7:23)

To conclude his reply to the messengers of John, Jesus makes a statement in the form of a beatitude in which he declares "blessed" (μακάριος) whoever is not scandalized (σκανδαλισθῇ) by him. The interpretation of the beatitude has been as problematic as John's question. Opinions differ as to whether the statement is an exhortation or a warning, and whether it is directed at John, his disciples, or the crowd in general. Furthermore, among those commentators who regard the beatitude as a warning, views vary as to what the cause of the scandal is that Jesus is trying to prevent: (1) an erroneous assessment of Jesus' mission; (2) impatience; (3) despair over Jesus' humble and unexpected ministry; or (4) a contradiction or conflict between Jesus' messianic manifestation and a

---

(7:21), perhaps to compensate for the fact that up to this moment in the narrative Jesus has not yet healed anyone from blindness (see 18:35–43).

85. Poirier ("Elijianic Figure," 351) claims that at the pre-Lukan stage 4:16–30 contained a layer of Elijianic Christology.

86. Sanders, "Isaiah 61 to Luke 4"; Busse, *Nazareth-Manifest*, 46–47.

87. For Luke, Jesus is fulfilling prophetic expectations, even if the OT passage did not originally mean this; see Fitzmyer, *Luke*, 1:534.

88. In light of the expectation at the time of Jesus "to the effect that the coming of God's Messiah would be accompanied by such marvelous events, in fulfillment of Isaiah's prophecies," Jesus' answer would have been obvious to John; see Dunn, *Jesus Remembered*, 449; Puech, *Qumran Cave 4.XVIII*, 1–38.

A Narrative-Critical Interpretation of 7:18-28

nationalist, political, or eschatological view of the Messiah.[89] The meaning of this puzzling verse is best understood by taking into consideration its context as well as its literary structure.

Prior to the beatitude, Luke has used the term μακάριος to refer to several characters and character groups.[90] During Mary's visit with Elizabeth, Mary was called μακαρία (1:45; cf. 11:27), and in the Sermon on the Plain Jesus called all those who are poor, hungry, weeping, and hated μακάριοι (6:20-22). In these and other circumstances the term usually refers to the inner happiness of those who either already enjoy some sort of good fortune (10:23; 11:27-28; Acts 26:2) or will do so in the future (12:37-38, 43; 14:14-15; 23:29; Acts 20:35). But in 7:23 the promised happiness is contingent on not being scandalized by Jesus (μὴ σκανδαλισθῇ ἐν ἐμοί). The contrast between the felicity of μακάριοι and the moral connotation of σκανδαλίζω connotes the implicit warning of the phrase. Although Luke rarely uses σκανδαλίζω, he applies other phrases to convey the conflict that Jesus' ministry generates.[91]

In the infancy narratives, Simeon predicted that Jesus would be the cause for "the fall [πτῶσις] and rise of many" and a "sign of contradiction" (σημεῖον ἀντιλεγόμενον, 2:34). Although Simeon did not spell out the reasons for the "fall" and "contradiction," as Jesus begins his public ministry some take offense at his words and actions. After he reads from the scroll in the synagogue of Nazareth, the reactions of his compatriots change from acceptance to cynicism to incredulity, and finally to hostil-

---

89. These interpretations have usually lumped together the testimony of all the Gospels without sufficiently taking into account the particular narrative thrust of each evangelist. For a convenient summary of interpretations, see Sabugal, *Embajada*, 7-27.

90. Aside from Mary, who is the only character specifically called "blessed," all other uses of the expression apply to anonymous subjects with a sense of contingency attached to them. Μακάριοι is often used during Jesus' paraenetic speeches to urge people to adopt the values of the kingdom; see Hauck, "μακάριος," 367-70; Fitzmyer, *Luke*, 1:632-33.

91. Luke uses σκανδαλίζω—and its cognate σκάνδαλον—only once more in the Gospel (17:1-2), within the context of a warning. Jesus' beatitude in 7:23 implies an element of judgment (cf. 17:1-2). Kingsbury (*Conflict in Luke*, 84 n. 24) suggests that terms such as θαυμάζω, ἐξίστημι, and διαπορέω in some instances have a negative connotation in connection to the conflicts of Jesus with the religious authorities. In such instances the semantic range of those terms is similar to that of σκανδαλίζω. Dunn (*Jesus Remembered*, 450) notes: "[T]he verb (*skandalizō*, Aramaic *tql*) is well attested in the Jesus tradition in a variety of contexts, which together probably indicate Jesus' awareness of the 'scandalous' character of his mission." See also Lupieri, *Giovanni Battista*, 87-96.

ity (4:16–30).⁹² The episode suggests that the growing antipathy against Jesus arises from the inability of his fellow villagers to reconcile Jesus' prophetic claims with their acquaintance of him (cf. John 7:27, 41–42, 52). Likewise, when Jesus forgives the paralytic (5:21), the scribes and the Pharisees are scandalized; they regard his self-attribution of divine prerogatives as blasphemy (βλασφημίας), because only God can forgive sins (cf. John 10:33). Later, when he replies to accusations of violating the Sabbath with an implicit claim of superiority over David (6:1–5) and heals a man with a withered hand on the Sabbath (6:6–10), he infuriates the scribes and the Pharisees (ἐπλήσθησαν ἀνοίας), who "begin to plan how to deal with him" (6:11). Jesus' actions are met with increasing opposition (see also 7:39, 49), and the report that the disciples of John brought him (περὶ πάντων τούτων, 7:18) implies that John has heard not only the positive comments of the people (5:15; 6:17–19; 7:16–17) but also what his detractors have been saying (5:30, 6:11).⁹³

The warning about scandal in 7:23 comes after Jesus has performed a number of mighty works (7:1–10, 11–17, 21) that identify him with the prophetic expectations of his generation (7:16).⁹⁴ Hence, in light of the mounting hostility, and since the beatitude is not addressed to any one specifically (ὃς ἐάν), Jesus now warns not only John but also others against the potential of being scandalized by him.⁹⁵ Furthermore, since the adversaries of Jesus have been scandalized for several reasons, Jesus' warning should not be attributed to one particular cause.⁹⁶ Jesus, then,

---

92. Brawley, *Luke-Acts*, 6–27. The interpretation of the passage is complicated by its composite nature (Busse, *Nazareth-Manifest*, 13–67). Talbert (*Literary Patterns*, 39) highlights the thematic parallel between 4:16–30 and 7:18–30.

93. The use of the imperfects ἐγόγγυζον and διελάλουν denotes a continuous action.

94. Mighty works were presumed to be evidence of prophetic credentials as in Deut 18:15, 18; Isa 7:11; Luke 11:16, 29; 23:8; Acts 2:22, 43; 4:16, 30; 5:12; 6:8; 7:36; 8:6, 13; 14:3; 15:12. Based on this popular presumption, Luke uses the wonders performed by Jesus as evidence that he is God's agent; see Rengstorf, "σημεῖον," 208–25, 230–43; Achtemeier, "Miracles of Jesus," 158; Squires, *Plan of God*, 78–102.

95. The form of the beatitude, which patterns a Greek usage rare in the NT (i.e., the adjective [μακάριος] followed by the relative pronoun ὅς), hinders any attempt to identify a more specific addressee. Regarding the form associated with the use of μακάριος, see Fitzmyer, *Luke*, 1:632–33.

96. The narrative suggests various reasons for the potential scandal: inability to reconcile the acquaintance of Jesus with his prophetic claims, envy, and/or conflict over authority.

takes advantage of John's question to pronounce not only a blessing but a warning, which is universal in scope (as in the case of other uses of μακάριος). The theme of the scandal, which is so closely related to the conflicts of Jesus, will continue to resonate in the Acts of the Apostles as his followers spread his message and imitate his actions (Acts 4:2; 5:28; 6:11; 7:54; 22:22–23).

The lack of John's formal response to this final beatitude of Jesus has led some scholars to question the integrity and historicity of the present account. Commentators have sensed that there is something missing in the way the story is told. Such claims are fostered by the enigmatic style and the grammatical structure of the beatitude. The historical plausibility of the event is beyond the scope of the present study, but those who deny the historicity of the episode based on John's lack of response fail to take into consideration the literary form of the final saying. Although it has been common to refer to this statement of Jesus as an apothegm, the literary structure of the beatitude is more accurately described as an enthymeme.[97] The form of this rhetorical device, which often leaves out a premise or a conclusion, explains in part why many scholars have felt that an element of the story is lacking.[98] The formulation of the en-

---

97. While a syllogism best suits a deductive argument in logic, the abbreviated and/or simplified form of an enthymeme better serves a rhetorical argumentation aimed at persuading; see Aristotle, *Rhet.* 1.2.1357a.13–14; 2.22–26; 3.17.1418a.6–1418b.17; Quintilian, *Inst.* 5.10.1–4; 5.14.1–3; Demetrius, *De elocutione* 30–33; Burnyeat, "Enthymeme"; Kennedy, *Rhetorical Criticism*, 49–51. Several authors have emphasized the rhetorical function of 7:18–35 within the context of the Lukan narrative. For instance, Spencer (*Rhetorical Texture*, 101–2) describes the structure of 7:18–23 as an extended chreia, while Cameron ("Characterizations," 35–69), on the other hand, claims that the whole of 7:18–35 resembles an elaborate chreia. Theon (*Progymnasmata*, 96) points out that beatitudes are usually connected with chreias, and Kennedy (*Rhetorical Criticism*, 49–51) notes that enthymematic reasoning is commonly associated with beatitudes. In the case of 7:23 the enthymeme is best described as an asyndetic enthymeme because despite the initial καί it lacks the causal particles characteristic of many enthymemes (i.e., ὅτι or γάρ). Vinson ("Enthymemes," 119) points out, "Greek, of course, has many ways of showing cause, and the lack of a causal conjunction may not mean that an enthymeme was not intended." See also Robbins, "Enthymeme," 191–214.

98. Robbins ("Enthymeme," 191–92) notes: "A special characteristic of an enthymeme is to leave a premise or conclusion unexpressed, with a presumption that the premise or conclusion is obvious from the overall context. Enthymemic discourse, then, is discourse that presumes a context to fill out its meanings." Scholars continue to debate about what constitutes the formal structure of the enthymeme; see Aune, "Abuse of the Enthymeme," 299–320; Vinson, "Enthymemes," 119–41. For a critique of Aune and Vinson, see Spencer, *Rhetorical Texture*, 54–58 nn. 31, 33, 35. Despite the discus-

thymeme creates a natural gap that does not demand a reaction.⁹⁹ Since, in the preceding narrative, Jesus has been shown to be performing the actions that are to be associated with a forthcoming prophetic figure, the unstated conclusion presented here, in the form of a beatitude, is that Jesus is "the one who is to come."¹⁰⁰

The final beatitude counterbalances the question of John and expresses an uncertainty that is symmetrical to that conveyed by the question of the Baptist.¹⁰¹ Just as John is uncertain about Jesus' identity, Jesus is uncertain about who (John included) will ultimately recognize in him the eschatological agent of God. The literary gap produced by the enthymematic argumentation yields a sense of ambiguity that reinforces the previous narrative's insinuation of John's lack of thorough knowledge of Jesus.¹⁰² And, as Darr points out, the predicament as to whether John and his disciples will recognize in Jesus the expected prophetic figure serves yet another literary feature: "[T]he tension this creates helps to maintain reader interest in the matter until it is resolved much later, when Paul encounters the disciples of John in Ephesus [Acts 19:1-7]."¹⁰³

---

sions regarding the form and structure of the enthymemes, five characteristics of an enthymematic argument can be seen in Jesus' response to John in 7:22-23: (1) a missing conclusion, (2) juxtaposition of elements to demonstrate an argument; (3) the appeal to abductive reasoning (i.e., reasoning that begins with a suggestion rather than formal logic); (4) a desire to persuade; and (5) a pivotal marker in the speech. The missing conclusion of the argument is that since, according to the narrative, Jesus performs the actions attributable to a prophetic figure, he is the expected agent of God.

99. Kurz, *Biblical Narrative*, 31–36; Roth, *Character Types*, 216; Darr, *Character Building*, 75–76.

100. According to Becker (*Jesus of Nazareth*, 112–13) Jesus' contemporaries would have understood his actions in this way; see also Taylor, *Immerser*, 290–92; Dunn, *Jesus Remembered*, 449; Bird, *One Who Is to Come*, 98–104.

101. Bovon, *Luke 1*, 281.

102. Alter's explanation (*Biblical Narrative*, 153) of the "art of reticence" illustrates the effects of this final beatitude of Jesus: "In biblical narrative, this kind of purposeful ambiguity of a single statement may occur . . . in the selective reticences of the narrator's report and in the sudden breaking off of dialogue as well." And Alter adds, "We are compelled to get at character and motive through a process of inference from fragmentary data, often with crucial pieces of narrative exposition strategically withheld, which sometimes lead to multiple or even wavering perspectives on the characters" (126).

103. Darr, *Character Building*, 84.

Summary

The meaning of John's question in Luke is rooted in the infancy narratives' implicit assumption of an expected prophetic figure. In these early pages of his Gospel, Luke manifests, through the statements of different characters, the expectations of the people of Israel for a Messiah. Although from the narrator's point of view Jesus is the expected Messiah, the characters in the developing narrative still have to identify him with the eschatological prophet. It is within this context that the report of John's disciples arouse the Baptist's interest about whether Jesus is the "the one who is to come."

Unlike Matthew, where the Baptist's identification of Jesus with God's envoy and the contrast between John's expectation of "the stronger one" and Jesus' compassionate ministry furnish the main interpretative key, John's question in the Gospel of Luke invites a more nuanced interpretation. The sustained separation between John and Jesus, the plot of the context in which Luke introduces the question of John, and the unique character of the Baptist's eschatological preaching suggest that John's inquiry is an initial probe regarding Jesus' identity. John's question is prompted not so much by a striking difference between his own expectations of "the coming one" and Jesus as by John's lack of knowledge of, and permanent alienation from, Jesus' ministry. Like many other characters in the narrative, John now speculates about whether Jesus is the one who will fulfill the eschatological expectations.

Jesus responds to John's question by performing a number of healings that identify him with the prophetic expectations of his contemporaries. Jesus' healings strengthen the persuasive force of his verbal reply to John, improve the literary logic and style of the passage, add christological focus to the scene, and recall Jesus' programmatic speech in the synagogue of Nazareth (4:16–30). His reply to the messengers of John clarifies the plot of the narrative and serves as an interpretative framework within which to understand Jesus' ministry and identity. Jesus urges the Baptist to recognize him as the envoy of God who is to be associated with an age of salvation and concern for the needy.

The final beatitude of Jesus is both a blessing and a warning addressed to anyone who may listen. The beatitude, which is part of an enthymematic argumentation that forms a natural gap in the narrative, is aimed at persuading those who may hesitate to accept Jesus' claim that he is indeed God's eschatological agent. Since, in the ongoing narrative,

Jesus has been portrayed as performing the actions associated with the arrival of a prophetic figure, the unstated conclusion of the enthymeme is that he is "the one who is to come." The final beatitude counterbalances the uncertainty of John, reinforcing the narrative's implicit insinuation of a lack of mutual knowledge between John and Jesus, but it also expresses Jesus' hope that the people (including John) may recognize him as the promised agent of God.

Second Subunit: Jesus' Encomium of John the Baptist (7:24–28)

THE FIRST RHETORICAL QUESTION: THE MORAL FIBER OF JOHN (7:24)

The second subunit begins with the departure of the messengers of John (7:24). As in the previous episode (7:18–23), there is no description of the setting, and Luke, like Matthew (11:7), mentions only that Jesus' interlocutors have departed (ἀπελθόντων). Luke links more clearly than Matthew the beginning of this subunit to the previous one by specifying that the "messengers of John" (τῶν ἀγγέλων Ἰωάννου) have just left.[104]

Jesus, who has been addressing the disciples of the Baptist, begins (ἤρξατο) to speak to "the crowds" (τοὺς ὄχλους). In the previous subunit, Luke referred only indirectly to a crowd that remained as silent witnesses to the exchange between the disciples of John and Jesus until the narrator remarked that Jesus began to heal "many" (πολλούς) from their infirmities (7:21). The narrative suggested then that the crowd was comprised of a large group of people suffering from different diseases, although this did not necessarily mean that they were all ill. The proximity of that episode to the present scene and the purported unity of the narrative indicate that the "crowds" here are the same. Thus far in the narrative, Luke has portrayed the crowds (ὄχλοι) as curious bystanders who come to be baptized and instructed by John (3:7, 10) and to follow Jesus to hear his words (4:42; 5:1, 3; 6:17; 7:9, 11) and be cured (5:15, 19; 6:19).[105] Through the rest of the subunit, the crowd will remain as silent listeners to Jesus' encomium of the Baptist. As character types, they are

---

104. Luke's reference to the emissaries of John has varied from οἱ μαθηταί (7:18) to οἱ ἄνδρες (7:20), to τῶν ἀγγέλων (7:24). The style of Luke's transitional verse is better than Matthew's; see Nolland, *Luke*, 335; Fitzmyer, *Luke*, 1:673.

105. Tannehill (*Luke-Acts*, 1:144) points out that there is continuity between crowds that follow John and those who follow Jesus; see also Kingsbury, *Conflict in Luke*, 28–31; Brawley, *Luke-Acts*, 133–54.

A Narrative-Critical Interpretation of 7:18–28

anonymous and without the capacity to make moral choices.[106] But the passive presence of the crowd facilitates the christological focus of the narrative.

When Jesus begins to speak to the crowd, the topic of his address is John (περὶ Ἰωάννου). Jesus addresses the audience with three consecutive rhetorical questions regarding the identity of John (7:24, 25, and 26).[107] Each question has two parts. The first part of the questions begins with an identical phrase (τί ἐξήλθατε . . . ;) followed by a second part that presents the audience with a possible answer in the form of yet another rhetorical question. The alternatives of the first two rhetorical questions represent almost hyperbolically a false portrayal of John. Therefore, they are to be rejected. The final question, however, contains the right answer.

Jesus first asks the crowd what they went out into the desert to see (τί ἐξήλθατε εἰς τὴν ἔρημον θεάσασθαι).[108] His question regarding the desert (ἔρημος) recalls Luke's remarks about John's habitat in the infancy narratives. In 1:80, Luke notes that John lived in deserted places (ἐν ταῖς ἐρήμοις) from his childhood until his manifestation to the people of Israel. Luke also points out that when the word of God came to John and he inaugurated his public ministry, he was in the desert (3:2, 4). But Jesus' rhetorical question also evokes his own trips into the desert, where he went to face the temptations of the devil (4:1), seek solitude (4:42), and pray (5:16).

In the second part of the first rhetorical question, Jesus asks the crowd if they went out into the desert to see a reed shaken by the wind (κάλαμον ὑπὸ ἀνέμου σαλευόμενον). In the NT, the image of the shaken reed appears only here and in the parallel passage of Matt 11:7.[109] In Luke's narrative, the image stands in contrast to Jesus' metaphor of the

---

106. Roth, *Character Types*, 215.

107. Spencer (*Rhetorical Texture*, 105) remarks: "The rhetorical arrangement—questioning followed by the corresponding answer—is a common Greco-Roman rhetorical device"; Aristotle, *Rhet.* 3.18; *Rhet. Her.* 4.23–24.

108. The interrogative pronoun τί could also be translated (as in the *Gospel of Thomas*) as "why" to accentuate the reason rather than the object of the people's journey into the desert (Fitzmyer, *Luke*, 1:673; Marshall, *Luke*, 293–94).

109. Theissen ("Schwankende Rohr," 26–44) posits that the image of the reed was meant to evoke Herod Antipas's symbol on a coin. Theissen presents numismatic evidence to bolster his claim that Jesus is contrasting the unwavering convictions of John with the accommodating principles of Herod Antipas.

person who builds the foundation of his house on a rock (6:48). In that parable the house not shaken by the river that bursts against (ὁ ποταμὸς ... οὐκ ἴσχυσεν σαλεῦσαι αὐτήν) it stands for the person who listens to the word of God and puts it into practice, i.e., the person who, by being coherent with his/her principles, is able to withstand the difficulties of life (cf. 21:26).[110] In 7:24, the image of the shaken reed illustrates the opposite behavior. More than an ironic allusion to a worthless journey into the wilderness to contemplate a common spectacle, the image of the shaken reed represents the erratic behavior of someone who is not coherent with his/her beliefs.[111] Thus, the answer to Jesus' rhetorical question is "no," because John, whose life and mission has been sanctioned by God (1:15–17, 44, 76–77) and who has been portrayed as a zealous and unflinching emissary of his word (3:1–20), cannot be represented by such a flimsy image. But Jesus leaves the question unanswered, and it is up to the crowd to supply the response.

THE SECOND RHETORICAL QUESTION: THE AUSTERITY OF JOHN (7:25)

In the second rhetorical question, Jesus asks the crowd if they went out to see "a man dressed in soft clothing." Jesus supplements this image with a second remark that elaborates and to a certain extent explains the meaning of the rhetorical question by adding that "those with glorious clothing and living in splendor are in the royal palaces."

These statements appear in almost identical form in Matt 11:8. But whereas Matthew uses μαλακός twice to describe those who wear fine garments, Luke complements the picture of the "man dressed in soft clothing" with the image of "those with glorious clothing" (οἱ ἐν ἱματισμῷ ἐνδόξῳ) and "living in splendor" (τρυφῇ ὑπάρχοντες).

Since Luke lacks Matthew's description of John dressed in camel's hair, wearing a leather belt, and eating locusts and wild honey (Matt 3:4), the second rhetorical question of Jesus does not have the obvious referent that Matthew's characterization of the Baptist has. However, since

---

110. The form of the Lukan parable is different from Matthew's version (7:24–27); see Nolland, *Luke*, 310. In the Acts of the Apostles, Peter applies to Jesus the theme of the righteous person who is not shaken (σαλεύω) by difficulties: "I saw the Lord ever before me, with him at my right hand I shall not be shaken [μὴ σαλευθῶ]" (2:25; Ps 16:8 [LXX]).

111. Schürmann, *Lukasevangelium*, 416; Marshall, *Luke*, 294. Fitzmyer (*Luke*, 1:673–74) points out that John is in prison precisely because he did not compromise his principles.

A Narrative-Critical Interpretation of 7:18–28

the point of the comparison is the austerity and asceticism of John,[112] Jesus' question recalls Luke's portrayal of the Baptist as an abstemious and austere figure in the preceding narrative. When the angel of the Lord appeared to Zechariah, the angel said that John would taste neither wine nor strong drink and that he would be endowed with the spirit and the power of Elijah (1:15–17). The presentation of John as a sober herald of God, his identification with the spirit of Elijah (a paradigmatic, austere prophet), and the information about John's dwelling in the desert (1:80; 3:2, 4) all contribute to his portrayal as an ascetic, spirit-filled prophetic figure (cf. 5:33).[113] Consequently, Jesus' question presumes that John is the antitype of those dressing in fine clothing. On the contrary, John is more concerned with sharing clothing with the destitute (3:11) than with wearing fine linen. Taken together, Luke's description of those wearing "soft clothing," "glorious clothing," and "living in splendor" illustrates an exuberant lifestyle (cf. 16:19) that contrasts with the previous characterization of John. Moreover, Luke's pleonastic description and variation in vocabulary depicts more vividly than Matthew's Jesus' intended comparison and creates a starker contrast between the lavish lifestyle of the rich and the Baptist.[114] In a Gospel in which the concerns for the poor and proper administration of wealth play such an important role, these minor changes are intended to stress the reproach against those who are wealthy.[115]

Jesus completes the imagery with the final remark that those with such luxurious tastes abide in royal palaces (ἐν τοῖς βασιλείοις εἰσίν).[116] Jesus' reference to the refined tastes of those living in palaces contrasts not only with John's habitat (ἔρημος) but also with Jesus' own proclama-

---

112. Marshall, *Luke*, 294.

113. Darr, *Character Building*, 84.

114. If the variations are attributed to Luke's redaction, they might be considered a case of ecphrasis. According to Spencer (*Rhetorical Texture*, 103), 7:24–35 "is replete with ecphrasis and synkrisis." Theon (*Progymnasmata* 118–20) defined ecphrasis as "descriptive language, bringing what is portrayed clearly before the sight," and noted that it was concerned with "clarity and vivid impression of all-but-seeing what is described."

115. Nolland, "Money and Possessions," 178–93; Karris, "Poor and Rich," 112–25; Schmidt, *Hostility to Wealth*, 135–62. According to Gagnon ("Double Delegation," 142–43), concerns about the proper use of wealth are present in this section of the Gospel.

116. The expression ἐν τοῖς βασιλείοις is elliptical and it means "in the royal palaces."

tion of the kingdom (βασιλεία) of God, in which the poor (οἱ πτωχοί), not the wealthy, are blessed (6:20).

The first and the second rhetorical questions of Jesus play an important function in the development of the narrative. They not only build up an expectation in anticipation of the correct answer, but they also with some irony shape the true character of John, which Jesus validates in the next rhetorical question.

The Third Rhetorical Question: John the Prophet (7:26a)

Jesus begins the third rhetorical question as he did the two previous ones: τί ἐξήλθατε ἰδεῖν;. This time, however, the second part of the inquiry contains the correct answer. The momentum that has been building up since the first rhetorical question now leads to an inexorable conclusion: John the Baptist is a prophet, and even more than a prophet (περισσότερον προφήτου).[117] Jesus' remarks about the Baptist's prophetic character are framed within the context of the discussion about Jesus' own prophetic status (7:16; 39). But his identification of John as a prophet harks back to what the infancy narratives suggested about John.

As noted earlier, during the annunciation to Zechariah the angel of the Lord foretold that John would be endowed "with the spirit of Elijah (1:17)," the embodiment of the OT prophet par excellence.[118] Luke reinforced that characterization of John in the canticle of Zechariah, where John is portrayed as the "prophet of the Most High" (προφήτης ὑψίστου κληθήσῃ) and cast in the role of the prophetic forerunner of the Lord (1:76). This image is developed further by Luke's formulaic presentation of the beginning of John's ministry in a form characteristic of OT prophets (i.e., ἐγένετο ῥῆμα θεοῦ ἐπὶ Ἰωάννην τὸν Ζαχαρίου υἱόν, 3:2; 1 Kgs 12:22; Jonah 1:1; Isa 38:4; Jer 1:4; Ezek 1:3; Mic 1:1; Zech 1:1). Moreover, the prophet-like portrayal of the Baptist is emphasized by the way Luke presents John in the rest of chapter 3 as an itinerant preacher of repentance and salvation (3:3–18). Although Jesus portrays himself as a prophet (4:24–27) and the people regard him as such (7:16; 24:19; Acts 3:22–23; 7:37), he now depicts John in the role of someone who is more (περισσότερον) than a prophet.[119] The sense in which John is more than

---

117. Green, *Luke*, 298.
118. Wink, *John the Baptist*, 42.
119. Luke's association of the Baptist with prophetic figures continues to echo throughout the narrative (9:7–8, 19; 20:6), although such characterization ceases in the

A Narrative-Critical Interpretation of 7:18–28

a prophet will receive further elaboration in 7:27–28. In the meantime, Jesus' confirmation of John's prophetic role is significant for the plot of the narrative because for the first time in the Gospel the most important character of the story confirms Luke's characterization of John.

JOHN THE FORERUNNER OF THE LORD (7:27)

To support his affirmation that the Baptist is more than a prophet, Jesus quotes the Scriptures: "Behold, I send my messenger ahead of you, who will prepare your way before you." Jesus' reference to what is "written" (γέγραπται) to explain John's role supports Luke's characterization of Jesus as someone who knows and quotes the word of God (4:4, 8, 12; 6:3–4; 18:31; 19:46; 20:17; 21:22, 37; 24:27, 44–46). The quotation also recalls Luke's own use of Scripture citations—either new ones or those inherited from the tradition—to elucidate particular aspects of the narrative (2:23; 3:4). Here, Jesus' reference to the Scripture harks back to Mal 3:1 and identifies John as his forerunner (cf. Exod 23:20).[120] Luke began this portrayal of John in the infancy narratives, when the angel of the Lord announced to Zechariah that John would go before "him" (αὐτοῦ) and "prepare [κατασκευάζω] for the Lord a people fit for him"

Acts of the Apostles. There is some discussion about whether περισσότερον means here "something greater" or "someone greater" (Nolland, *Luke*, 336). The comparative appears three other times in Luke: 12:4, 48; 20:47. Regarding Luke's characterization of John as a prophetic figure, Poirier ("Elijianic Figure," 353–58) has argued recently that there are indications in the OT as well as in both Second Temple and rabbinic writings to support the view that Elijah was more widely identified with a priestly figure than with a prophetic one. Poirier's remarks, however, are not concerned with the narrative level but with the pre-Lukan stage.

120. Luke's quotation may be a conflation of Mal 3:1 and Exod 23:20 (Nolland, *Luke*, 336; Marshall, *Luke*, 295–96). The difference between the "me" (μου) in Mal 3:1(LXX) and the "you" (σου) in Luke's quotation may be attributed to an adaptation of the OT text (Fitzmyer, *Luke*, 1:671). Luke's characterization of John as the forerunner of the Lord implies the notion of the Baptist as Elijah *redivivus*, whom Mal 3:23–24 identifies as the agent whom God will send at the end of time (2 Kgs 2:11; see also Luke 1:17); Marshall, *Luke*, 296; Fitzmyer, *Luke*, 1:671–74; Nolland, *Luke*, 337. Conzelmann (*Theology*, 25) denied John's role as the forerunner of Jesus, but his interpretation—explained by his neglect of the infancy narratives—has been widely refuted (Wink, *John the Baptist*, 53–54; Fitzmyer, *Luke*, 1:671–72; Tannehill, *Luke-Acts*, 1:24). On the other hand, although Wink accepts Luke's portrayal of John as the forerunner, he claims that Luke has divested John of the role of Elijah *redivivus* (ibid., 43). But this portrayal of John is already implicit in the infancy narratives, as many authors agree (Brown, *Birth*, 275–79; Webb, *John the Baptizer*, 62 n. 42; Spencer, *Rhetorical Texture*, 105).

(1:17).¹²¹ Later, Zechariah proclaimed in his canticle that John would go "before the Lord to prepare [ἑτοιμάσαι] his way" (1:76).¹²² Luke further strengthens John's portrayal as the forerunner of the Lord by using Isa 40:3–5, which depicts the Baptist as one who "prepares [ἑτοιμάσατε] the way for the Lord" (3:4; see Mark 1:3). Luke's presentation of the people's speculation about whether or not John would be the Messiah (3:15), followed by John's implicit denial (3:16–17), emphasizes the preparatory role of the Baptist's ministry in expectation of "the stronger one" (ὁ ἰσχυρότερος).¹²³

In 7:27, God speaks to Jesus—the implicit eschatological figure—and announces that he has commissioned his ἄγγελος (i.e., John) to prepare (κατασκευάσει) the way before him.¹²⁴ Jesus recapitulates with a Scripture quotation the infancy narratives' portrayal of the Baptist as the forerunner of the Lord. Luke's early characterization, along with his presentation of John's baptism and proclamation of repentance, receives Jesus' endorsement.¹²⁵ Through the Scripture quotation Jesus grants to John a role that no one else has occupied in salvation history: to be the prophetic figure associated with "the one who is to come." John's privilege is corroborated even further in the next verse, but now it begins to be clearer why he is "more than a prophet."

---

121. In Mal 3:1, αὐτοῦ refers to God, but the pronoun could also refer to Jesus in Luke's allusion to the Scripture quotation (Marshall, *Luke*, 58–59).

122. Since the infancy narratives have been composed retrospectively with regard to the rest of the Lukan Gospel, and furthermore since in 1:43 Mary has been identified as "the mother of my Lord," in 1:76 κυρίου should be understood as referring to Jesus (Fitzmyer, *Luke*, 1:385–86).

123. Wink, *John the Baptist*, 53–54.

124. Fitzmyer, *Luke*, 1:674; Nolland, *Luke*, 337.

125. Conzelmann (*Theology*, 20) claimed that the Baptist was not a kingdom preacher. But Wink (*John the Baptist*, 52–53) asserts that the use of εὐαγγελίζω in 3:18 to describe John's proclamation of the "coming king" is what Luke considers the "good news" in John's message. Given the link between the missions of John and Jesus as well as Luke's almost synonymous use of εὐαγγελίζω, κηρύσσω, and διδάσκω (Tannehill, *Luke*, 1:47–53, 78), a sharp distinction should not be drawn between the messages of the Baptist and Jesus. John was not so much a preacher of "good news"—in the sense that Jesus was—but a preacher of repentance whose message included elements of the kingdom (3:10–14).

The Greatness of John and the Kingdom of God (7:28)

To summarize for the crowd (λέγω ὑμῖν) the importance of John, Jesus points out that "among those born of women there is no one greater [μείζων] than John."[126] The future greatness (μέγας) of John had been foretold even before his birth (1:15, 32).[127] Despite John's prophesied greatness, although both he and Jesus have been born of women (γεννητοῖς γυναικῶν), the infancy narratives left no doubt that Jesus was superior because his birth belonged to a higher order.[128] The superiority of Jesus allows him now as the preeminent character of the story to certify John's status among those "born of women."

John's status as more (περισσότερον) than a prophet receives here an added rationale. As Nolland points out, John's greatness stems from his place in salvation history: "In the whole sweep of human history from the beginning to the eschatological coming of God, John has been assigned that most exalted of roles."[129] Jesus' statement thus echoes and supplements his previous remark regarding John's preeminence with respect to the prophets (7:26). The encomium of Jesus helps to summarize John's significance within the thread of the narrative and functions as a final epitaph upon the Baptist's brief but important career.[130] Jesus' high esteem for John here does not imply that a definite relationship had developed between John and Jesus. Rather, Jesus is echoing the people's high regard for John (3:15; 5:33; 9:7; 20:6). Finally, Jesus' followers will later argue about who is the greatest (μείζων) among them (9:46–48; 22:24–27), but he will try to persuade them to adopt a different set of criteria by which to measure the true meaning of greatness.

---

126. This clause has been interpreted often as an early Christian community's attempt to restrict Jesus' praise of John in the church's polemic against Baptist sectarians (Bultmann, *History*, 164–65). In addition, although μείζων is comparative, its effect is superlative (Marshall, *Luke*, 296); see also Viviano, "Least in the Kingdom," 41–54.

127. Brown, *Birth*, 273.

128. The expression γεννητοῖς γυναικῶν underlines the ordinary origin of the person; see also Job 11:2, 12; 14:1; 15:14; 25:4; Gal 4:4; 1QS 11.21; Büchsel, "γεννητός," 672. As Böhlemann (*Jesus und der Täufer*, 20) points out: "Jesus ist nicht größer als Johannes, sondern bein ihm is Größe ein absolutes und damit göttliches Wesensmerkmal, während Johannes „Größe" nur in Relation zu anderen Menschen besitzt."

129. Nolland, *Luke*, 338. In Matt 11:14, the issue was solved by Jesus' immediate affirmation that John was Elijah, ὁ μέλλων ἔρχεσθαι. But since—as many agree—Luke has transposed part of that tradition to 16:16, the explanation of John's superiority in this sense is left implicit.

130. The next reference to the Baptist (9:7) presumes that he has been put to death.

In the second part of the statement, however, Jesus qualifies his high regard for John by pointing out that "the least [μικρότερος] in the kingdom of God is greater [μείζων] than he [John]." Scholars have often discussed whether μικρότερος should be understood as a comparative or a superlative and whether it refers to Jesus or someone else.[131] If the term is taken as a comparative referring to Jesus, several interpretations are possible; Jesus is "less" because (a) he is younger than John; (b) he is a disciple of John; (c) or his baptizing role is less important than John's. If μικρότερος is taken as a comparative, Jesus would be making a personal comparison between John and himself in order to emphasize his present subordination to the Baptist vis-à-vis Jesus' future greatness, i.e., smaller now but greater in the kingdom.[132] However, these interpretations attribute a sense to μικρότερος that is alien to the context. It also runs counter to the rest of the passage (7:29–35), in which Jesus puts the Baptist's ministry on a par with his own. On the one hand, Jesus always uses μικρότερος with the article as a generic category that epitomizes those of a lower rank or those who have adopted the values of the kingdom (9:48; 12:32; 17:2; cf. ὁ νεώτερος, 22:26). On the other hand, Luke's concern for the "little ones" has already been featured in the narrative (1:48, 52–53; 4:18; 7:22) as well as their special claim on the kingdom (6:20).[133] Therefore, μικρότερος is better understood as a superlative in relation τῇ βασιλείᾳ τοῦ θεοῦ, which stands in contrast to γεννητοῖς γυναικῶν in the previous clause. This contrast indicates that the true meaning of the comparison is not a personal one but one dealing with categories.[134]

As in the other Synoptics—albeit with some differences in nuance—Jesus' proclamation of the "kingdom of God/heaven" constitutes

---

131. Dibelius ("Kleinere," 190–92) argues that μικρότερος refers to Jesus. The comparative use of μείζων in this clause is specified by the dependent genitive (αὐτοῦ) that follows, but μικρότερος could be translated either as a comparative ("less") or as a superlative ("least"). Here μικρότερος stands in antithetical parallelism to the first use of μείζων as a superlative in the previous clause. Given this contrast and biblical Greek's encroachment into the domain of the superlative, μικρότερος should be translated as a superlative (i.e., "the least"); Wallace, *Greek Grammar*, 296–305; Blass et al., *Greek Grammar*, §§ 60–62, 244–45.

132. Nolland, *Luke*, 338; Fitzmyer, *Luke*, 1:675.

133. The greater-to-lesser and lesser-to-greater argumentation was a common feature in classical rhetoric (Aristotle, *Rhet.* 2.23.1397b.12–29; Spencer, *Rhetorical Texture*, 106).

134. Taylor, *Immerser*, 303–4; Viviano, "Least in the Kingdom," 53.

his central message.¹³⁵ Luke begins to emphasize the importance of this concept in the infancy narratives when the angel of the Lord announces to Mary that her son will sit on the throne of David his father and his "kingdom" (βασιλεία) will have no end (1:33).¹³⁶ As Jesus inaugurates his public ministry, Luke refers to the "kingdom of God" in a summary statement that implies that Jesus' previous activity has been concerned with the proclamation of the kingdom (4:43; see 8:1).¹³⁷

While Jesus never systematically explains what the kingdom is, its meaning can be drawn out from the multiplicity of references to that concept. Hence, Jesus is concerned with the proclamation of the kingdom (8:1; 9:11; 11:2; Acts 1:3), which is a growing reality (13:18–21) that involves both a present (16:16; 17:21) and a future phase (13:28–29; 22:30). The destitute, not the rich, will inherit the kingdom (6:20), because worldly riches are relative to its demands (18:24–25; see also 12:31). Its mysteries are revealed only to the disciples (8:10), who participate in the proclamation of the kingdom (9:2; 10:9, 11). The demands of the kingdom are great (9:60, 62; 13:28–29; Acts 14:22), and they must be accepted with the confidence of a child (18:16–17). Although its arrival is imminent, the precise moment of its manifestation is unknown (9:27; 11:20; 18:29–30; 21:31; 22:16–18; Acts 1:6–7) because it does not come by way of physical observation (17:20).¹³⁸

Therefore, it is in relation to this "kingdom of God," which so much concerns Jesus, that anyone, even "the least" (μικρότερος), is greater that John. Despite the outstanding career of John, the "kingdom of God" emerges as a new reality that surpasses his achievements and opens the doors to a new era. To the extent that the present phase of the kingdom has begun, "the least" who "see and hear" the signs and words of Jesus

---

135. Luke-Acts contains 45 references to the "kingdom of God," even if the expression does not appear in full (4:43; 6:20; 7:28; 8:1, 10; 9:2, 11, 27, 60, 62; 10:9, 11; 11:2, 20; 12:31, 32; 13:18, 20, 28, 29; 14:15; 16:16; 17:20 [x2], 21; 18:16, 17, 24, 25, 29; 19:11; 21:31; 22:16, 18, 29, 30; 23:42, 51; Acts 1:3; 8:12; 14:22; 19:8; 20:25; 28:23, 31). Luke never uses the characteristic Matthean phrase "kingdom of heaven"; see Caragounis, "Kingdom," 425–29; McKnight, "Matthew," 537; Hahn, "Kingdom and Church," 294–326.

136. With regard to the use of this concept in the infancy narratives, Böhlemann (*Jesus und der Täufer*, 21) notes: "Mit dem Reich und der Herrschaft Gottes sind so grundlegende Begriffe der lukanischen Eschatologie bereits genannt."

137. Caragounis, "Kingdom," 428.

138. In the Acts of the Apostles Jesus' followers will continue to proclaim the "kingdom of God" as an essential element of their message (Acts 8:12; 14:22; 19:8; 20:25; 28:23, 31).

(cf. 10:23–24) are greater than John, who in prison is isolated from Jesus' proclamation of the "kingdom of God."[139] Jesus' reference to the kingdom of God elevates the discussion to a new level, to which the conversation about the successful ministry of John must now yield. The introduction of this theme gives Luke the opportunity to put into perspective this concept in relation to the ministry of John. Luke will seize Jesus' overture, and in the next two subunits (7:29–30, 31–35) he will elaborate how the kingdom's underlying purpose (the will of God) has been operative through the Baptist's ministry.

Summary

In the second subunit of the passage, Jesus addresses a crowd in a monologue that, within the broader context of the narrative, recapitulates and defines John's role and identity. Luke records the departure of the Baptist's disciples and notes that Jesus addresses a crowd that until then had been present as a silent witness to the exchange between Jesus and the messengers from John. With the skill of a rhetorician and not without some irony, Jesus interrogates the members of the crowd as to what they had gone out into the desert to see.

First, he presents the crowd with two seemingly absurd options about who John was. In the first question, Jesus asks the crowd if they went to see a reed shaken by the wind. The comparison, which aims at portraying John as a man without a moral compass, fails in the face of Luke's characterization of John. The metaphor of a reed shaken by the wind, which stands for the person who wavers in the face of difficulties, does not correspond to the true character of John. The Baptist, who has been divinely sanctioned and whose rigorous lifestyle has been previously emphasized, is more like the image of the house unshaken by the rising waters mentioned in the preceding narrative.

---

139. Nolland, *Luke*, 338. There has been a long-standing argument about whether 7:28 (// Matt 11:11, 13; cf. Luke 16:16) adds to the view that John is excluded from the kingdom of God (Conzelmann, *Theology*, 25). The Baptist is excluded from the present stage of the kingdom because of his imprisonment. However, he is not excluded from the future and final stage of the kingdom. As Acts 1:22 shows, through his role as the forerunner of the Lord, John stands as a transitional figure at the dawn of a new era. John's ministry triggers the ultimate manifestation of the kingdom and his role is best understood as a preparatory one. Luke's portrayal of John as "greater than a prophet" places him well within the boundaries of the kingdom (13:28); Wink, *John the Baptist*, 54–57; Fitzmyer, *Luke*, 1:184–85; 2:1115–16.

In his second rhetorical question, Jesus asks the crowds if they had gone out to the desert to see a man who lived surrounded by luxury. Again, the crowd is confronted with a characterization of John that, in light of the previous story, seems incongruent. John is an ascetic figure, whose moderate eating and drinking habits, desert dwelling, and concern for the needy identify him as the antitype of someone who would be surrounded by luxuries and living in a palace.

In the third and final rhetorical question, Jesus asks the crowds if they went out to see a prophet. This time Jesus presents the audience with the correct option: John is a prophet and more than a prophet. John is the one who the angel said would come in the spirit of Elijah, the embodiment of the OT prophet par excellence, the "prophet of the Most High," to prepare the way of the Lord. John is more than a prophet, then, because he has been assigned the role associated with the coming of the Lord.

John has ushered in the dawn of a new eschatological era, and therefore no one born of women is greater than he. But despite John's great achievements, Jesus is concerned first and foremost with the manifestation of the "kingdom of God." Now is the time when the "blind regain their sight, the lame walk, lepers are cleansed, the deaf hear, the dead are raised, the poor have the good news proclaimed to them." Following Jesus' implicit affirmative response to the question of John, the Baptist's importance is put in perspective in relation to the ultimate goal of his career: the preparation of the arrival of the kingdom of God. Therefore, anyone who accepts the manifestation of the kingdom, even the "least" who "sees and hears" the signs and words of Jesus, is greater than John. The Baptist's subordination to the members of the kingdom is explained by the fact that his imprisonment has temporarily alienated him from its present manifestation. Luke notices Jesus' reference to the "kingdom of God," and in the next subunit he will unveil the logic of the concept's underlying purpose (the will of God), its relevance in the ministry of John, and its meaning for the plot of the story.

4

A Narrative-Critical Interpretation of 7:29–35

PRELIMINARY REMARKS

IN THE GOSPELS OF Matthew and Luke the accounts of John the Baptist and Jesus' indictment of the religious leaders follow very similar story lines until the end of Jesus' encomium of John (Matt 11:11 // Luke 7:28). Prior to this point, only minor differences have surfaced between the two versions, and these have not substantially altered the basic meaning of the tradition that the evangelists used. Hence, there is little disagreement among proponents of the two-source theory that a common source lies behind the parallel passages in Matthew and Luke. However, from the end of Jesus' encomium of John (Matt 11:11 // Luke 7:28) to the beginning of the parable of the children in the marketplace (Matt 11:16–19 // Luke 7:31–35), both evangelists differ significantly from each other. As each Gospel displays its own specific material (Matt 11:12–15 // Luke 7:29–30), the narrative agreement that has prevailed thus far between Matthew and Luke ends, and so does the scholarly consensus regarding the origin of these verses.

In chapter 2, I analyzed how the differences between Matthew and Luke functioned within each Gospel. The goal of that analysis was not to attempt a reconstruction of the original source but to understand how the differences between the two evangelists could illuminate the meaning of each pericope. The exegesis of Luke 7:29–30 calls for further detailed analysis that may shed some light onto why the similarities in wording and sequence between the two passages are suddenly interrupted (Matt 11:12–15 // Luke 7:29–30). This investigation will help us to evaluate which of the two may have followed his source more closely or who may have changed it to achieve a different narrative objective. Therefore, before beginning the exegesis of 7:29–30, I will consider two distinct but related issues regarding these verses. First, taking into consideration the redactional and compositional tendencies of Matthew and Luke, I will examine Matt 11:12–15 and Luke 7:29–30 as well as other related passages (i.e., Matt 21:31b–32; Luke 16:16) in order to understand what their content and context tell us about the history of their transmission. Second, I will consider another disputed topic: whether 7:29–30 ought to be understood as a direct speech of Jesus or as a narrative commentary. A more in-depth analysis of these issues will help us to understand better the meaning of Luke 7:29–30.

REDACTIONAL AND STYLISTIC ISSUES IN LUKE 7:29–30

The History of Transmission of Matt 11:12–15 and Luke 7:29–30

More than in any other place within the parallel passages of Matt 11:2–19 and Luke 7:18–35, the differences between Matt 11:12–15 and Luke 7:29–30 press the question about the original form of the source. Whereas in the Gospel of Matthew the testimony of Jesus about John is followed by the words about the kingdom and the identification of the Baptist with Elijah (11:12–15), Luke follows Jesus' remarks about the Baptist with a statement that highlights the diverse responses of the Jews to the ministry of John (7:29–30). The differences between these two passages are so great that the possibility that a common source lies behind both texts should be ruled out. At issue then is whether Matthew or Luke preserves the more authentic form of the traditional source or whether each evangelist may have coincidentally introduced his own material at this particular point. The number of variables that could account for the differences between Matthew and Luke is illustrated in Figure 3 below.

FIGURE 3: Possible Redactions/Sources of Matthew 11:12–15 and Luke 7:29–30

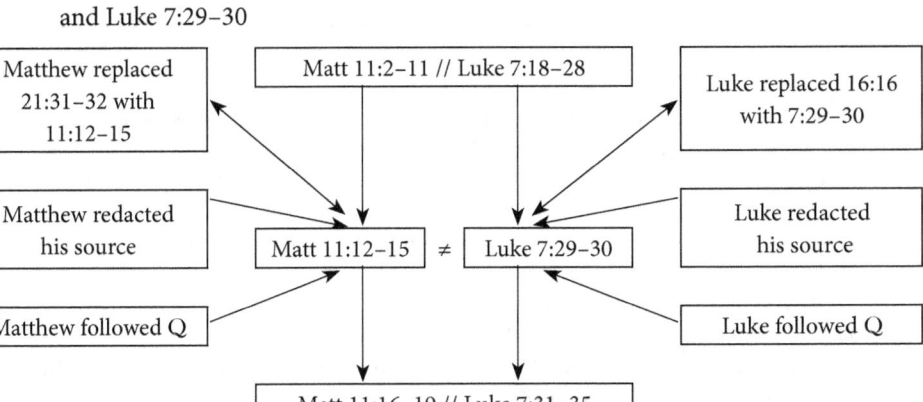

To these six possible scenarios, one can add the prospect that Matthew and Luke may have incorporated simultaneously their own particular alterations into the source. The following analysis will explore these possibilities.

In chapter 2 we saw that although an exact parallel to Matt 11:12–15 does not appear in Luke, some of these verses (Matt 11:12–13) can be found in another context within the Lukan Gospel (16:16).[1] This raises the prospect that either Matthew or Luke may have preserved the wording and the context of an existing tradition.

With respect to wording, Matt 11:14 can be classified as redactional because, although Luke implicitly and explicitly links John to Elijah (e.g., 1:17; 7:27), neither Luke nor any of the other evangelists except for Matthew (see Matt 17:13) ever directly identifies the Baptist with Elijah.[2] Likewise, Jesus' remark in Matt 11:15, "Whoever has ears to hear, should hear," can be viewed as a floating tradition that has been attached to many of his sayings.[3] However, the parallel verses about the Law, the Prophets, and John (Matt 11:12–13 // Luke 16:16)—the so-called *Stürmmerspruch*—offer greater difficulty. A comparison of these verses shows the similarities and differences between them:

TABLE 6: Matthew 11:12–15 and Luke 16:16

Matthew 11:12–15: ἀπὸ δὲ τῶν ἡμερῶν Ἰωάννου τοῦ βαπτιστοῦ ἕως ἄρτι ἡ βασιλεία τῶν οὐρανῶν βιάζεται καὶ βιασταὶ ἁρπάζουσιν αὐτήν. (13) πάντες γὰρ οἱ προφῆται καὶ ὁ νόμος ἕως Ἰωάννου ἐπροφήτευσαν· (14) καὶ εἰ θέλετε δέξασθαι αὐτός ἐστιν Ἠλίας ὁ μέλλων ἔρχεσθαι. (15) ὁ ἔχων ὦτα ἀκουέτω.	Luke 16:16: Ὁ νόμος καὶ οἱ προφῆται μέχρι Ἰωάννου· ἀπὸ τότε ἡ βασιλεία τοῦ θεοῦ εὐαγγελίζεται καί πᾶς εἰς αὐτὴν βιάζεται.

1. Regarding the interpretation and the difficulties associated with these verses, see Cameron, *Violence and the Kingdom*, 1–133; Kloppenborg, *Q Parallels*, 58 n. on 7:29–30; Fitzmyer, *Luke*, 2:1114–18; Meier, *Marginal Jew*, 2:156–63; Hoffman, *Studien*, 50–79; Ernst, *Johannes der Täufer*, 63–72; Luz, *Matthew 8–20*, 136–44.

2. Meier, *Marginal Jew*, 2:156. Having said that, given the association of the Baptist with Elijah elsewhere (Luke 1:17) as well as the belief among the people in some sort of return from the dead (Mark 8:28; Luke 9:7), it is not impossible that this verse may have been an early saying about the Baptist preserved in Q.

3. Matt 13:9, 43; 25:29 (similar); Mark 4:9; 7:16 (similar); Luke 8:8; 14:35; see also Rev 2:7, 11, 17, 29; 3:6, 13, 22; 13:19.

As the comparison shows, the Matthean version is not only longer than the Lukan version but their statements appear in a different order: Matt 11:12 corresponds to Luke 16:16b and Matt 11:13 corresponds to Luke 16:16a.[4] On the one hand, the asyndetic juxtaposition of the Lukan passage in contrast to the Matthean use of two coordinating conjunctions (δε, and γάρ) points to Matthew's editorial effort.[5] Luke's use of ἀπὸ τότε, a phrase that he uses nowhere else in his work, suggests its authenticity in comparison to the redactional character of Matthew's ἀπὸ δὲ τῶν ἡμερῶν.[6] Matthew's unique use of the "kingdom of heaven" (βασιλεία τῶν οὐρανῶν) is widely recognized as a sign of his editorial hand.[7] Moreover, Matthew's formulation of "the Prophets and the Law" (οἱ προφῆται καὶ ὁ νόμος) does not follow the traditional pattern of "the Law and the Prophets" (e.g., 2 Macc 15:9; Sir 1:1; Matt 5:17; 7:12; 22:40; Acts 13:15; Rom 3:21). The order of Matthew's phrase as well as his use of ἐπροφήτευσαν point to his redaction.[8] On the other hand, Luke's salvific-historical sequence of "the Law and the Prophets" followed by the "kingdom of God" points to the primacy of his composition.[9] However, his use of the combination εὐαγγελίζεται and βιάζεται, which fits his universal view of the church's mission, seems secondary next to Matthew's more violent arrangement of βιάζεται, βιασταί, and ἁρπάζουσιν.[10] Aside from this final observation, the analysis suggests that Luke has preserved the more authentic wording of the logion.

Regarding the context of the logion, on the surface the Matthean version seems to have better preserved what probably originated as a

4. Many commentators argue that Luke has kept the more original sequence of the saying (Cameron, *Violence and the Kingdom*, 124 n. 192; Ernst, *Johannes der Täufer*, 66 n. 113).

5. Ernst, *Johannes der Täufer*, 64.

6. Meier, *Marginal Jew*, 2:159; Luz, *Matthew 8–20*, 137. Dibelius (*Überlieferung*, 24) considers ἀπὸ δὲ τῶν ἡμερῶν more original. Ernst (*Johannes der Täufer*, 66), regards Luke's temporal delimitation μέχρι Ἰωάννου ... ἀπὸ τότε redactional.

7. Caragounis, "Kingdom," 425–29; McKnight, "Matthew," 537; Luz, *Matthew 1–7*, 167; Foster, "Kingdom of Heaven," 487–99.

8. Meier, *Marginal Jew*, 2:158; Luz, *Matthew 8–20*, 137. Ernst (*Johannes der Täufer*, 66), however, considers Matthew's less traditional phrasing οἱ προφῆται καὶ ὁ νόμος as well as the use of ἐπροφήτευσαν authentic.

9. Commentators often grant Luke the original order of the saying (Ernst, *Johannes der Täufer*, 66 esp. n. 113).

10. Cameron, *Violence and the Kingdom*, 129–33; Meier, *Marginal Jew*, 2:159, Hoffmann, *Studien*, 51; Ernst, *Johannes der Täufer*, 65.

collection of sayings about the Baptist. However, on this issue scholars are more divided.[11] While some favor Matthew's position because they find no reason why he would have inserted the logion in its present location had it not been there in the first place,[12] others do not see why Luke would have moved the verse to its current context had he found it within a section dealing with the Baptist.[13] Still, others suggest that both settings are artificial and that the original arrangement of the tradition cannot be recovered.[14]

The question about the original position of Matt 11:12-15 // Luke 16:16 has often been limited to the examination of the present contexts of each saying. But an examination of the present context of Luke 7:29-30 has seldom been part of the discussion. An evaluation of whether Luke 7:29-30 belongs in its present position or not is relevant for the discussion of whether Matthew or Luke may have found the *Stürmmerspruch* (Matt 11:12-15 // Luke 16:16) in its current context.[15] As Schürmann notes: "Daß in Lk und Mt jeweilig am gleichen Ort ein verschiedenes Logion eingefügt ist, legt schon der Verdacht nahe, daß einer der beiden Evangelisten das vom andern bewahrte ausgetauscht hat."[16] The possibility that both evangelists may have introduced their own material in this particular place would entail a remarkable coincidence.[17] Working

11. Among those who favor that Luke has retained the original Q context are Crossan, *Aphorisms*, 345; Schürmann, *Lukasevangelium*, 422; Marshall, *Luke*, 297; Nolland, *Luke*, 342; Robinson et al., *Critical Edition*, 464. Commentators who favor the authenticity of the Matthean context include Harnack, *Sayings*, 15-16; Easton, *St. Luke*, 249; Beare, *Earliest Records*, 87-88; Lührmann, *Redaktion*, 27-28; Fitzmyer, *Luke*, 2:671.

12. Luhrmann, *Redaktion*, 27-28.

13. Cameron, *Violence and the Kingdom*, 134-41.

14. Kloppenborg, *Q Parallels*, 56 n. on Q 16:16.

15. Weiss's (*Predigt Jesu*, 192-97) claim, "Es ist kein Grund ersichtlich, warum Lk ihn dort weggenommen und an einem anderen Platze so ungeschickt untergebracht haben sollte" (quoted from Cameron, *Violence and the Kingdom*, 74), seems unconvincing on the face of Luke's redaction of the Baptist material in Mark. Luke omits or transposes the following material: (1) the reference to John's attire (1:6); (2) the explicit reference to Jesus' baptism by John (1:9); (3) one of the two references to the fasting done by the disciples of John and those of the Pharisees (2:18); (4) the report of John's death (6:17-29); (5) Jesus' intimation of John's role as Elijah *redivivus* (9:9-13); and (6) the two references to Elijah at the scene on the cross (15:35, 36), which come after Jesus' implicit identification of John with Elijah; see Wink, *John the Baptist*, 42-86.

16. Schürmann, *Lukasevangelium*, 422.

17. Such a break would be unprecedented where Matthew and Luke agree in the sequence of the alleged source; cf. Hawkins, *Horae Synopticae*, 108-9.

A Narrative-Critical Interpretation of 7:29–35

independently from each other, Matthew and Luke would have had to break the sequence of a common tradition at the exact same location to insert their own choice of material, while keeping much of the remaining source intact. The singularity of this occurrence suggests that only one of the two evangelists has kept the original setting of the logion.

As most commentators acknowledge, Luke 16:16 fits very inadequately in its present location (*connexio difficilior*), whereas most admit that Matthew's position is more suitable for the logion. The poor context of Luke 16:16 results probably not so much from Luke's desire to incorporate it into its current place as from his need to preserve it somewhere, after having removed the saying from the location in which he found it in his source. Several factors make this observation possible: (1) In Luke 4:14—9:50 the evangelist omits or transposes three other references to the Baptist found in his source (Mark 2:18; 6:17–29; 9:9–13) to focus the narrative on the response of different characters to the ministry of Jesus;[18] (2) Luke's literary improvements in 7:18–35 (excluding momentarily 7:29–30) show his marked christological interest in the use of the tradition;[19] and (3) the reference to the "plan of God" (τὴν βουλὴν τοῦ θεοῦ) in 7:30 hints at Luke's intention to reassess the Baptist's role in view of an important theological theme in Luke-Acts. These three factors suggest that Luke's need to remove the *Stürmmerspruch* from its original context in the source in order to meet his compositional goal may have outweighed the need to preserve it, even if it meant accommodating it in a poorly fitting context.

Before making any final determination, however, we have yet to consider whether Matthew has moved the original location of the logion. For some, an alleged parallelism between Matt 21:31b–32 and Luke 7:29–30 reflects such a possibility. A comparison of both texts shows the similarities as well as the differences between them:

---

18. See ch. 2, 67–83.
19. See ch. 2, 44–50, 57–60.

TABLE 7: Matthew 21:31b–32 and Luke 7:29–30

Matthew 21:31b-32 ἀμὴν λέγω ὑμῖν ὅτι οἱ τελῶναι καὶ αἱ πόρναι προάγουσιν ὑμᾶς εἰς τὴν βασιλείαν τοῦ θεοῦ. (32) ἦλθεν γὰρ Ἰωάννης πρὸς ὑμᾶς ἐν ὁδῷ δικαιοσύνης, καὶ οὐκ ἐπιστεύσατε αὐτῷ, οἱ δὲ τελῶναι καὶ αἱ πόρναι ἐπίστευσαν αὐτῷ· ὑμεῖς δὲ ἰδόντες οὐδὲ μετεμελήθητε ὕστερον τοῦ πιστεῦσαι αὐτῷ.	Luke 7:29-30 Καὶ πᾶς ὁ λαὸς ἀκούσας καὶ οἱ τελῶναι ἐδικαίωσαν τὸν θεὸν βαπτισθέντες τὸ βάπτισμα Ἰωάννου· (30) οἱ δὲ Φαρισαῖοι καὶ οἱ νομικοὶ τὴν βουλὴν τοῦ θεοῦ ἠθέτησαν εἰς ἑαυτοὺς μὴ βαπτισθέντες ὑπ' αὐτοῦ.

As far as vocabulary is concerned, there are only two identical words (τελῶναι and τοῦ θεοῦ) between the two passages, and one similar reference to John (Matt: Ἰωάννης, Luke: Ἰωάννου). In terms of content, while Matthew repeatedly speaks about believing (ἐπιστεύσατε, ἐπίστευσαν, πιστεῦσαι) in John, Luke talks about being baptized (βαπτισθέντες, βάπτισμα) by John. While Matthew refers to toll collectors (οἱ τελῶναι) and prostitutes (αἱ πόρναι), Luke talks about the people (ὁ λαός) and toll collectors (οἱ τελῶναι). Matthew mentions the kingdom of God (τὴν βασιλείαν τοῦ θεοῦ), whereas Luke speaks about the plan of God (τὴν βουλὴν τοῦ θεοῦ). While the religious leaders are addressed but never mentioned in Matthew, Luke specifically names the Pharisees (οἱ Φαρισαῖοι) and the scholars of the Law (οἱ νομικοί). Matthew attributes the way of righteousness (ὁδῷ δικαιοσύνης) to John, whereas Luke refers to the people and toll collectors as those who have declared the righteousness of God (ἐδικαίωσαν τὸν θεόν). While both passages talk about the rejection of John, they do so in different terms (Matt: οὐκ ἐπιστεύσατε / οὐδὲ μετεμελήθητε, Luke: ἠθέτησαν). Regarding the context, unlike Luke, who places this tradition after the question of John and Jesus' encomium of the Baptist, Matthew locates his passage as an addendum following the first of his three parables of judgment on Israel at the end of Jesus' ministry in Jerusalem.

While the differences between these two passages are considerable, they should not be exaggerated because several commentators have found strong parallels between the two pericopes.[20] Both texts pit social and religious outcasts against the Jewish authorities and make the Baptist "the touchstone by which all these groups are judged."[21] Nevertheless,

---

20. Bultmann, *History*, 164–65.
21. Meier, *Marginal Jew*, 2:168.

A Narrative-Critical Interpretation of 7:29–35 131

the differences in vocabulary, grammatical structure, and content suggest that we are not dealing with Q but with two different traditions.²² If Matt 21:31b–32 has not come from Q, then either Matt 11:12–15 reflects an original or a slightly modified form of the source—which Luke has partially transposed elsewhere (16:16)—or Luke 7:29–30 preserves the authentic form of the tradition, which Matthew has omitted completely.

The foregoing discussion has shown that to some extent both evangelists have edited their source at Matt 11:12–15 and Luke 7:29–30 in order to fit their theological interests. Regarding the form of the *Stürmmerspruch*, the analysis indicates that Luke probably retained the most original wording of the logion (except for his more neutral combination of εὐαγγελίζεται and βιάζεται). With respect to the original context of the saying, Luke's frequent omissions and/or transpositions of the Baptist's references in his source, as well as the poor context of 16:16, suggest that he had compositional reasons for removing the *Stürmmerspruch* from its original context. Moreover, the differences between Matt 21:31b–32 and Luke 7:29–30 are such that it seems unlikely that we are dealing here with Q material. In sum, the variables involved in the analysis of why—within almost identical traditions (Matt 11:2–19 // Luke 7:18–35)—the differences between Matt 11:12–15 and Luke 7:29–30 are so great suggest that Luke made the most significant changes to the original source. Even under the presumption that the essence of 7:29–30 was part of the tradition, these verses would have to be attributed to Luke, since the redaction of the subunit shows substantial Lukan modifications.²³ Therefore, the exegesis of 7:29–30 will proceed under the assumption that the subunit reflects Luke's own theological perspective.

The Narrative Voice of 7:29–30

From a contextual reading, Luke 7:29–30 will strike any reader as a passage in which the narrative tempo and the content of the statement change the pace of the story. Such an experience raises the question of whether one ought to read the verses as a continuation of Jesus' previous statements about John or as a narrative commentary. According to Schürmann, 7:29–30 is sort of an afterthought that follows Jesus'

---

22. Ibid., 167–70.
23. Fitzmyer, *Luke*, 1:671; Nolland, *Luke*, 342; Klein, *Lukasevangelium*, 287.

remarks about John: "Es redet die Volkscharen nicht mehr direkt an, vielmehr bekommt seine Rede etwas von der Art eines abgesetzten Selbstgespräches, bevor sie dann vv 33f zu anredender Anklage wird."[24] But for Fitzmyer these verses ought to be interpreted as "a comment of the evangelist."[25] The issue remains disputed.[26] The lack of clear grammatical clues to signal a change of narrative style between the end of Jesus' encomium of John 7:28 and 7:29 obscures the assessment of how one should read 7:29–30. This ambiguity hampers the perception of the narrative voice, which is the essential element for locating and defining a narrative commentary.[27]

For Sheeley, who has analyzed narrative asides in Luke from the perspective of rhetoric and narrative criticism, four elements characterized narrative commentaries: (1) they interrupt either the syntax of the narrative, the plot, or both; (2) they address a different audience from that addressed by the narration proper; (3) they establish a relationship between the narrator and the reader; and (4) they move the reader from the story world to the narrative world.[28] Of these four criteria, the first two are the most crucial ones for determining a change of narrative voice.[29] Because neither of these two principal character-

---

24. Schürmann, *Lukasevangelium*, 421.

25. Fitzmyer, *Luke*, 1:670.

26. Among those who interpret the verses as a statement of Jesus are Plummer, *St. Luke*, 205–6; Lagrange, *Luc*, 221; Schürmann, *Lukasevangelium*, 1:421. Those who interpret them as a narrative commentary include Bovon, *Luke*, 1:284 n. 51; Nolland, *Luke*, 342; Fitzmyer, *Luke*, 1:670; Sheeley, *Narrative Asides*, 114–15.

27. Sheeley, *Narrative Asides*, 32.

28. Ibid., 34. Sheeley defines a narrative aside as a "parenthetical remark addressed directly to the reader which interrupts the logical progression of the story, establishing a relationship between the narrator and the narratee which exists outside the story being narrated" (36). Although Sheeley outlines the elements that characterize narrative commentaries and identifies 7:29–30 as such, he never explains how these elements are present in the form of 7:29–30.

29. The first two criteria are those more directly related to *parenthesis*, which has been the criterion that different authors have more consistently identified as the single most important element of a narrative commentary. For Tenney ("Footnotes," 350–51), who does not address the grammatical or syntactical clues of narrative commentaries, the *parenthesis* or footnotes are "... [s]entences or paragraphs of explanatory comment, interjected into the running narrative of the story, and obviously intended to illumine some casual reference, or to explain how some important statement should be understood." Meanwhile, for O'Rourke ("Asides," 211), "the criterion for determining the presence of such asides is this: Their omission would not affect greatly the flow of the

istics is evident in 7:29-30, the alleged change in narrative voice must be more a function of content and context than of grammatical form. Therefore, I will compare first the content of 7:29-30 with the rest of the narrative to see if any of the words in these verses exclude the possibility that either Jesus or the narrator may have given voice to them. Second, I will analyze the syntactical structure of 7:29-30 within its immediate literary context to determine whether a contextual contrast suggests a change in narrative voice.

Several key words in 7:29-30 are used interchangeably in the rest of the Lukan narrative either by the narrator or by Jesus as a character in the story. The word τελώνης is used by Jesus (7:34; 18:10, 11, 13) as well as by the narrator (3:12; 5:27, 29, 30). Both the Lukan narrator (3:3; Acts 1:22; 10:37; 13:24; 18:25; 19:3-4) and Jesus (12:50; 20:4) employ the term βάπτισμα. The verb δικαιόω is also employed by the narrator (10:29; Acts 13:38-39) and Jesus (7:35; 16:15; 18:14). Both the narrator (5:17; 6:2, 7:36; 11:37; 13:31; 14:1; 15:2; 16:14; 17:20; Acts 5:34; 15:5; 23:6; 26:5) and Jesus (11:39-43; 12:1; 18:10-11) use the term Φαρισαῖος. Similarly, νομικός is employed by the narrator (10:25; 11:45; 14:3) and Jesus (11:46, 52). In sum, there is no exclusive use of these terms by either the narrator or Jesus.

However, two other words in 7:29-30 are used elsewhere exclusively by either the narrator or Jesus. The term ἀθετέω appears only once more in the whole of Luke-Acts in a saying attributed to Jesus (Luke 10:16 [used 4 times]). Meanwhile, βουλή is never used by anyone other than the Lukan narrator, specially in the Acts of the Apostles, where Luke is believed to have been less constrained by his sources (Luke 23:51; Acts 2:23; 4:28; 5:38; 13:36; 20:27; 27:12, 42). Moreover, it is noteworthy that all uses of the circumstantial participle ἀκούσας are employed by the narrator (Luke 7:3, 9, 29; 8:50; 14:15; 18:22, 23, 36; 23:6; see also Acts 7:12; 23:16).[30]

With regard to context, at first sight nothing in 7:29-30 appears patently incompatible with the surrounding material. The narrative leading to this subunit focuses on the Baptist, who continues to be men-

---

narrative, but should be noted that some asides may be important for the achievement of an important goal of the evangelist, as, for example, his remarks about fulfillment."

30. Only in 6:49 is ἀκούσας used by Jesus, but in this case it is used substantively. Acts 22:26 has the only circumstantial use of ἀκούσας by a character (Stephen) besides the narrator.

tioned in these verses. Although in 7:29–30 a new element—the baptism of John—is introduced in the story, this is not unusual, since throughout 7:25–28 Luke has continuously recalled different aspects of the Baptist's ministry (e.g., reference to his moral character, dressing habits). But other elements are more conspicuous, because they introduce a new thematic strand into the passage. The mention of the people (ὁ λαός) not as interlocutors (ὄχλους, 7:24) but as objects of the statement adds a new dimension to the narrative. This new dimension is further highlighted by the references to toll collectors, the Pharisees, and the scholars of the Law. The mention of these characters changes the focus of the story and shifts the emphasis of the passage away from John. Although a clear textual marker does not indicate a change of narrative voice in 7:29, the beginnings of v. 28 and v. 31 contrast with v. 29. Whereas in v. 28 the emphatic λέγω ὑμῖν and in v. 31 the phrase τίνι οὖν ὁμοιώσω have Jesus as the speaker, the conjunction καί in v. 29 makes no obvious allusion as to who is making the statement.

The presence of peculiarities in vocabulary as well as discreet contrasts in syntactical structure suggests not only a thematic shift but also a change in narrative voice. This subtle change in narrative voice is one of those instances in Luke-Acts in which the narrator has chosen to be prudent and hide his identity behind a shroud of ambiguity. Luke does not trumpet his presence. Rather, he intrudes into the story ever so inconspicuously.[31] However, the fact that Luke has not deliberately emphasized the change of narrative voice suggests that he may have intended to synchronize unobtrusively his own point of view with that of Jesus (cf. 11:39–54; 12:1; 16:15; 20:46–47). By using this rhetorical strategy, Luke emphasizes an important aspect of his theology without distracting the narrative flow. Therefore, although most commentators agree that 7:29–30 ought to be read as a narrative commentary that provides an inside view into the thoughts of the characters and supplies material necessary to understand the plot of the story, the statement should also be interpreted as one in which Luke and Jesus speak in unison.[32]

---

31. Sheeley, *Narrative Asides*, 97–98.

32. Green, *Luke*, 300. Arguably, 7:29–30 may be considered a comment, a digression, or an elaboration from the perspective of the *Progymnasmata* tradition. With respect to these three applicable literary forms, Theon (*Progymnasmata* 103) points out, "We can add a comment, appropriately and briefly approving what is said in the chreia, to the effect that it is true or noble or beneficial, or that other famous men have thought the same." He also notes, "One should, moreover, avoid inserting long digressions in the

Summary

After the preceding analysis of 7:29–30 and related passages, several points are worth emphasizing:

(1) Luke has probably better preserved the original wording of the *Stürmmerspruch* (Matt 11:12–15 // Luke 16:16). Despite the fact that in both evangelists the verses show signs of editing, the sequence and conciseness of the Lukan form represent with a higher degree of probability the authentic wording of the logion.

(2) The Matthean context of the *Stürmmerspruch* seems to be a more accurate reflection of its original setting in the source. Although the *connexio difficilior* has often been invoked as the main reason for attributing the original context of the *Stürmmerspruch* to Luke, the previous analysis suggests that the altered location of the logion in his Gospel is the result of Luke's selective editing of his sources.

(3) The analysis of Matt 21:31b–32 and Luke 7:29–30 indicates that the material does not proceed from a common source (Q). My examination of Luke 7:29–30 also revealed that the verses contain distinct signs of Lukan style. Moreover, since the immediate context is almost identical in Matthew and Luke, and Matthew seems to have better preserved the original form of the source, the verses in Luke 7:29–30 should be attributed to Luke.

(4) In 7:29–30, Luke has worked in his own point of view by merging it with Jesus' preceding statement about John the Baptist. By doing so, Luke has attempted to align his narrative commentary with Jesus' own voice in order to heighten an important theological theme (the plan of God) in a way that was rhetorically effective and did not distract from the flow of the narrative.

In the final analysis, whether in this particular segment of the pericope Luke substantially modified the tradition about John and Jesus or just

---

middle of a narration. It is not necessary simply to avoid all digressions, as Philistus does, for they give the hearer's mind a rest, but one should avoid such a lengthy digression that it distracts the thought of the hearers and results in the need for a reminder of what has been said earlier..." (80), and moreover, "Elaboration is language that adds what is lacking in thought and expression.' What is 'lacking' can be supplied by making clear what is obscure; by filling gaps in the language or content" (110).

slightly edited the source, 7:29–30 reflects his own theological perspective and ought to be attributed to him.

EXEGESIS OF LUKE 7:29–35

Third Subunit: The People and the Religious Leaders: Different Responses to the Plan of God (7:29–30)

THE BAPTISM OF JOHN AND THE GLORIFICATION OF GOD (7:29)

At the end of the previous subunit (7:24–28) Jesus emphasized the privileged role of John in ushering in the dawn of a new eschatological era (i.e., the kingdom of God). Jesus put into perspective the importance of the Baptist in relation to this key concept of Jesus' message and ministry. The mention of this concept now leads Luke to evaluate within the plot of the narrative how the revelation of this new reality has played out among the people of Israel in relation to the ministry of the Baptist.

Luke begins his narrative commentary by asserting that "all the people who listened, including toll collectors, and who were baptized with the baptism of John acknowledged the righteousness of God" (7:29). The reference to "all the people" (πᾶς ὁ λαός) includes more than just the crowd who overheard the exchange between Jesus and the disciples of John, received the benefits of his healing ministry (7:18–23), and were addressed by Jesus (7:24–28). "All the people" refers to the multitudes who, as a character group, have reacted favorably to God's initiative as manifested in the messages and ministries of John and Jesus throughout the plot of the narrative.[33]

As a character group, the people (ὁ λαός) play an important and complex literary function in the Lukan narrative.[34] In the infancy narratives, the people first appear as a pious group praying outside the temple (1:10, 21). They are the object of a divine initiative, which aims, through

---

33. Klein (*Lukasevangelium*, 289) specifies, "Mit, 'Volk' meint er das glaubende, gottesfürchtige Israel."

34. In the Gospel of Luke, the terms λαός and ὄχλος are virtually synonymous. However, λαός has a special connotation. The term appears twice in Mark, 14 times in Matthew, but 84 times in Luke-Acts (36 times in Luke and 48 times in Acts). In the LXX, λαός designates the distinctive character of the people of Israel. According to Strathmann ("λαός," 29, 32), "the word is now a specific term for a specific people, namely Israel, and it serves to emphasize the special and privileged religious position of this people as the people of God." See also Dahl, "People," 324–26; Minear, "Audiences," 81–87; George, "Israël," 482–86; Kodell, "*LAOS*," 327–28, 338–40, 343.

A Narrative-Critical Interpretation of 7:29-35

the incipient ministries of John and Jesus, at preparing them for the manifestation of the Lord. In this initial phase of the story, the people are portrayed as a hopeful yet uncommitted group that awaits the fulfillment of God's salvific plan (1:17, 68, 77; 2:10, 31–32).[35]

When John begins to preach in the desert, despite his initial unflattering address to the crowd (3:7) the people respond receptively to his message (3:10, 15, 18, 21). Later, when Jesus travels throughout Galilee and Judea, the people flock to him to be healed and listen to his words (4:42; 5:1, 3, 15, 19, 26, 29; 6:17–19; 7:1, 9, 11, 16). As the role of John begins to wane, Luke recalls the reaction of the people to his ministry in 7:29 and credits them for having responded favorably to God's initiative through the Baptist. In the rest of the Gospel, Luke continues to develop this sympathetic portrayal of the people into a pattern whereby he juxtaposes their readiness to listen to Jesus (e.g., 8:40; 9:11, 43; 11:14; 19:47–48; 21:38—22:2; 23:27, 34, 48) to his rejection by the religious leaders (e.g., 7:39; 9:22; 13:17; 20:19; 22:2; 23:2).[36] Some commentators see this pattern of acceptance and rejection as a dramatic disappointment of the hope of Israel.[37] A similar pattern appears in the Acts of the Apostles (3:11–26; 4:1, 4; 5:14, 17; 6:7; 13:42, 45; 14:2; 17:5, 12; 21:20), where Luke depicts the true people of God (i.e., the true Israel) as the portion of the Jews who believe in the message of Jesus—they are a "people in crisis."[38] However, the complexity of the people's role can be understood only by paying close attention to their various reactions and transformations that they undergo as the story develops.[39] Brawley best summarizes the complex portrayal and function of the crowds in Luke-Acts as follows:

---

35. The special reference to the people in 2:31-32 (i.e., πάντων τῶν λαῶν) and the juxtaposition of εἰς ἀποκάλυψιν ἐθνῶν to λαοῦ σου Ἰσραήλ reflects the universalistic sotereological perspective of Luke.

36. This pattern, however, does not exclude Luke's occasional characterization of the people as apprehensive of Jesus (19:3, 7) and individual religious leaders as sympathetic (8:41, 50; 23:50-52); see Kingsbury, *Conflict*, 28–31; Johnson, *Function of Possessions*, 121–26.

37. Tannehill, "Tragic Story," 69–85.

38. Jervell, *People of God*, 41–74; idem, *Theology*, 34–43; George, "Israël," 492–95; see, however, Tyson, "Jewish Public," 83.

39. Tannehill, *Luke-Acts*, 1:103–39, 143–66; Kingsbury, *Conflict*, 28–31; Brawley, *Luke-Acts*, 133–54; Roth, *Character Types*, 215–21; Strathmann, "λαός," 50–57; Meyer, "ὄχλος," 586–90.

[O]n occasion Luke has some sense of continuity in the identity of the crowds, but he can also create them without any interrelationship. Moreover, the crowds frequently are distinguished by coming under the sway of other more clearly defined characters. Even when the crowds are identical, Luke can differentiate them by having them undergo a transformation. Therefore, the role of the crowds is fluid and they wear different masks.[40]

As part of the intricate characterization of the people, in 7:29 Luke singles out one specific group: toll collectors (οἱ τελῶναι).[41] The group is first mentioned during John's ethical exhortation as one of the groups who approach the Baptist in search of moral instruction (3:12).[42] Luke mentions them again when Jesus calls Levi, his fourth disciple and a toll collector who, after a brief encounter with Jesus, leaves everything and follows him without hesitation (5:27–28).[43] After this encounter, Levi celebrates a meal in which Jesus eats with a crowd of toll collectors (ὄχλος πολὺς τελωνῶν) and sinners (ἁμαρτωλῶν) (cf. Mark 2:15). This leads the Pharisees (οἱ Φαρισαῖοι) and the scribes (οἱ γραμματεῖς) to criticize Jesus for sharing a meal with those whom they considered to be social outcasts.[44] The passage juxtaposes the Pharisees and the scribes

---

40. Brawley, *Luke-Acts*, 139. The people will continue to play an important role in the plot of the Gospel. They will seek Jesus and show a good disposition towards him, sometimes verbally (8:42–48; 9:43, 44; 11:14; 19:47–48; 21:38—22:2), other times silently (23:24–25, 27, 34, 48). In the Acts of the Apostles, their response is mixed. A degree of differentiation between the people and religious leaders allows for the rejection of offers of salvation (2:23, 36; 3:14–15; 6:9–14; 25:24) as well as for acceptance (4:2, 29).

41. Commentators have often noted that the syntactical position of οἱ τελῶναι after the participle ἀκούσας reads as a later addition (Fitzmyer, *Luke*, 1:676). The toll collectors were those Jews responsible for collecting different kinds of taxes throughout Palestine on behalf of the Roman authorities. They were despised for collaborating with the occupying power and for their alleged fraudulent practices (Donahue, "Tax Collectors and Sinners," 39–61; Michel, "τελώνης," 88–105). Luke mentions toll collectors 10 times in his Gospel (3:12; 5:27, 29, 30; 7:29, 34; 15:1; 18:10, 11, 13), but they are never mentioned in Acts.

42. Aside from the parable of the Pharisee and the toll collector (18:10–14; which probably comes to Luke from another tradition [L]), Luke's reference to toll collectors is not the result of a personal concern for this particular segment of the Jewish society but of his use of sources (cf. Matt 5:46; 9:10–11; 10:3; 11:19; 18:17; 21:31–32; Mark 2:15–16).

43. In contrast to Peter's initial hesitation (5:8), Levi follows Jesus without uttering a word (5:28).

44. Sanders (*Jesus and Judaism*, 200–208) suggests that Jesus' association with toll collectors and sinners would have offended the Jews not because he broke purity laws but because he called into question the adequacy of the Law.

on one side and toll collectors and sinners on the other—a juxtaposition that foreshadows 7:29-30 (see 15:1-2). In 7:29, toll collectors are credited along with the people for having responded favorably to God's initiative. In the rest of the passage as well as elsewhere (7:34; 15:1), toll collectors and sinners will be portrayed as sympathetic to the message of Jesus and recipients of God's salvific purpose. Despite being deprecated by the Pharisees and the scholars of the Law, the toll collectors and sinners with their humble attitude win the admiration and praise of Jesus (18:10-14).

As Luke evaluates the response of the people and toll collectors to the ministry of John, he states that these two groups have *acknowledged the righteousness* (ἐδικαίωσαν) of God. In Luke-Acts, the word group associated with δικαιόω reflects the LXX notion of a correct relationship with God through the fulfillment of the Law.[45] Luke takes for granted that his audience understands the concept and, beginning with the infancy narratives, he associates it with the fulfillment of the divine purpose. Accordingly, he describes the parents of John as righteous (δίκαιοι) before God and blameless in following every righteous decree (δικαιώμασιν, 1:6). Luke recalls this concept when the angel announces that John will turn the disobedient to the understanding of the righteous (δικαίων, 1:17). In the canticle of Zechariah, Luke links the people's duty to live in holiness and righteousness (ὁσιότητι καὶ δικαιοσύνῃ, 1:75) to the birth of John and the fulfillment of OT promises. The notion of righteousness comes into view again when Luke portrays Simeon as a righteous and devout (δίκαιος καὶ εὐλαβής, 2:25; see 23:50; Acts 10:22) Jew who awaits the consolation of Israel. Thus, Luke's statement that the people and toll collectors have acknowledged the righteousness (ἐδικαίωσαν) of God (7:29) means that by accepting the baptism of John they have vindicated God, i.e., they have recognized that God is righteous and has been faithful to his promises.[46] By doing so, not only

---

45. Schrenk, "δίκαιος," 182-225; Doble, *Paradox of Salvation*, 93-160.

46. Schrenk, "δίκαιος," 214-15. Green (*Luke*, 301) defends an even more literal translation of ἐδικαίωσαν τὸν θεόν (i.e., "justified God") arguing that within the framework of Luke's discourse the situation is appropriate to say that God requires vindication. Nolland (*Luke*, 342), however, notes that the meaning here is more similar to "they glorified God." See ἐδόξαζον τὸν θεόν and similar phrases: 2:20; 5:25, 26; 7:16; 13:13; 17:15; 18:43; 23:47; Acts 4:21; 11:18; 21:20. Despite the differences in nuance, both phrases are related to Luke's theological program; see also Doble, *Paradox of Salvation*, 25-69. In essence, this is but another way of saying that the people and toll collectors

have they recognized the holiness of God, they have also become associated with his uprightness. The way in which the people and toll collectors have acknowledged the righteousness of God will be illuminated further by the reference to the baptism of John in relation to God's salvific plan (7:30) and by its relation to the divine wisdom (7:34). In the meantime, by recognizing the positive response of the people and toll collectors to John's ministry, Luke exonerates them from any wrongdoing in this part of the narrative and confirms Jesus' previous statement that he has not come to call the righteous (δικαίους), but sinners (5:32; see also 15:7).

As the narrative continues, the people's and toll collectors' acknowledgement of the righteousness of God is contrasted with those who try to justify (δικαιόω) themselves without being concerned for their neighbors (10:29), overestimate material possessions (16:15), or despise the people (18:9). At the conclusion of the Gospel, and as the message about Jesus enters a new phase in the Acts of the Apostles, true righteousness will be understood not so much in terms of observance of the Law as in terms of the redemption achieved through the death and resurrection of Jesus, the upright one (Luke 23:47; Acts 3:14; 7:52; 13:38–39; 22:14).

Luke proclaims the acknowledgement of the righteousness of God by people and toll collectors by their acceptance of John's baptism (βαπτισθέντες τὸ βάπτισμα Ἰωάννου). His initial presentation of John noted that he preached a baptism of repentance for the forgiveness of sins (βάπτισμα μετανοίας εἰς ἄφεσιν ἁμαρτιῶν, 3:3).[47] His baptism stood at the dawn of God's impending judgment, and it required an authentic change of conduct—one that would result in good works (3:7–14). To this demand, the people as well as toll collectors responded positively by accepting John's baptism (3:7, 12, 21). Although John's baptism anticipates another baptism with a holy spirit and fire that will be administered by the stronger one (3:16), for the time being John's ritual is sufficient to fulfill all righteousness (cf. Matt 3:15). In 7:29 Luke intimates that by letting themselves be baptized by John the people and toll collectors have heeded the Baptist's call to repentance. By accepting the baptism of John, they have aligned themselves with God's salvific

---

have acknowledged that God has been faithful—an important Lukan concern (Matera, *Theology*, 59).

47. The origin, form, and meaning of John's baptism continue to be a matter of discussion; see Meier, *Marginal Jew*, 2:100–116; Webb, *John the Baptizer*, 95–216; Taylor, *Immerser*, 49–100.

A Narrative-Critical Interpretation of 7:29–35

purposes, begun to prepare the way for the Lord, and fulfilled the expectations of the Baptist's ministry as outlined in the infancy narratives (1:17, 77).

In the Acts of the Apostles, Jesus will refer again to the baptism of John in anticipation of the baptism of the Holy Spirit (Acts 1:5; see also 1:22; 10:37). After the message of Jesus spreads throughout Judea and beyond, the baptism of John resurfaces as an incomplete ritual in need of further legitimacy (13:24–25; 18:25; 19:3–4).

The Frustration of the Plan of God (7:30)

Luke contrasts the praiseworthy reaction of the people and toll collectors with that of the Pharisees (οἱ Φαρισαῖοι) and the scholars of the Law (οἱ νομικοί).[48] Unlike Matt 3:7–12 (cf. Mark 1:5), where the Pharisees and the Sadducees are present during John's preaching, Luke's account of John's public ministry does not mention the presence of the religious leaders (3:7–18). Instead, in Luke the Pharisees first appear as part of a crowd that gathers from different parts of Palestine to see and listen to Jesus (5:17) as his popularity spreads (4:14–15, 31–32, 36–37, 44; 5:1, 15). Sitting side by side with the Pharisees are the "teachers of the Law" (νομοδιδάσκαλος, 5:17)—Luke' alternative designation for the scribes (γραμματεῖς) and the scholars of the Law (οἱ νομικοί).[49] After Jesus

---

48. Levine ("Luke's Pharisees," 129–30) provides a convenient summary of Pharisee's portrayal in Luke; see also Meyer and Weiss, "Φαρισαῖος," 11–48; Bowker, *Jesus and the Pharisees*, 1–52; Ziesler, "Luke and the Pharisees," 161–72; Neusner, *Pharisees*, 301–19; Powell, "Religious Leaders," 93–110; Saldarini, *Pharisees*, 277–97; Sanders, *Jews*, 84–131; Gnilka, *Jesus of Nazareth*, 51–54; Carroll, "Pharisees," 604–21; Fitzmyer, *Luke*, 1:580–81; Darr, *Character Building*, 85–126; Grangaard, *Conflict and Authority*, 36 n. 14; Meier, *Marginal Jew*, 3:311–88; Kilpatrick, "Scholars of the Law," 56–60.

49. Luke uses νομοδιδάσκαλος once more in Acts 5:34. The terms νομικός (7:30; 10:25; 11:45, 46, 52; 14:3) and γραμματεύς, which is a technical differentiation, refer to one and the same group. According to Meier (*Marginal Jew*, 3:549–60) the term "scribe" had a wide range of meanings applied to a number of persons whose activity involved writing documents, such as marriage contracts, legal records, or personal correspondences. Some performed clerical work in government and religious institutions or acted as judges, teachers in the Mosaic Law, or Jewish bureaucrats (see also Saldarini, *Pharisees*, 241–76; Leaney, "ΝΟΜΙΚΟΣ," 166–67). Besides the Pharisees and the scribes, Luke also mentions other religious groups (e.g., οἱ ἀρχιερεῖς, οἱ πρῶτοι τοῦ λαοῦ, οἱ πρεσβύτεροι, οἱ Σαδδουκαῖοι, and οἱ ἄρχοντες) who, with different degrees of culpability, constitute the opponents of Jesus in the Lukan narrative. Without prejudice regarding their participation in different parts of the narrative, I subsume their role as a character group under the term "religious leaders" (so Kingsbury, *Conflict*, 21–22; Grangaard, *Conflict and Authority*, 23).

forgives a paralytic (5:20), the Pharisees and the scribes are scandalized and begin among themselves to censure his conduct (5:21). When Jesus shares a meal with a group of toll collectors and sinners, the Pharisees and the scribes ask his disciples why he eats with people whom they consider religious outcasts (5:30).[50] While they are not yet explicitly confrontational, the Pharisees and the teachers of the Law (scribes) appear as those who most strictly scrutinize Jesus. The exchange between the religious leaders and Jesus continues as they question him about why the disciples of John and the Pharisees fast and pray often while his disciples eat and drink (5:33). Jesus replies to their concerns and the episode concludes without further consequences.[51]

Later, the Pharisees ask Jesus why he does what is unlawful on the Sabbath (6:2). Again, Jesus answers their concerns and the scene ends without an explicit confrontation. But in the next episode (6:6–11) Luke gives the first clear indication that the tension between Jesus and the religious leaders is escalating. As a man with a withered hand enters the synagogue where Jesus is teaching, Luke reports that the Pharisees and the scribes watch him closely (παρετηροῦντο αὐτόν) to see if they can find a reason to accuse him (κατηγορεῖν αὐτοῦ, 6:7). The way in which Luke describes Jesus' perception of the religious leaders (6:8), the ironic question with which he replies (6:9), his defiant gesture (περιβλεψάμενος πάντας αὐτούς, 6:10; cf. Mark 3:5), and Luke's final remark (6:11) confirm the growing tension between them. The reactions of the religious leaders begin to shape the plot of the ensuing narrative, in which the opposition of the Pharisees and scribes to Jesus becomes increasingly hostile. Hence, after Jesus acknowledges the importance of John in relation to the kingdom of heaven (7:28), Luke seizes the opportunity to emphasize how the reaction of the religious leaders, represented by the Pharisees and the scholars of the Law, has played out in relation to the ministry of the Baptist.

---

50. The first encounters between Jesus and the religious leaders occur within the context of eating and drinking scenes, which provide the narrative framework for three successive pronouncement stories (5:27–32; 5:33–39; and 6:1–5); see Heil, *Meal Scenes*, 21–37.

51. While at this stage of the narrative the encounter between Jesus and the religious leaders is not openly confrontational, it is not entirely neutral. The meeting between Jesus and the religious leaders is colored by the hostile encounter between Jesus and his fellow villagers (4:17–30) as well as by certain hints of emerging antagonism in the narrative (e.g., ἐγόγγυζον, 5:30).

Luke accuses the Pharisees and the scholars of the Law of rejecting for themselves (ἠθέτησαν εἰς ἑαυτούς) the plan of God (τὴν βουλὴν τοῦ θεοῦ).[52] Unlike the people and toll collectors, the Pharisees and the scholars of the Law have not accepted the baptism (μὴ βαπτισθέντες) of John. As noted above, prior to 7:30 the Lukan narrative does not record any reaction of the religious leaders to the ministry of John (3:7–18). They are absent from the scene and, despite John's harsh language, the reaction of those who are present seems receptive. Aside from Herod's imprisonment of John (3:19–20), the Baptist does not face opposition from the religious leaders or anyone else. The only opposition that Luke reports is that of Nazareth's villagers, the Pharisees, and scholars of the Law against Jesus. If anything, after John's incarceration the religious leaders seem sympathetic to the Baptist's cause (5:33). In line with 3:7–18, Jesus' remarks in 7:24–28 about the people's interest in John do not mention the religious leaders, and the scene can only be construed as an approval of the Baptist's ministry.

Now, for the first time in the story, Luke states in 7:30 that the religious leaders have in fact rejected[53] the baptism of John, which is but a metonymy for the whole of his message.[54] Aided by the narrative parallel he has so carefully crafted between John and Jesus, Luke intimates that the reaction of the religious leaders to the ministry of John was the same as their response to Jesus' ministry. Through this literary device, Luke is able to transfer the religious leaders' reaction from Jesus to John and fill an important narrative gap. "The disclosure of this information at this point in the narrative works to unite the ministries of Jesus and John the Baptist: both are inextricably related to the purpose of God, with

---

52. The phrse εἰς ἑαυτούς has been understood either as modifying ἠθέτησαν, thus emphasizing the responsibility of the religious leaders, or in relation to the plan of God. The difference is minimal (Fitzmyer, *Luke*, 1:676; Nolland, *Luke*, 343).

53. Throughout the narrative, Luke expresses similar rejection and hostility to Jesus by the use of other terms (e.g., ἐξουθενέω, παροτρύνω, ἀπειθέω, ἀντιτάσσω), phrases (e.g., ἐπέβαλον αὐτοῖς τὰς χεῖρας, ἐπλήσθησαν ζήλου, ἐκάκωσαν τὰς ψυχὰς τῶν ἐθνῶν), and narrative means (e.g., interaction of the religious leaders with Jesus, interaction of the religious leaders with other characters, and narrative comments); see Tyson, "Conflict," 314–26; Kingsbury, *Conflict*, 30–31.

54. Green, *Luke*, 300. Müller (*Charakterzeichnung*, 241) notes that the rejection of John by the religious leaders is "eine neue Thematik, da diese Gruppen in Lk 3 nicht erwähnt warden." In her comments on 7:29–30, Taylor (*Immerser*, 201–3) claims that, historically, John would not have expected Pharisees to repent, since he would have considered them already righteous.

the result being that those who jettison the baptism of John the Baptist reject the purpose of God."⁵⁵ The surveillance, murmuring, scrutiny, and conspiracies that the Pharisees and the scholars of the Law have leveled against Jesus are but a reflection of their rejection of the Baptist. By rejecting John's baptism they have rendered invalid and nullified his ministry, and by doing so they have behaved insolently and offensively.⁵⁶ The religious leaders' rejection of the baptism of John is an affront against God and an act of arrogance. "By refusing John's baptism, the religious authorities affirmed in effect that they had no need of repentance and forgiveness (15:7). The reason they had no such need is that, as they see themselves, they are already righteous (5:32; 18:9)."⁵⁷ Luke's assessment of the religious leaders' rejection of John will be supported by Jesus' own remarks in the parable of the children in the marketplace (7:33). Moreover, this accusation is corroborated later when Jesus reminds the religious leaders that they did not believe in John (20:1–8).

Luke's remark about the reaction of the religious leaders is important for the development of the narrative on three counts. First, given the previous narrative silence about how the religious leaders have responded to the ministry of John, Luke's remark fills an important narrative gap.⁵⁸ Second, by corroborating that the Pharisees and the scholars of the Law have rejected John, Luke's commentary improves the logic of the narrative and paves the way for the interpretation of the parable of the children in the marketplace not only as a reproach against "this generation" but as a condemnation of the religious leaders. Third, within the narrative, the rejection of John by the Pharisees and the scribes foreshadows how the religious authorities will ultimately respond to the ministry of Jesus.

As the story continues, the rejection of the religious leaders will prove to be lethal.⁵⁹ Ironically, while the Pharisees and the scholars of

---

55. Spencer, *Rhetorical Texture*, 107.

56. BDAG, "ἀθετέω," 24. Luke uses ἀθετέω four more times in 10:16, a verse in which Jesus links the rejection of his disciples to his rejection and that of God's initiative.

57. Kingsbury, *Conflict*, 23.

58. Whether this gap results from Luke's redaction of Q (τῶν Φαρισαίων καὶ Σαδδουκαίων, Matt 3:7) is difficult to decide (Marshall, *Luke*, 139; Fitzmyer, *Luke*, 1:467).

59. Nolland, *Luke*, 342–43; Kingsbury, *Conflict*, 23–24; Powell, "Religious Leaders," 96, 98.

the Law consider themselves righteous, they stand in the wrong relationship with God.⁶⁰ Although the religious leaders' attitude toward Jesus is mixed, for the most part in the Gospel of Luke their behavior is confrontational. Despite their occasional demonstrations of respect (8:41–42; 13:31; 17:20; 18:18; 20:26; 20:39), the religious authorities show disdain toward Jesus. Jesus himself predicts these confrontations (9:22, 44; 12:50; 17:25; 18:31–33; cf. 24:7, 25–27). Thus, after Jesus' parable of the children in the marketplace (7:31–35), the Pharisees impugn his legitimacy (7:39), put him to the test (10:25; 20:20–25; 20:27–38), question his religious practices (11:38), plot against him (11:53–54; 19:47; 20:9–19; 20:40; 22:2–6), become angry at him (13:14), watch him closely (14:1–3), murmur about him (15:1–2), ridicule him (16:13–14), object to his recognition (19:39), confront him (20:1–18), accuse him (22:66–71; 23:2, 5, 10), and mock him (23:55; 22:63–65). The antagonism between the religious leaders and Jesus intensifies as the story unfolds and leads to his final demise.

In the Acts of the Apostles, the followers of Jesus will experience similar rejections from the religious leaders. The confrontations between Peter and the temple authorities highlight the hostility of this character group to the followers of Jesus (Acts 4:1–21; 5:17–18, 26–40).⁶¹ The conflicts between Stephen and the Sanhedrin precipitate his death (6:12—8:1), and when Paul turns from a persecutor of the church (8:3; 9:1–2) to its most fervent advocate, he experiences similar opposition and rejection (9:23; 12:3–4; 13:45, 50; 14:2, 5, 19; 17:5–9; 18:5–6, 12–13; 21:27–31; 23:12–15; 24:1–9; 25:2–3, 7; 28:24–28).⁶²

The rejection of John's baptism by the Pharisees and the scholars of the Law is in reality a rejection of the plan of God (τὴν βουλὴν τοῦ θεοῦ). The reference to the "plan of God" is Luke's first explicit allusion to a motif that runs deep throughout his two-volume work.⁶³ His use of this

---

60. Kingsbury, *Conflict*, 23.

61. Tannehill, *Luke-Acts*, 2:63.

62. Toward the second part of Acts, Luke favors the use of *the Jews* to identify the adversaries of the church. Luke's complex characterization of *the Jews* includes the religious leaders, who, throughout the narrative, have been portrayed as the principal antagonists of the Baptist, Jesus, and the church (Sanders, *Jews*, 71–72).

63. This is so despite the fact that, as Schulz ("Gottes Vorsehung," 104–16) points out, "Lukas gibt zwar keine ausdrückliche Darstellung dieses Vorstellungskomplexes, aber er setzt nichtsdestoweniger eine feste Konzeption voraus"; see also Squires, *Plan of God*, 1; Fitzmyer, *Luke*, 1:179–81; O'Toole, *Theology*, 26–28; Conzelmann, *Theology*, 149–57; Bovon, *Theologian*, 1–85; Matera, *Theology*, 56–57.

concept in this part of the narrative is also telling for the way in which he views and shapes this tradition about John and Jesus. In Luke-Acts, the "plan of God" has many different thematic strands. "In Luke's view the definite plan or purpose of God underlies the 'event' he narrates. The plan is evident from vocabulary such as 'the plan' or 'purpose' of God (*hē boulē tou theou*), the divine necessity that certain things 'must' (*dei*) happen, the manner in which God 'appoints' or 'determines' (*horizō*) what happens or must be 'fulfilled' (*pleroō*)."[64] To appreciate the significance of Luke's allusion to the "plan of God" in 7:30 it is necessary to understand the role of this concept in the whole of Luke-Acts.[65]

In the Luke-Acts narrative, God is the one who enables all the events that take place in the travails of human history.[66] God has predetermined the course of human affairs and, even though the circumstances may seem to contradict the fulfillment of those divine purposes, his designs will come to fruition.[67] The events of which Luke wants to make Theophilus aware—those related to Christ—are inscribed in the ancient and ongoing story of God's dealing with humanity. In fulfillment of his purposes, God has chosen Jesus to be the Messiah[68] and through him to bring salvation to all humanity—Jews, Gentiles, and the marginalized alike.[69] As the principal agent of God's plan of salvation, Jesus reveals God's radical requirements and moral demands, which from Jesus' point of view can be summed up in the primacy of love.[70] Inscribed in this plan is also the necessity that he must suffer, die, and be raised from

---

64. Matera, *Theology*, 56–57. Other terms such as θέλημα (22:42; Acts 13:22), τελέω (12:50; 18:21: 22:37; Acts: 13:29), and τελείωσις (1:45) also outline the concept of God's plan. According to Squires (*Plan of God*, 24–25, 58–77) Luke indicates the providential dimension of his story through phrases such as "the things concerning Jesus," "the things that God has done," and "the things we have heard and seen," phrases that are meant to put into perspective the events that have unfolded among the Christian community.

65. Cadbury, *Luke Acts*, 303–6.

66. Acts 1:7; 17:26.

67. Luke 7:29–30; 11:2; 22:42; Acts 1:16, 20; 4:26–28; 5:38–39; 20:27; 21:14.

68. Luke 1:26–28; Act 3:20; 22:14.

69. Luke 2:11; 3:6; 4:18–21; 7:22; Acts 2:40–41, 47; 4:12; 16:31. God's plan of salvation entailed the deliverance of human beings from evil and eternal damnation as well as the forgiveness of sins, the bestowal of peace, life, justification, and an intimate relationship with Jesus. Regarding the effects of salvation and its universal dimension, see Fitzmyer, *Luke*, 1:187–92, 221–26.

70. Luke 6:20–38; 7:47; 10:25–28.

A Narrative-Critical Interpretation of 7:29–35

the dead.[71] But God has predestined that Jesus should become the judge of the living and the dead after his resurrection.[72] For the implementation of this plan, God has chosen some people, such as John the Baptist and Paul, to participate and cooperate in the fulfillment of God's divine purposes.[73]

This profound Lukan conviction is evident from the opening verses of the Gospel. Beginning with the prologue, he intimates that the events that have unfolded among the Christian community have taken place in fulfillment (πεπληροφορημένων) of divine purposes.[74] The infancy narratives are filled with examples in which these events occur according to divine guidance. God's underlying activity is manifested in the angel Gabriel's announcement to Zechariah (1:11–20) as well as in the fulfillment of the events promised to him (1:24, 60–64). The epiphany of the angelic choir to the shepherds confirms the providential character of Jesus' birth (2:9–14). Simeon's divinely inspired confirmation of Jesus' messianic identity (2:26–32) as well as his prophetic announcement regarding Jesus' destiny and that of Mary (2:34–35) is yet another example of the plan of God. When Jesus' parents look for him in the temple, he explains that it is necessary (δεῖ) that he be in his Father's house (2:49).[75] The prophecies and angelic epiphanies of the infancy narratives establish a number of predictions that create an expectation for fulfillment as the narrative develops.[76] These celestial interventions amplify the theme of divine guidance and provide a deeper insight into the way God will be at work in the story.[77] Squires highlights the formative function of the infancy narratives concerning the divine providence motif:

71. Luke 9:22, 44; 13:33; 17:25; 18:31–33; 22:22; 24:7, 25–27; Acts 2:23; 3:18; 4:28; 13:27; 17:3.

72. Acts 10:42; cf. 17:31.

73. Luke 1:13–17; 3:4–6; Acts 9:6, 16; 10:41; 13:36; 16:10; 23:11; 26:16; 27:24.

74. Dillon ("Luke's Project," 205–27) emphasizes Luke's interest in the plan of God in the use of διήγησις, καθεξῆς, ἀσφάλεια, and πληροφορέω. Other concepts, such as περὶ τῶν πραγμάτων, περὶ λόγων, evoke the theme of fulfilled prophecy (Squires, *Plan of God*, 23–24).

75. The term δεῖ appears 18 times in Luke and in some instances implies the divine necessity that some events must come to pass. Relevant uses of the term for the discussion of the plan of God are 2:49; 4:43; 9:22; 13:33; 17:25; 21:9; 22:37; 24:7, 26, 44 (Grundmann, "δεῖ," 21–25).

76. Squires, *Plan of God*, 29; Marshall, *Luke*, 49–50; Aune, *Prophecy*, 146–47; Minear, "Birth Stories," 118–19.

77. Squires, *Plan of God*, 29.

> [T]he prologue establishes without any doubt the way in which God is active in the events that take place. Events subsequent to this prologue are thus introduced and interpreted as taking place under God's guidance. Epiphanies, prophecies, an indication of divine necessity and an insistence on the divine initiative throughout these two chapters indicate that providence is to be a major theme of Luke's story. Through the miraculous events, epiphanies, predictive prophecies and declarations of necessity which will follow throughout the Gospel, Luke will build a case for viewing everything which he narrates as part of the overall plan of God.[78]

Thus, as John and Jesus begin their public ministries, God's designs remain the moving force behind the development of the story in ever subtle ways.[79] When John calls the people to repentance, he urges them to prepare for the coming wrath (τῆς μελλούσης ὀργῆς, 3:7), an allusion to God's predestined judgment.[80] In the baptism of Jesus (3:22), God "personally" enters the story to identify Jesus as his "Son" and sanction his ministry. Later, when Jesus reveals himself as God's anointed agent in the synagogue of Nazareth, he notes that this is occurring in fulfillment of the Scripture (πεπλήρωται ἡ γραφή, 4:21).[81] After he begins his public ministry, Jesus tells his disciples that it is necessary (δεῖ) that he go to other cities to preach the kingdom of God, because for this purpose (ἐπὶ τοῦτο) "I have been sent" (ἀπεστάλην, 4:43). In the course of his ministry, Jesus performs a number of mighty works (e.g., 5:17–26; 7:11–17), which are a continuing manifestation of God's plan (cf. Acts 2:22–23).[82]

Now in 7:30, after John has resurfaced as one of the characters who wonders about the identity of Jesus and receives his homage (7:18–28), for the first time in the narrative Luke takes the opportunity to assess how the responses of the people and the religious leaders to the minis-

---

78. Ibid., 31.

79. Dibelius (*Studies*, 181) underlines that Luke demonstrates his convictions through means that are more subtle than direct.

80. The term μέλλω appears 12 times in Luke. Relevant for the discussion of plan of God are 3:7; 9:31, 44; 21:36; 22:23; 24:21.

81. The term πληρόω appears 9 times in Luke. Significant passages include 1:20; 4:21; 9:31; 21:24; 22:16; 24:44. Moreover, God's plan is hinted at in this passage by the remark that he is well pleased with Jesus (εὐδοκέω, 3:22; 12:32; see also εὐδοκία, 10:21).

82. Squires, *Plan of God*, 90–91.

try of John fare in relation to the plan of God (7:29–30). Within God's grand scheme of salvation, the Baptist has played a monumental role, which the religious leaders in their shortsightedness have failed to comprehend. Luke's narrative commentary exposes their ineptitude and lack of wisdom to discover underneath the appearance of the ministry of John—and by extension that of Jesus—the providential hand of God. Luke's remarks serve as an indictment against the religious leaders who have gradually become hostile to Jesus.

Ironically, the conspiracies (the plans) of the religious leaders (6:11; 11:53–54; 19:48; 20:19–20; 22:2) stand in contrast to the salvific purpose of God's overarching plan.[83] But even as the religious leaders fulfill their plot against Jesus, God's purpose is neither frustrated nor sabotaged. In the Acts of the Apostles, the inner logic of God's plan is revealed in a deeper and more complete sense. Thus, in his first speech, Peter claims that Jesus' betrayal occurred as part of God's definite plan and knowledge (τῇ ὡρισμένῃ βουλῇ καὶ προγνώσει τοῦ θεοῦ, 2:23). In their prayer, the early believers acknowledged that the plot against Jesus had taken place by what the hand and plan (βουλή) of God had determined to occur (προώρισεν γενέσθαι, 4:28). Gamaliel cautions the Sanhedrin to consider what they are going to do to the followers of Jesus, lest the religious leaders find themselves fighting against the plan (ἡ βουλή) of God (5:38–39). In his first reported sermon, Paul credits David with serving the plan of God (τῇ τοῦ θεοῦ βουλῇ, 13:36). Finally, as Paul bids farewell to the Ephesian community, he declares that he did not shy away from proclaiming the entire plan of God (πᾶσαν τὴν βουλὴν τοῦ θεοῦ, 20:27).[84]

---

83. The plans of the religious leaders against Jesus have neither the depth nor the efficacy of the plan of God. Yet by their attempts to sabotage the fulfillment of God's designs the religious leaders unknowingly become co-conspirators in a deeper and wider conflict between Jesus and Satan (4:13; 22:3–4, 31, 53).

84. Other indications of the plan of God in the Acts of the Apostles include Paul's obedience to the will of God (21:14; 22:14) and terms that imply the divine necessity that some events must come to pass: δεῖ (Acts 1:6, 21; 3:21; 4:12; 5:29; 9:6, 16; 14:22; 16:30; 17:3; 19:21; 20:35; 23:11; 24:19; 25:10; 26:9; 27:24) and μέλλω (Acts 11:28; 17:31; 26:22, 23). As in the Gospel, Luke understands events in the church as the fulfillment (πληρόω) of God's plan (Acts: 1:16; 2:28; 3:18; 13:27; 14:26; 19:21) and depicts the manifestations of God's plan through a number of epiphanies (Acts 1:3, 9–11; 2:3; 5:19–20; 9:3–6; 10:3–7, 10–16, 30–32; 11:5–10, 13–14; 12:7–11, 23; 16:9–10; 18:9; 22:6–8, 17–21; 23:11; 26:13–18; 27:23–24). Finally, a cluster of προ- compounds and related verbs point to God's purpose throughout the narrative: πρόγνωσις (Acts 2:23),

Summary

As a summary of the way in which different character groups have responded to the ministry of John, 7:29-30 highlights the response of the multitudes who have reacted favorably to God's initiative as manifested in the messages and ministries of John and Jesus. Along with the people, Luke singles out toll collectors, a group that, although despised by the religious leaders, is portrayed benevolently in the narrative. By accepting the baptism of John they have shown repentance and acknowledged the righteousness of God, i.e., they have vindicated God and demonstrated that God is faithful. In doing so, not only have they become associated with his uprightness, they have also fulfilled God's salvific expectations as outlined in the infancy narratives.

Luke juxtaposes the people and toll collectors with the Pharisees and the scholars of the Law, two character groups that, as the narrative develops, show increasing hostility toward Jesus. Although the previous narrative has not noted any controversies between John and the religious leaders, Luke states for the first time in the narrative that they have rejected the baptism of John. Aided by the narrative parallel between John and Jesus, Luke insinuates that the religious leaders have responded to John in much the same way that they have responded to Jesus. With this statement, Luke fills an important narrative gap and paves the way for the interpretation of the parable of the children in the marketplace as a condemnation of the religious leaders. More importantly, Luke shows how the reaction of both groups, the people and toll collectors as well as the Pharisees and the scholars of the Law, fares in relation to the "plan of God," an important Lukan motif. By asserting that the religious leaders have rejected the baptism of John, Luke exposes their shortsightedness and lack of wisdom. Moreover, Luke's indictment foreshadows the future development of the narrative, in which the religious leaders' presumed righteousness ironically results in their gradual alienation from the kingdom.

As an added commentary to Jesus' epitaph on John, Luke's remarks on 7:29-30 function as an important thematic threshold to the short but important career of the Baptist. Within the structure of the Gospel,

---

προκαταγγέλλω (Acts 3:18; 7:52), προορίζω (Acts 4:28), προχειρίζομαι (Acts 3:20; 22:14; 26:16), προχειροτονέω (Acts 10:41), προστάσσω (Acts 17:26); see also πληροφορέω (Luke 1:1), τάσσω (Acts 13:48; 22:10), τίθημι (Acts 1:7; 13:47, 48; 19:21; 20:28), and ὁρίζω (Luke 22:22; Acts 2:23; 10:42; 17:26, 31).

A Narrative-Critical Interpretation of 7:29–35

Luke's commentary brings closure to the role of John and sets the narrative on a decisive christological path. If in the following narrative the religious leaders' response to God's offer of salvation broadens the "division" within the people of Israel, Luke's explicit verdict in 7:29–30 ought to be viewed as seminal for the development of this theological perspective.

Fourth Subunit: The Parable of the Children in the Marketplace (7:31–35)

JESUS AND THE PRESENT GENERATION (7:31)

While some authors are unsure whether the statements in 7:29–30 should be attributed to the narrator or Jesus, no one doubts that as the narrative continues it is Jesus who speaks in the parable of the children in the marketplace (7:31–35). Almost every aspect of the parable—from its origin to its meaning—has been the subject of extensive debate.[85] Regardless of what may have been the history of the parable's composition and its original setting, Luke envisions Jesus' remarks as part of an ongoing speech in which Jesus continues to address a crowd of people.[86] Therefore, the setting is connected to the previous episodes and, with little movement or description of location recorded, the setting of the scene remains the same and as vague as before (7:18–20, 24).

The parable begins with a soliloquy in which Jesus wonders to what he should compare the people of this generation (7:31).[87] Jesus starts with a double rhetorical question (τίνι οὖν ὁμοιώσω ... καὶ τίνι εἰσὶν ὅμοιοι;) designed to involve the addressees in search of an answer.[88] Throughout the narrative, Luke has portrayed Jesus as an

---

85. A number of questions regarding the history of transmission of the parable, the figure of the children's game, and the extent to which allegorical interpretations are appropriate, complicate the meaning of the parable; see Plummer, *St. Luke*, 206–9; Dibelius, *Überlieferung*, 15–20; Jeremias, *Parables of Jesus*, 160–62; Mussner, "Kairos," 599–612; Linton, "Children's Game," 159–79; Zeller, "Bildlogik," 252–57; Fitzmyer, *Luke*, 1:677–82; Cotter, "Parable of the Children," 289–304; Meier, *Marginal Jew*, 2:144–56.

86. Many find behind its current form a parable (7:31–32), an explanation of the parable (7:33–34), and a wisdom saying (7:35) (e.g., Kloppenborg, *Formation of Q*, 115–17). Others, however, think it could have existed in its present form from the beginning (Perrin, *Rediscovering*, 121).

87. The conjunction οὖν is probably Lukan and, in light of 7:29–30, the parable is meant to follow as consequence of those statements (Plummer, *St. Luke*, 206).

88. Schürmann, *Lukasevangelium*, 423. The introductory formula is also found in rabbinical parables (Jeremias, *Parables of Jesus*, 101 n. 54).

engaging speaker. He has often addressed the crowd with rhetorical questions (7:24, 25, 26) and comparisons (ὅμοιος, 6:47–49) to illustrate his points (see also ὁμοιόω, 13:18, 20).[89] In line with this pattern, Jesus addresses the crowd with two rhetorical questions that seek a suitable example with which to compare the people of this generation (τοὺς ἀνθρώπους τῆς γενεᾶς ταύτης).

The phrase "this generation," a biblical idiom which in this case modifies the people (ἀνθρώπους),[90] often carries a pejorative connotation (Deut 32:5; Judg 2:10; Ps 78:8; Jer 2:31). However, as a generic designation for the people, the negative meaning of the phrase is not absolute in the Lukan narrative.[91] The people of Mary's generation (γενεαί) as well as future ones are destined to consider her blessed (1:48). They (γενεάς) are also in a position to receive the mercy of God, who bestows it upon those who fear him (1:50). When Jesus initially called Peter and his companions, he hinted that he was making them participants in a ministry aimed at the people (ἀνθρώπους, 5:10). Even if the people (ἀνθρώπους) have the potential to oppose his ministry (6:22), Jesus occasionally views them as victims of unscrupulous religious leaders (11:46). The present generation is sometimes portrayed as conspirators against God's chosen ones (11:50–51; 17:25), self-servingly shrewd (16:8), faithless and perverse (9:41; 11:29–32; Acts 2:40), but also as neutral bystanders in the course of events (Acts 8:33; 13:36; 14:16; 15:21). Nevertheless, the pejorative nuance prevails in 7:31.

As part of the rhetorical strategy in Jesus' introductory double question, the mention of "the people of this generation" has a twofold function. First, as part of a statement conceived to draw the audience into identifying themselves with one of the aforementioned character groups (i.e., "the people and toll collectors" or "the Pharisees and the scholars of the Law"), it is an inclusive expression. In other words, the phrase re-

---

89. Some authors have discussed in the past whether the passage should be considered an allegory, a similitude, or a parable. For a clearer distinction between these three literary means, see Boucher, *Mysterious Parable*, 3–25.

90. Note that I translate here ἀνθρώπους with the same English word ("people") that I translated ὁ λαός ("the people") in 7:29. However, these two terms do not entirely correlate. While in 7:29 "the people" are portrayed favorably as those who have acknowledged the righteousness of God, in 7:31 "the people of this generation" stand predominantly for those who have rejected the message of God through the ministries of John and Jesus.

91. Nolland, *Luke*, 343; see also Meinertz, "'Dieses Geschlecht,'" 283–89.

A Narrative-Critical Interpretation of 7:29-35

fers to the people (ἀνθρώπους) in general, all those who have accepted the message of John and Jesus as well as those who have rejected it.[92] Second, in a more literary sense, to the extent that "this generation" has a predominantly pejorative connotation, the phrase refers to all those who in the previous narrative have opposed the ministry of John and Jesus. Since in the foregoing scenes Luke has progressively shown the religious leaders to be the adversaries of Jesus, the phrase has them particularly in view. Whereas in Matt 11:16 the expression has no immediate referent, after Luke has unequivocally identified "the Pharisees and the scholars of the Law" as those who have frustrated the plan of God (7:30), the phrase refers to the religious leaders. By the proximity of the narrative commentary, Luke has transformed what may have originally been a condemnation of the people in general into a criticism of the religious leaders. Therefore, as the parable unfolds in the Lukan version they will be the main objects of Jesus' reproach and this is how the reference to "the people of this generation" should be understood.[93]

The Children Playing in the Marketplace (7:32)

To illustrate the way in which the people of this generation have behaved, Jesus appeals to a familiar scene and compares them to children (παιδίοις) sitting in the marketplace (ἐν ἀγορᾷ καθημένοις, 7:32).[94] The figure of the parable has been a matter of much discussion. Most commentators agree that the parable contemplates two sets of children, but they disagree about what type of imagery it suggests. With different emphases and nuances, some authors take the figure of the quarreling children to mean that the two groups cannot agree about what kind of game to play; one group wants to play a game involving dancing and another group a game involving mourning.[95] Other commentators un-

---

92. The temporal-spatial connotation of the phrase includes not only Jesus' opponents and his contemporaries, but Jesus himself; see Spencer, *Rhetorical Texture*, 108; Plummer, *St. Luke*, 206.

93. Regarding Luke's identification of "the people of this generation" with the religious leaders and the significance of this identification for the sinful woman and the Pharisee scene (7:36-50), see Kilgallen, "John the Baptist," 677-78.

94. As in other NT writings, Luke uses other terms besides παιδίον to refer to children (e.g., υἱός, 6:35; τέκνον, 1:17; νήπιος, 10:21; παῖς, 8:51) without any discernable difference. Cotter ("Parable of the Children," 298-302) interprets the phrase ἐν ἀγορᾷ καθημένοις and the parable as referring to a judicial process.

95. Hoffmann, *Studien*, 225-27. One of the reasons for this interpretation is the use

derstand the parable in the sense that one group invites the other to play two different types of games but the latter group refuses to join in either one of them.[96] In the former interpretation, there is an element of mutual recrimination—both groups are at fault. Hence, Jesus would be reproaching the people of this generation for their mutual conflicts and for not being able to agree among themselves. In the latter interpretation, only one group is at fault. Jesus' criticism would be aimed at the people of this generation for refusing to play despite the efforts of the second group to find an acceptable game. A variant of these interpretations understands the children sitting in the marketplace as the ones who call out the games and complain to Jesus and John for not joining in their dancing and mourning, i.e., not accommodating their lifestyles to the customs of the people of this generation.[97]

From the perspective of the narrative, Jesus' reference to the children (παιδία) in the marketplace recalls that the announcement of John's birth brought hope for the return of rebellious (ἀπειθεῖς) children to the wisdom of the just (1:17; cf. Acts 2:39; 13:33).[98] However, although the people of this generation consider themselves children of Abraham (3:8), the rejection of the religious leaders frustrated (7:30) the fulfillment of the angel's promise. Jesus' reproach in 7:31–32 reminds them that they are not like the children of Abraham but like sullen children sitting in the marketplace who refuse to play. In contrast to Jesus, who as a child sat in the temple among the teachers to listen and ask them questions (2:46), the people of this generation sit in the marketplace and behave like stubborn children. Jesus' criticism foreshadows his future reproach of the Pharisees, who seek the seats of honor in synagogues and greetings in the marketplaces (ἀγοραῖς, see also 20:46). The parable's view of children reflects the opinion of Jesus' contemporaries who held children in low esteem along with other weaker members of society.[99]

---

of the reciprocal pronoun ἀλλήλοις.

96. Mussner, "Kairos," 600; Jeremias, *Parables of Jesus*, 161.

97. Linton, "Children's Game," 175; Green, *Luke*, 303.

98. Given the OT portrayal of the people of Israel as disobedient children (e.g., Isa 1:2–4; 30:1), and Mal 3:24 (MT; cf. LXX), ἀπειθεῖς could be interpreted as referring to the disobedient children to whom John is sent to turn their hearts to the understanding of the righteous (Brown, *Birth*, 278–79). For the interpretation of φρονήσει (1:17) as "wisdom," see Fitzmyer, *Luke*, 1:327.

99. Bakke, *Children*, 16–55. Because of their vulnerability and physical weakness, children were held in low esteem and became symbols of human limitations. The belief

But in the rest of the Lukan narrative, Jesus also witnesses to the positive value of the children (11:13; 13:34). He regards children worthy of emulation (9:47–48) and presents them as the epitome of those who are fit to enter the kingdom of God (18:16–17).

Before this more benevolent view of children appears, Jesus compares them to the people of the present generation because the flute has been played (αὐλέω) but they have not danced (ὀρχέομαι); there has been mourning (θρηνέω), but they have not cried (κλαίω).[100] In a literal sense, Jesus' comparison contrasts circumstances of joy and sorrow.[101] The problem remains, however, of how we should understand the parable in a metaphorical sense.

When all the different ways in which the parable has been interpreted are considered, one must acknowledge the difficulty imposed by the intrinsic ambiguity characteristic of a "riddle-speech, which is naturally open to multiple interpretations."[102] It is easy to understand why a microscopic analysis of the parable, which focuses on the grammatical, structural, and/or chronological inconsistencies of the passage, can complicate its interpretation.[103] However, when one looks at the broader context it becomes clearer how each individual element of the parable fits the narrative's characterization of those it intends to portray. From this perspective, the invitation to mourn in the parable agrees with Luke's characterization of John as a prophet who emphatically calls the people to a radical and urgent change of lifestyle (3:3–18). Likewise, the joyful melody of a flute recalls the portrayal of Jesus as the enthusiastic herald of God who brings hope through his preaching and healing ministry (4:16—7:17). Meanwhile, the obstinate children of the parable resemble

---

that they lacked reason was widespread, which prompted many to consider them the opposite of what every adult ought to become; see Osiek et al., *Woman's Place*, 68–94; see also Rawson, *Children*, 115–335.

100. The translation of the relative clause ἃ λέγει has caused confusion. While some take παιδίοις as its antecedent and understand it as "what (one) says," others have interpreted the phrase simply as "who say." The difference has little relevance for the meaning of the text; see Bovon, *Luke*, 1:286; Nolland, *Luke*, 343. Αὐλέω and ὀρχέομαι are *hapax* in Luke-Acts. Θρηνέω occurs once more in 23:27 (cf. πενθέω 6:25). Κλαίω occurs 11 times in Luke-Acts (6:21, 25; 7:13, 32, 38; 8:52; 19:41; 22:62; 23:28; Acts 9:39; 21:13).

101. Fitzmyer, *Luke*, 1:680.

102. Meier, *Marginal Jew*, 2:147.

103. Brown (*Introduction*, 26) makes the point about the problems created by "microscopic" analysis of a given passage versus a simplified look at a narrative that takes much for granted.

the religious leaders, who have raised their objections every step of the way and have refused either to heed John's call to repentance or Jesus' offer of hope and celebration. Like children everywhere, who are always asking questions (e.g., why? warum? ¿porqué?), the religious leaders have been portrayed as pesky children who are constantly objecting and asking "why?" or "who?" (τίς, 5:21, διὰ τί, 5:30; τί, 6:2; see Exod 12:26; Deut 6:20; Josh 4:6, 21) in order to avoid accepting God's offer of salvation.[104]

Therefore, at a metaphorical level, the complaints of the children allude to the celebratory character of Jesus' ministry and the austere message of John.[105] Although the parable may have existed as an independent proverbial saying,[106] in its current context the two groups of children correspond to the messages of John and Jesus on one hand and to rejection of the religious leaders on the other. Accordingly, within the Lukan Gospel, the parable serves as an indictment aimed particularly at the Pharisees and the scholars of the Law for failing to respond—like the obstinate children of the parable—to the different messages of salvation.[107] Just as they have remained on the sidelines and have responded neither to the invitations to be baptized nor to the overtures of the king-

---

104. Note that a widespread manuscript tradition (A, Ψ, 33, M) renders the difficult phrase ἃ λέγει as καὶ λέγουσιν ὑμῖν. This variant supports the interpretation here. These manuscripts understand the parable as part of a speech in which Jesus addresses those who have rejected his message and that of John. With this variant, the children's complaints are directed at those whom Jesus is presumably addressing. Since here the antecedent of ὑμῖν (as in the case of λέγετε, 7:33–34) can only refer to the religious leaders (7:30), they cannot be the ones raising the complaints. Therefore, in the parable the religious leaders remain silent, just as they have remained silent (except for the childish objections they have periodically raised) in the narrative. Linton ("Children's Game," 173) has to regard Matthew's λέγουσιν (11:18–19) as the original over against Luke's λέγετε (7:33–34) to avoid this interpretation. Although Spencer (*Rhetorical Texture*, 109) has a different understanding of who are the children in the parable, his observation about the enthymematic argumentation of the passage is helpful. The unstated conclusion of the parable is that the other children (i.e., the religious leaders) raised objections to the games and refused to play. The religious leaders' voices, omitted in the parable, are heard in Jesus' recapitulation of their complaints against John and himself (7:33–34).

105. The sequence of the parable, however, reverses the salvation-historical sequence from Jesus to John (Bovon, *Luke*, 1:287). Bovon also points out that the prophets related apocalyptic times with the silencing of music (Isa 16:10; Jer 7:34; 16:9; 25:10; 48:33; Ezek 26:13; see ibid., esp. n 73).

106. Nolland (*Luke*, 344) notes: ". . . [T]he refrain has all the marks of being a fixed piece . . . and not as ad hoc protest"; see also Fitzmyer, *Luke*, 1:680; Meier, *Marginal Jew*, 2:148.

107. Ambrosius, *Lucam*, 175–76.

dom, the children sitting in the marketplace remain passively unwilling to respond to the various invitations to play.[108]

THE FALSE ACCUSATIONS AGAINST JOHN AND JESUS (7:33–34)

As the reason (γάρ) for comparing the people of this generation to children, Jesus recalls the manner in which they have reacted to his ministry and that of John. First, Jesus notes the reaction to the ministry of John. In recalling the response to John's offer of salvation, Jesus notes that the Baptist came neither eating food nor drinking wine and they said he had a demon (7:33). After a thematic shift in which the story moved the emphasis from John to the "plan of God" and to the way in which the people of this generation have responded to the different calls for salvation (7:24–30), the Baptist reappears on the scene. But this time John returns in a supportive role. Whereas in 7:18–28 the plot of the pericope focused on John, after Luke's narrative commentary in 7:29–30 the Baptist no longer dominates the scene. John becomes a supporting character because, although the Baptist remains an important figure in the story, the real focus of Jesus' explanatory remarks is the way in which the people of this generation—with special emphasis on the religious leaders—have reacted to the ministries of John and Jesus.[109]

Jesus' assertion that John came (ἐλήλυθεν) neither eating food nor drinking wine (μὴ ἐσθίων ἄρτον μήτε πίνων οἶνον) recalls the angel's words to Zechariah that John would drink neither wine nor strong drink (οἶνον καὶ σίκερα οὐ μὴ πίῃ, 1:15).[110] Although Luke omits Mark's remarks about John eating only locusts and wild honey (Mark 1:6), the infancy narratives' reference to his drinking habits succeeds in portraying John's future ministry as one that will be characterized by ascetic practices.[111] The portrayal of John as an austere herald of God who is

---

108. Dibelius (*Überlieferung*, 17) points out, "Das Gleichnis handelt also nicht von den spielenden Kindern, sondern von den nicht spielenden, von denen, die über lauter Zank nicht zum Spiele kommen."

109. Hence, perhaps Luke's need to mention him with his fuller designation, i.e., Ἰωάννης ὁ βαπτιστής, as if to emphasize the significance of his role (cf. Matt 11:18).

110. Luke's double use of ἐλήλυθεν (7:33–34; cf. Matthew's ἦλθεν, 11:18–19) expresses the prophetic commissioning of his ministry (Bovon, *Luke*, 1:287).

111. Heil, *Meal Scenes*, 13–14. Although ἄρτος and οἶνος may just be stock terms for food (Fitzmyer, *Luke*, 1:680–81), Bovon (*Luke*, 1:287) suggests that the phrase μὴ ἐσθίων ἄρτον indicates that John only ate raw food unprepared by human hands; see also Böcher, "Johannes der Täufer," 90–92; Meier, *Marginal Jew*, 2:48–49.

endowed with the spirit of Elijah (1:17) and who lives in the desert (1:80; 3:2, 4; 7:24–26) serves to dramatize his call to conversion in light of God's imminent appearance.[112] Jesus' mention of the eating and drinking habits of John (7:33)—which differ from Jesus' own conduct—recapitulates this characterization and serves as the basis for his reproach of the religious leaders. Within the broader narrative, these eating habits of John stand in sharp contrast to the sumptuous feasting of the rich (14:2, 16:19).

To the Baptist's asceticism the religious leaders responded by saying that he has a demon (λέγετε, δαιμόνιον ἔχει). The extent to which Luke has adapted the tradition dealing with John and Jesus in 7:18–35 to fit his literary aim can be appreciated in the small but significant way in which he has modified his source in 7:33–34. Whereas in Matt 11:18–19 the double use of λέγουσιν makes Jesus' remarks a general reproach against the people of this generation, Luke's double use of the second-person plural form λέγετε makes it a more direct statement. By using λέγετε, Luke transforms Jesus' summary of the opponents' accusations into a direct address, which presumes that those who levy the charges against the Baptist and Jesus, i.e., the Pharisees and the scholars of the Law, are among the audience.[113]

Jesus denounces the religious leaders because they have considered John a possessed man (δαιμόνιον ἔχει). Since the early parts of the Gospel, Luke has portrayed demons as well as other evil forces as powerful and cunning adversaries that seek to derail the mission of Jesus, and afflict human beings.[114] Consequently, as Jesus begins his public minis-

---

112. Darr, *Character Building*, 84.

113. Some consider λέγετε Lukan (Bovon, *Luke*, 1:280 n. 19; Nolland, *Luke*, 345); others regard it as original (Schürmann, *Lukasevangelium*, 426 n. 132; Robinson et al., *Critical Edition*, 144–47; Ernst, *Johannes der Täufer*, 73). Theon (*Progymnasmata* 87) is aware that different types of speech forms can be used to achieve different purposes: "Since we are accustomed to setting out the facts sometimes as making a straightforward statement and sometimes as doing something more than making a factual statement . . . , sometimes [by] addressing the participants . . . , it is possible to produce varied narrations in all these ways."

114. Luke uses δαιμόνιον about twice as many times (23 times; once in Acts 17:18) as Mark (13 times) and Matthew (11 times). Luke refers to these evil forces with other terms: πνεῦμα δαιμονίου ἀκαθάρτου (4:36; 6:18; 8:29; 9:42; 11:24; Acts 5:16; 8:7); and πνευμάτων πονηρῶν (7:21; 8:2; 11:26; Acts 19:12, 13, 15, 16). His understanding of δαιμόνιον corresponds to the general NT usage, which views demons as closely associated with other powerful demonic figures (διάβολος [4:2, 3, 6, 13; 8:12; Acts 10:38; 13:10], Σατανᾶς [10:18; 11:18; 13:16; 22:3, 31; Acts 5:3; 26:18], and Βεελζεβούλ [11:15, 18, 19]) who are actively at work in the world to afflict human beings and make them

try (4:1–13), the devil tries to impede the fulfillment of God's purposes in the ministry of Jesus, which is foretold in the infancy narratives. As the episode of the possessed man in the synagogue of Capernaum illustrates (4:33–36; see also 4:41), demonic characters will emerge time and again showing extraordinary knowledge, tormenting humans, and enticing them to conspire against Jesus (8:2, 27–39; 9:1, 38–42, 49–50; 10:17–20; 11:14–26; 13:16, 32; 22:3, 31, 53). The portrayal of the demons as the chief adversaries of God's purposes makes the religious leaders' claim that John has a demon (δαιμόνιον) all the more slanderous and offensive (cf. Mark 3:28–30; Luke 12:10). While evil spirits can recognize Jesus as God's anointed one (4:3, 9, 34, 41; 8:28), the religious leaders fail to recognize the manifestation of God's plan in John. Ironically, the religious leaders' accusation against the Baptist stands in stark contrast to the greatness of John announced in the infancy narratives (1:15, 17), the importance of his role as the forerunner of the Lord (1:76–77), and his recognition by the people as a prophet (20:6). Moreover, the religious leaders' poor judgment of John contradicts Jesus' identification of the Baptist as a prophet and as the greatest among those born of women (7:26–28). By criticizing the asceticism of John as unreasonable and worthy of a lunatic (δαιμόνιον ἔχει)—perhaps because his detractors thought that John's practices exceeded the prescriptions of the Mosaic Law—the religious leaders show their lack of wisdom in a scene that foreshadows similar charges against Jesus (11:14–20).[115]

After explaining why the people of this generation are like children because of the way in which they have responded to John, Jesus illustrates why they have behaved like children with respect to his own ministry. While they have called John a possessed man for his ascetic practices, they have called the Son of Man a glutton and a drunkard (φάγος καὶ οἰνοπότης), a friend (φίλος) of toll collectors and sinners (7:34).[116] Whereas the complaint against John focuses on a single charge, i.e., he is possessed, the rumors against Jesus are twofold: he is

---

suffer. These evil forces often manifest themselves through sicknesses and temptations (πειρασμός—the term can refer to a "trial" or a "test" in which a person's fidelity, integrity, or virtue is proven, whether through internal desires or external circumstances); see Foerster, "δαίμων," 16–19; Bovon, *Luke*, 1:141–42; Brown, *Death*, 1:157–62; Seesemann, "πειρασμός," 23–36.

115. Marshall, *Luke*, 301; Fitzmyer, *Luke*, 1:681; Bovon, *Luke*, 1:287.
116. Miquel, *Esclavos, Prostitutas y Pecadores*, 284–91.

accused of eating and drinking in excess and of gathering around people of questionable repute.

Referring to himself as "the Son of Man" (ὁ υἱὸς τοῦ ἀνθρώπου), Jesus acknowledges that his ascetical practices are different from John's and that, unlike him, he has come (ἐλήλυθεν) "eating and drinking" (ἐσθίων καὶ πίνων).[117] The accusations regarding the eating habits of Jesus recall a frequent and important motif in the Lukan Gospel, which often portrays Jesus sharing in table fellowship.[118] As the popularity of Jesus spreads, he becomes a regular guest at meals and banquets. After Jesus calls Levi, Levi hosts a banquet in which Jesus shares with a group of toll collectors and sinners (5:29-39). At this meal, the Pharisees and the scribes raise questions about Jesus' eating practices and about the company he keeps.

First, the Pharisees and the scribes inquire why Jesus eats with toll collectors (τελῶναι) and sinners (ἁμαρτωλοί).[119] While the Pharisees and the scholars of the Law considered toll collectors and sinners social and religious outcasts, Jesus reaches out to them (5:31). Despite the religious leaders' loathing for toll collectors and sinners, the narrative portrays their repentant and humble attitude as worthy of emulation (3:12-13; 15:1; 18:10-14). In 7:29 toll collectors are recognized along with the people for having responded favorably to God's initiative. The charge against Jesus is therefore accurate, but the conclusion that his opponents reach subverts the true meaning of his initiative. For the religious leaders Jesus is a friend (φίλος) of undesirable people.[120] They

---

117. The title "Son of Man" appears here for the third time. Luke uses it 25 times in the Gospel: 5:24; 6:5, 22; 7:34; 9:22, 26, 44, 58; 11:30; 12:8, 10, 40; 17:22, 24, 26, 30; 18:8, 31; 19:10; 21:27, 36; 22:22, 48, 69; 24:7. Jesus' preferred way of self-identification, "the Son of Man," has divine and human connotations and its meaning is associated with the figure in Dan 7, *1 En.*, and *4 Ezra* as a person of sovereign authority, a Messiah, the Son of God, and the Elected One (Fitzmyer, *Wandering Aramean*, 143-60; Marshall, "Son of Man," 775-81). The claim that the use of "Son of Man" here is secondary has been refuted (Dunn, *Jesus Remembered*, 744-45).

118. 5:27-39; 6:1-5; 7:36-50; 9:10-17; 10:38-42; 11:37-54; 14:1-24; 15:1-32; 19:1-10; 22:7-38; 24:28-35; 24:41-43; Heil, *Meal Scenes*, 1-8; Karris, *Eating*, 13-24.

119. The word ἁμαρτωλός appears in Luke 18 times (never in Acts). As in other NT writings, it designates someone who does wrong or whose behavior does not conform to expected moral standards; see Sanders, *Jesus and Judaism*, 174-211; BDAG, "ἁμαρτωλός," 51-52.

120. The term φίλος denotes a close association or relationship with another (e.g., 7:6; 11:5, 6, 8; Acts 10:24; 19:31); BDAG, "φίλος," 1058-59.

insinuate that by befriending toll collectors and sinners, Jesus is as corrupt as they consider them to be.

Second, during Levi's banquet the religious leaders ask Jesus why the disciples of John and the Pharisees fast and pray while his disciples eat and drink—implying that they do so in imitation of Jesus (5:33). The implication is that Jesus' eating and drinking habits violate Jewish customs.[121] Jesus' meal at Levi's house as well as the subsequent eating scene in which his disciples pick grains on a Sabbath (6:1-5) troubles the religious leaders, who begin to plot against him (6:11). While at these meal scenes Luke does not record the verbal response of the religious leaders, Jesus now voices what their reactions would have been then: he is nothing but a glutton (φάγος) and a drunkard (οἰνοπότης, cf. Deut 21:18-21; Prov 23:20-21).[122] "The accusation against Jesus is that in his eating and drinking (and in his selection of table companions) he is not acting like a wise person, but like a fool."[123] For the religious leaders, his eating habits are proof of his licentious lifestyle and of his false pretenses as an agent of God.

However, the religious leaders' charges against Jesus distort the truth because, as the narrative has shown, Jesus is not only a temperate but a compassionate man. Although his eating habits are different from John's, Jesus knows how to moderate them—even more than the Baptist—when the moment calls for it (4:2-4). From the point of view of Luke, the charges of gluttony and drunkenness contradict the lifestyle of Jesus, who not only never engages in such conduct but reproves it in his teachings (12:45; 21:34). If Jesus partakes in numerous meals, it is not to indulge himself but to share with the people his joyous message of salvation.[124] In their lack of wisdom, the religious leaders have missed the deeper significance of Jesus' table sharing:

---

121. Fasting was prescribed for the expiation of sins, for penitence, and for mourning; see Fitzmyer, *Luke*, 1:596.

122. Both φάγος and οἰνοπότης appear only here and in Matt 11:19 in the NT. In normal Palestinian meals, wine, mixed with three parts water, was the main drink; see Broshi, *Bread*, 121-43, 144-72. As possible background for the pair of words (φάγος and οἰνοπότης) Deut 21:20 and Prov 23:20-21 have been cited (Dunn, *Jesus Remembered*, 599 n. 253). According to Kee ("Glutton and Drunkard," 391) Jesus recognizes in the accusation against him (i.e., φάγος καὶ οἰνοπότης) the reason for his future execution.

123. Karris, *Eating*, 27.

124. Jesus disapproves of drunkenness in 12:45; 21:34.

> ... [J]esus' meals with the toll collectors and sinners, too [like those in Judaism], are not only events on a social level, not only an expression of his unusual humanity and social generosity and his sympathy with those who were despised, but had an even deeper significance. They are an expression of the mission and message of Jesus (Mark 2.17), eschatological meals, anticipatory celebrations of the feast in the end time (Matt. 8.11 par.), in which the community of saints is already being represented. The inclusion of sinners in the community of salvation, achieved in table-fellowship, is the most meaningful expression of the message of the redeeming love of God.[125]

Jesus' meals with toll collectors and sinners are a sign of the "inclusive meal fellowship of God's great final feast."[126] Ironically, while the religious leaders accuse Jesus of having a questionable friendship (φίλος) with toll collectors and sinners, from the point of view of the narrator the Pharisees are the ones who have entered into a wrong relationship by becoming friends of money (φιλάργυροι, 16:14). Jesus' reiteration of the religious leaders' accusations in 7:34 sets the stage for his eventual teaching on how to celebrate a banquet from the perspective of the kingdom's values (14:12–14).

Wisdom Prevails (7:35)

As a corollary to the explanation of the parable of the children in the marketplace (7:33–34), a wisdom saying concludes the subunit (7:31–35) and brings to a climax the entire passage about John and Jesus (7:18–35). Several issues of translation and interpretation continue to be debated in this verse. Commentators have almost unanimously attributed this final aphorism to Jesus and interpret the reference to σοφία as an allusion to divine wisdom in light of the OT and other Jewish writings. This widespread consensus, however, has been recently challenged.[127] According

---

125. Jeremias, *Theology*, 115–16.
126. Heil, *Meal Scenes*, 37; see also Perrin, *Rediscovering*, 102–8.
127. Phillips, "Background of the Human Wisdom," 385–96. Whereas most scholars interpret the use of σοφία in this verse against the OT tradition of divine wisdom, Phillips argues that it ought to be understood in light of a Greco-Roman cultural background, particularly in light of the discussions of drunkenness and wine drinking in Philo and Seneca. Moreover, Phillips claims that the introductory καί in 7:35 should be read not as adversative but rather in its more common connective function (ibid., 395; see also Gathercole, "Justification of Wisdom," 482; for the adversative use of καί, see Carson, "Test Case," 142). According to Phillips, "The proverb can be understood as the

to Thomas E. Phillips, σοφία refers to human wisdom and should be interpreted against a Greco-Roman cultural background, and the final aphorism ought to be read as the conclusion to Jesus' summary of his opponent's charges. Phillips echoes the concern of other commentators for whom the sudden appearance of wisdom in this final verse of the passage creates suspicion about the origin of the tradition and difficulty regarding the exact meaning of the verse. However, although wisdom is not a pervasive theme in the Lukan Gospel, its affinity to the plan of God emphasizes the importance of that theme in this part of the narrative. When read within the broader scope of the narrative, its appearance at the conclusion of the pericope is neither jarring nor unprecedented.

Already in the infancy narratives, Luke alludes to wisdom as a distinctive trait of those whom God has chosen, i.e., John and Jesus. At the conclusion of John's birth story, Luke notes that John was growing in spirit (1:80), a notion closely associated with wisdom.[128] Twice Luke portrays Jesus as a child favored by God, who grew strong and full of wisdom (σοφία, 2:40, 52).[129] Through these stereotyped expressions, Luke articulates his conviction that God has sanctioned the lives of John and Jesus by endowing them with one of God's innermost qualities. In a context filled with allusions to the providential interventions of God in human history, these references to wisdom foreshadow the close association between God's plan and wisdom in 7:30–35. Hence, after illustrating the way in which the people of this generation have failed to discover the providential hand of God in the ministries of John and himself, Jesus emphasizes how the wisdom of God prevails over apparent setbacks. In 7:35, wisdom appears almost as coterminous with God's eternal plan.[130]

---

final portion of Jesus' summation of his detractors' words: '... you say, "Behold, a glutton and a drunkard, a friend of toll collectors and sinners and [human] wisdom is justified by all her children."' If one regards 7:35 as part of the allegations against Jesus, the tradition preserved in Matt 11:2–19 // Luke 7:18–35 would end with a total negative sense that lacks a proper resolution (Nolland, *Luke*, 346). Moreover, this interpretation not only disregards the symmetrical structure of the parable and its explanation in the form of antithetical parallelisms, it also goes against the virtual unanimous interpretation of the verse. The decisive issue is whether σοφία refers here to divine or human wisdom as Phillips claims. An analysis of how Luke understands the reference to wisdom here in relationship to God's plan will clarify this point.

128. Cf. Luke 2:40, 52; Acts 6:3, 10; 7:10; see also Brown, *Birth*, 469, esp. n. 74.

129. Regarding the use of stereotyped language, which reflects the Samuel story (1 Sam 2:21, 26) in this part of the infancy narratives, see Brown, *Birth*, 468–69.

130. As Meier (*Marginal Jew*, 2:152) notes: "In this context, then, 'wisdom' (*sophia*)

The concept is personified as a mother, who is recognized by those who belong to her and it is contrasted with the implied foolishness of the religious leaders.[131] Therefore, in virtue of its close association to the plan of God, the mention of wisdom in this passage supports and reiterates a dominant theme of the Lukan Gospel.

Jesus' reference to wisdom anticipates his criticism of the religious leaders for their lack of understanding in the rest of the Gospel. Thus, although they consider themselves wise (σοφοί), they are unable to recognize Jesus' greater wisdom (11:31). This shortsightedness of the religious leaders had been foreseen by God (11:49) and, in contrast to this, Jesus will give his disciples a wisdom that their adversaries will be unable to refute (21:15). This expectation is fulfilled in the Acts of the Apostles, where wisdom is not only a prerequisite for those who aspire to serve in the church (6:3), but, as in the stories of Joseph and Moses (7:10, 22), it manifests itself in the ministry of Stephen (6:10).

Jesus points out that wisdom has been justified (ἐδικαιώθη) by all her children (ἀπὸ πάντων τῶν τέκνων αὐτῆς).[132] His reference to the justification of wisdom echoes the previous claim that the people and toll collectors have declared the righteousness of God (7:29). As in that instance, justification is to be understood in terms of a vindication of wisdom that holds true to a correct relationship with God and the

---

probably refers to God's wise, well-ordered plan of salvation, which is now reaching its climax." See also Green, *Luke*, 304; Nolland, *Luke*, 347.

131. According to the OT and other Jewish wisdom traditions (Job 28; Prov 1:20–33; 8:1—9:6; Sir 1:24; Bar 3; 4; *1 En.* 42; *4 Ezra* 5:10; *2 Apoc. Bar.* 48; Wis 7:22—11:1; 11QPsa 18), which personify wisdom as a heavenly being eager to reveal God's knowledge and deliver his message to humans, John and Jesus are portrayed as messengers of wisdom (Fohrer and Wilckens, "σοφία," esp. 516; Marshall, *Luke*, 303; Nolland, *Luke*, 346; for a longer list of proponents of this interpretation, see Phillips, "Background of the Human Wisdom," 386 n. 6). Here, however, the emphasis is not so much on a personal being as on a personified attribute of God (Bovon, *Luke*, 1:287; Schüssler Fiorenza, *Sophia's Prophet*, 139–43; however, cf. Scott, *Sophia*, 75–77).

132. Ἐδικαιώθη has here a timeless or gnomic force (cf. BDF § 333). The preposition ἀπό has been translated in a variety of ways: "from" (Plummer, *St. Luke*, 209); "apart from" ("fern von"; Dibelius, *Überlieferung*, 19 n. 2); "in view of" (Jeremias, *Parables*, 162 n. 43); "by" (Marshall, *Luke*, 303; Fitzmyer, *Luke*, 1:681; Green, *Luke*, 294). The preferred sense of the preposition, which defines the precise meaning of ἐδικαιώθη, is the last. It should also be noted that the grammatical range of ἀπό as well as the redactional preferences of Matthew (ἔργων, 11:19) and Luke (τέκνων, 7:35) are two of the reasons why some scholars reject as unnecessary Jeremias's (*Parables*, 160–62) suggestion of an original Aramaic source behind the parable; see Meier, *Marginal Jew*, 2:214 n. 169; Fitzmyer, *Luke*, 1:681.

Law. Those who have heeded the call of the Baptist and Jesus have declared that God is in the right. Their actions bear testimony that, despite the rejection of the religious leaders, the events of human history will unfold according to God's plan.

Those who have justified wisdom have been all her children (πάντων τῶν τέκνων αὐτῆς). Whereas the people of this generation have behaved like stubborn children (παιδία) in the marketplace, the children (τέκνα) of wisdom have shown their prudence.[133] Like all the people (πᾶς ὁ λαός) who received the baptism of John (7:29), all the children (πάντων τῶν τέκνων) of wisdom are those who have accepted God's offers of salvation through the ministries of John and Jesus.[134] As witnesses to God's envoys, these little ones, like the least one (μικρότερος) in the kingdom of God (7:28),[135] have sided with those that God has chosen and have given credit to his wisdom. In the rest of the Gospel, the response of wisdom's children foreshadows Jesus' praise to God for revealing his true wisdom to those who are like children (νήπιοι, 10:21).

Summary

In the final subunit of the pericope (7:31–35), Jesus compares the people of this generation to children sitting in the marketplace. After the religious leaders have been singled out as those who rejected the message of the Baptist, the pejorative connotation of "the people of this generation" has in view all those who oppose Jesus throughout the narrative, especially the Pharisees and the scholars of the Law.

To illustrate the way in which they have treated John and himself, Jesus appeals to a familiar scene in which children sitting in a marketplace refuse to play. Jesus' characterization of the behavior of "the people

---

133. The "children of" image reflects a Hebraic formulation that describes the quality of a person and the sphere to which that person belongs; Prov 8:32; Sir 4:11; Luke 16:8; John 12:36; 1 Thess 5:5; Eph 5:8. Although some see no link between the "children" of v. 32 and those of v. 35 (e.g., Nolland, *Luke*, 347), the link between both terms is not by "catchword bonding, but by sense" as Fitzmyer (*Luke*, 1:681) correctly notes; see also Meier, *Marginal Jew*, 2:153 n. 170.

134. As Mussner ("Kairos," 611) notes, "Dadurch [the acceptance of John's Baptism] erwiesen sich die Zöllner und Sünder als „Kinder der Weisheit", durch die sie gerechtfertigt wurde."

135. As noted earlier, Jesus always uses μικρότερος with the article as a generic category that epitomizes those of a lower rank or those who have adopted the values of the kingdom (9:48; 12:32; 17:2; cf. ὁ νεώτερος, 22:26).

of this generation" recalls previous references in the narrative in which the Jewish people have been portrayed as rebellious or conceited children in need of correction. The parable reformulates these images and depicts the people of this generation as petulant children who refuse to join in games that represent God's various offers of salvation. The invitations to mourn and to dance are meant to recall John's call for a radical and urgent change of lifestyle and Jesus' enthusiastic preaching and healing ministry. However, like peevish children who can only raise questions and objections, the people of this generation have refused to heed the call to repent and celebrate, thus rejecting the different offers of salvation.

To illuminate the parable, Jesus sums up the accusations of the religious leaders against his ministry and John's. After he depicts John as one who neither "ate food nor drank wine," Jesus denounces with an ironic twist the religious leaders' lack of judgment for claiming that John was a possessed man. While they considered John a lunatic, the religious leaders criticize Jesus for being a glutton and a drunkard and a friend of toll collectors and sinners. For them, Jesus' eating and socializing habits are a proof of his licentious lifestyle and of his false pretenses as an agent of God. However, the religious leaders' charges against John and Jesus are but a distortion of the truth that runs counter to the evidence of the narrative. From the point of view of the narrator, John is God's envoy who, in the spirit of Elijah, has been chosen to prepare the way for the Lord (Jesus). His message has been sanctioned by the people and he is indeed more than a prophet, the greatest of all born of women. Meanwhile, Jesus has been shown to be not only a temperate and compassionate man, but also the son in whom God delights. In their lack of wisdom, the religious leaders have missed the deeper implications of the ministries of John and Jesus.

Jesus concludes with a saying that emphasizes that the wisdom of God prevails despite the rejection of the people of this generation. Wisdom is personified as a mother who is vindicated by those who belong to her, and it is contrasted with the implied foolishness of the religious leaders. She is justified by all her children, i.e., all those who have heeded the call of the Baptist and Jesus. Like the people and toll collectors, the children of wisdom have shown that God is in the right and that, despite the apparent setbacks, the inexorable realization of God's plan will come to fruition amid the travails of human history. As witnesses to John and Jesus, these little ones emphasize what the unfolding narrative will later affirm: that God has revealed true wisdom to those who are like children.

What began with an inquiry for "the one who is to come" by one of the most important characters in the story has ended in the chastisement of those who, unlike John, have not wondered but condemned. As the narrative moves into the next scene (7:36–50), the religious leaders will be seen manifesting the same attitude that the author has already censured. In the wake of John's passing role it is now time to gather the fruits of this investigation and outline just how the question of John and Jesus' indictment of the religious leaders (7:18–35) have contributed to the portrayal of the Baptist, to the depiction of the relationship between him and Jesus, and to the understanding of the narrative in general.

5

Conclusion

A Narrative-Critical Interpretation of Luke 7:18–35

INTRODUCTION

To conclude this investigation, I will summarize the most important findings and contributions of my exegetical analysis and provide a final synthesis of the passage's interpretation from a narrative-critical perspective. I will also explain the relevance of this investigation for some issues related to the role of John the Baptist in Luke-Acts and the other Gospels.

METHODOLOGICAL CONTRIBUTION: A NARRATIVE-CRITICAL FOCUS

Although Luke 7:18–35 (// Matt 11:2–19) is one of the most important passages in the Synoptic tradition, until now no single study has been devoted exclusively to a full analysis of this pericope. Of course, many contemporary works refer to the passage, since hardly any thorough exegetical inquiry dealing with the Synoptics can afford to disregard this important piece of tradition.

As we saw in chapter 1, historically oriented investigations, commentaries, specialized works on John the Baptist, and articles have referred to and interpreted the passage or portions of it.[1] From the Patristic period until now this passage has been a favorite of commentators, who have since applied different hermeneutical methods to the interpretation of the pericope. Commentators quickly became interested in the

---

1. See ch. 1, 2–41.

passage—and have been ever since—because of the apparent contradiction between some of its statements and other streams of tradition (e.g., Matt 3:14–15; John 1:36; 3:27–30). Since then, and throughout the long history of biblical interpretation, concerns about Luke 7:18–35 (// Matt 11:2–19) have shifted from moral and pastoral interests to more in-depth inquiries into the puzzling question of the Baptist, the history of the passage's transmission, and its historical reliability. In modern times, studies on the passage have focused predominantly on questions about the origin and the historical veracity of the tradition. Discussions about its *Sitz im Leben*, which many claim echo the controversies between John's followers and the early Christian community, have tended to dominate the contemporary interpretation of this tradition. Finally, interest in issues related to the Synoptic problem has led scholars to rely on exegetical reconstructions of the passage and the form it may have had originally in the hypothetical source known as Q.

All of these ways of interpreting Luke 7:18–35 (// Matt 11:2–19) have contributed to our understanding of the passage. They have also shed light on its origin and how it may have developed. However, although these different approaches have increased our understanding of this tradition, they have overlooked important aspects of the pericope's interpretation and imposed certain limitations on the way we look at it. Emphases on the reconstruction of an original Q form and the composite nature of the pericope have overshadowed the literary dimensions of how Matthew and Luke used this tradition in the composition of their Gospels. Furthermore, the extent to which the differences between the Matthean and the Lukan forms contribute to our understanding of how each evangelist interpreted and incorporated it into his overall literary work has been neglected.

Only recently have some studies shifted the focus of the research to consider the literary aspects of the passage. Issues such as character, setting, rhetorical function, and narrative plot have become the subjects of serious exegetical investigation. The relatively few analyses of Luke that have undertaken such interpretations have done so with an emphasis on the characterization of John the Baptist and other persons in the passage. None, however, has undertaken a thorough narrative-critical examination of the pericope within the context of Luke-Acts.

It is in light of this narrative-critical trend that the present work makes one of its principal contributions to the interpretation of the passage. This study interprets the passage as an essential element of the narrative and within its literary context. In this sense, it differs from other studies that interpret the passage based on a hypothetical reconstruction of Q and pay more attention to its individual parts than to the entire pericope. My study emphasizes literary features present in the passage such as characterization, setting, and plot to explain how they function within the Lukan narrative. This interpretation has shown how different elements of this tradition are foreshadowed in earlier parts of the story, how the rest of Luke-Acts reflects some of them, and how the passage contributes to and supports the entire narrative. In sum, without ignoring the contributions of other exegetical methods (such as historical, form, and redaction criticism) I have highlighted the literary features of the passage and explained how different elements of its composition contribute to the overall development of the story.

Before summarizing the ways in which the specifics of this narrative-critical analysis contribute to our understanding of this passage in Luke-Acts, I will outline the most significant findings of the comparative analysis of Matt 11:2–19 and Luke 7:18–35 and explain how this analysis sheds light on the origin, redaction, and literary function of the passage.

CONTRIBUTIONS TO THE DISCUSSION ABOUT THE ORIGIN AND TRANSMISSION OF LUKE 7:18–35

Exegetical methods whose approaches aim at ascertaining the source and original form of the tradition in Matt 11:2–19 // Luke 7:18–35 have generally agreed on the fragmented character of the material. As many scholars point out, the tradition may have arisen from separate sayings about John the Baptist that were later gathered into a single source in order to preserve them.[2] Accordingly, Matt 11:2–6 // Luke 7:18–23, Matt 11:7–11 // Luke 7:24–28, and Matt 11:16–19 // Luke 7:31–35 may have had their origin as separate traditions. Moreover, some claim that individual portions of the passage (e.g., Matt 11:6 // Luke 7:23, Matt 11:19c // Luke 7:35) may have originated as individual sayings that were later developed into stories about John and Jesus.[3]

---

2. Dibelius, *Überlieferung*, 6–22.
3. Bultmann, *History*, 21.

A Narrative-Critical Interpretation of Luke 7:18–35

Nothing in the comparative analysis of Matt 11:2–19 and Luke 7:18–35 contradicts this widespread consensus about the fragmented origin of the tradition. Indeed, the analysis of the pericope shows the existence of four different literary subunits (Matt 11:2–6 // Luke 7:18–23; Matt 11:7–11 // Luke 7:24–28; Matt 11:12–15 ≠ Luke 7:29–30; Matt 11:16–19 // Luke 7:31–35) delimited by various grammatical and thematic shifts. Within the Lukan Gospel, the diverse literary features of the four subunits and their narrative function tend to confirm the claims about the tradition's composite character.

As a result of the comparative analysis, it is pertinent to make certain observations regarding the origin and form of this tradition:

(1) Some commentators have insisted on the absolute heterogeneous origin of the material in Luke 7:18–23 (// Matt 11:2–6) and 7:24–28 (// Matt 11:7–11). While it is possible that the content of these verses may have had different origins, nothing in the structure of Matt 11:2–11 and Luke 7:18–28 precludes this material from having been originally conceived as a single unit. In terms of character, setting, plot, and overall theme, the passage shows considerable literary cohesion. Moreover, when one takes into account the enthymematic structure of the argumentation leading to Matt 11:6 // Luke 7:23, which does not necessitate a formal response (the lack of which has often been adduced as evidence of a break in the literary structure of the tradition), the possibility of the essential unity of both episodes (Matt 11:2–6 and 7–15 // Luke 7:18–23 and 24–28) increases. The fact that Luke 7:18–23 (// Matt 11:2–6) and 7:24–28 (// Matt 11:7–15) can be isolated and analyzed as self-contained subunits does not necessarily imply that they come from separate traditions. Whether or not the apparent unity of the material ought to be attributed to the literary skill of the original editor of the source or to historical circumstances is hard to decide, but from a narrative perspective it is not impossible that the material was received as a single tradition from the beginning.

(2) Something similar may be said regarding the claims about the original independence of the sayings in Luke 7:22–23 (// Matt 11:5–6) and 7:35 (// Matt 11:19c). These sayings could have existed as isolated statements of Jesus that were subsequently given a narrative framework. Nothing in the literary structure of these verses, however, excludes the possibility that they may have existed from the beginning in their present settings.

The literary correspondence of both statements with the previous narrative material suggests the integrity of their context. Unless one considers it impossible for the sayings of Jesus to have been preserved within the context of a story, the possibility that 7:22–23 and 7:35 have remained within their original settings should be kept open. Once again, it is virtually impossible to decide whether the present contexts of these sayings ought to be attributed to the creative genius of the original editor or to historical development.

(3) The composite origin of the material is more readily apparent after Jesus' encomium of John the Baptist (Matt 11:12–19 // Luke 7:29–35). This is especially obvious from the differences between Matt 11:12–15 and Luke 7:29–30. Moreover, the thematic change between this material and the subunits that follow (Matt 11:16–19 // Luke 7:31–35) evidences the composite nature of this part of the pericope. The parable of the children in the marketplace introduces a number of elements that, except for its characters (i.e., John and Jesus), has only a tangential connection with the previous material.

(4) With regard to the differences between Matt 11:12–15 and Luke 7:29–30, some final remarks are in order. First, of all the variables that would account for the differences between Matthew and Luke in this particular section of the passage, the possibility that both evangelists would have interrupted the sequence of a common tradition at exactly the same location to insert entirely extraneous material seems the least probable of the possibilities. This suggests that either Matthew or Luke has preserved the authentic form of the source. Second, my analysis indicates that it is Matthew who has preserved the more original sequence of the tradition. In comparison to Luke, whose narrative commentary (7:29–30) provides a smoother transitional summary into 7:31–35, the contextual dissonance of Matthew's material (11:12–15) appears to support the presumption that this tradition originated as a collection of sayings about John the Baptist. Third, this means that Matthew has kept the original context of the so-called *Stürmmerspruch* (Matt 11:12–13 // Luke 16:16), although not necessarily the correct wording. Luke has probably moved the saying to its present location (*connexio difficilior*) as a result of compositional choices that favored christological and literary goals over contextual integrity. Fourth, the contextual and grammatical analysis of 7:29–30 indicates that these verses ought to be attributed

to Luke and that they are essential for understanding the way in which he views and shapes this tradition about John and Jesus. These verses are crucial for appreciating how Luke incorporates this tradition into a section where the main literary concern is to outline the identity of Jesus and the diverse set of responses that his ministry evokes. As part of a dynamic movement that begins with the infancy narratives and continues through the Galilean ministry section and beyond, the response to God's initiative of salvation in the ministries of John and Jesus finds its first and more explicit formulation in 7:29–30. Through these verses, Luke reveals his theological perspective about how the plan of God may suffer apparent setbacks and still triumph.

Many specifics about the origin and/or authenticity of these verses must remain speculative and tentative since exegesis has not yet attained absolute certainty on some of these issues. However, with regard to 7:29–30, the analysis of its vocabulary, literary style, and theological affinity with other material not found in the sources commonly attributed to Luke (i.e., Mark and Q) provide further evidence to support the claim that these verses come from Luke's editorial hand. In this sense they are essential to assess how Luke has adapted this tradition about John and Jesus to fit his compositional goal and to understand how 7:18–35 should be interpreted in the Gospel of Luke.

THE QUESTION OF JOHN THE BAPTIST AND JESUS' INDICTMENT OF THE RELIGIOUS LEADERS (7:18–35): A NARRATIVE-CRITICAL INTERPRETATION

As an essential literary component of the story about Jesus in the Gospel of Luke, the tradition about the question of John the Baptist and Jesus' indictment of the religious leaders finds its most thorough interpretation in its context. This is important for the meaning of the tradition about John and Jesus in this Gospel because, as one scholar has noted, *where* something is said has as much relevance as *what* is said.[4] Therefore, the strategic location of this passage is significant for understanding what Luke intended to communicate by skillfully incorporating this tradition into his overall literary structure.

The passage about John and Jesus appears in the section dealing with Jesus' Galilean ministry (4:14—9:50). Within this section, Luke

---

4. Johnson, *Luke*, 124.

alternates Jesus' words and deeds with accounts about favorable and unfavorable responses of different characters in the story to his ministry.[5] The location of the pericope within this context is not a random act of creative writing but the result of a well-designed literary arrangement that is evident from the beginning of the Gospel. As a result of this compositional process, the pericope is integrated into a literary pattern within a section whose main goal is to clarify who Jesus is. In Luke, the pericope performs a number of important functions. First, it recapitulates the previous plot of the story by summarizing the ministry of Jesus thus far (7:22). Second, it keeps the section's thematic focus on the identity of Jesus (7:18–23) and on the way people react to his ministry (7:24–30). Third, it advances the emerging conflict motif by outlining for the first time in the story the negative reaction of the religious leaders to the ministries of John and Jesus (7:29–35).

The passage also serves as a transitional episode that highlights and qualifies the role of John for the ensuing narrative (9:7; 11:1; 16:16; 20:1–8) without distracting from the section's overriding christological concern. In addition, it supports the overall narrative by reiterating important themes in the Lukan Gospel, such as the plan of God, table fellowship, concern for the poor, the danger of riches, and the importance of hearing the word of God. Finally, the passage foreshadows the relevance of the Baptist for the growing Christian community in the Acts of the Apostles (1:5, 21–22; 10:37; 11:16; 13:24–25; 18:25; 19:4–5).

This systematic organization and location of the pericope betrays the skills of an accomplished writer who, at the beginning of his work, announced his intention to provide an orderly account of the "things fulfilled among us" (1:4).[6] Therefore, to understand the full meaning of the question of John the Baptist and Jesus' indictment of the religious leaders (7:18–35) in the Gospel of Luke it is necessary to interpret the passage as an essential part of this complex literary pattern.

Part of this literary trajectory is John's question (7:18–23) about the identity of Jesus. By the time John reappears in the story, the narrator has made sure that his readers are well acquainted with John's role and importance. They know that he was conceived under extraordinary circumstances, that his birth is the work of God, and that he has been chosen in the spirit of Elijah to precede the coming of the Lord. The au-

---

5. See ch. 2, 67–75.
6. See ch. 2, 77–79.

dience has heard the account of John's unrelenting message marked with threats and ethical exhortations about the importance of treating the neighbor with compassion—a message that Luke characterizes as good news (εὐηγγελίζετο, 3:18). The audience has also heard of the cruelty of Herod and of the ominous fate that has befallen John (3:20). But it has not yet heard of the initial encounter of John and Jesus.[7] Consequently, as the expectation about the identity of Jesus heightens, the Baptist appears on the scene to ask the question about "the one who is to come."

Although anonymous people (4:22, 36) and religious leaders (5:21, 30; 6:2) raise questions about Jesus' identity, the Baptist is the first character identified by name to ask about Jesus' identity. The question occurs because John's disciples arrive to tell him all the things that Jesus has been doing (περὶ πάντων τούτων, 7:18), a phrase that is meant to summarize not only the events previously reported (i.e., 7:1–10, 11–17) but the whole of Jesus' public ministry. The question of the Baptist is embedded in the previous narratives' expectation for a coming prophetic figure. As part of this plot, John's question expresses his uncertainty about whether Jesus is "the one who is to come." The Baptist's question emphasizes the situation in which many other characters in the story find themselves in this section of the Gospel: puzzled by Jesus' identity. This question seems motivated more by John's lack of knowledge about Jesus than by his perplexity about Jesus' ministerial activities.[8]

Unlike Matthew's Gospel, where the Baptist's question could be interpreted as being motivated by his disenchantment with Jesus' compassionate ministry, in the Gospel of Luke John's question calls for a more nuanced interpretation. In Luke's Gospel, John's question is neither a revision of his previous identification of Jesus as the Messiah nor a doubt provoked by an absolute contrast between an expected fiery reformer and Jesus' compassionate ministry. John's inquiry is the question of someone who, according to Luke's account, has not yet met Jesus. It is the question of someone who, because of his imprisonment, has been isolated from Jesus' ministry. Hence, the question of John is an initial attempt, motivated by the report of John's disciples and John's lack of personal knowledge of Jesus, to ascertain whether Jesus is "the one who is to come." Within the Lukan narrative, then, the question confirms that John had not yet recognized who Jesus was.

7. John and Jesus do not meet during the Baptism (3:1–22).
8. See ch. 3, 93–101.

Jesus responds to the question of the Baptist by performing a number of mighty works. The Lukan version of Jesus' response reveals Luke's literary sensibility. Instead of just *saying* who he is, Jesus replies by *doing* (cf. ποιήσατε, 3:8) deeds that reveal his identity in the presence of John's emissaries (7:21–22). Luke's report of Jesus' healings strengthens the persuasive force of his verbal reply, improves the literary logic and style of the passage, adds christological focus to the scene, and recalls Jesus' programmatic speech in the synagogue of Nazareth (4:16–30).

Jesus' answer is oblique but precise. Unlike Matthew's Gospel, in which the Baptist's eschatological expectations focused more narrowly on the fiery judgment of "the one who is to come," Luke's redactional and stylistic modifications in the parallel material (Matt 3:1–17 // Luke 3:1–18) yield a more nuanced characterization of John's expectations. For Luke, John's expectations concerning "the coming one" are associated with judgment and good works on behalf of one's neighbor.[9] Therefore, the deeds and words reported in 7:21–22 are a confirmation of John's hopes. By answering in this way, Jesus expects the Baptist to recognize him as the envoy of God who is to be associated with an age of salvation and concern for the needy.[10] Jesus' response to the messengers of

---

9. This is clear from Luke's special material in 3:10–14. Some commentators dismiss the verses as the work of Lukan redaction. While I consider this assessment accurate, I think that on the whole this material, along with the rest of 3:1–18, summarizes Luke's understanding of what the message of John the Baptist was about: the coming judgment and an ethical dimension that emphasized concern for one's neighbor. In this sense, 3:10–14 should be viewed as the speeches in the Acts of the Apostles. While they do not accurately reflect the verbatim content of the discourses, they indicate that the early Christians preached a message that included the basic elements of the primitive kerygma. In this regard, Dunn's (*Acts*, xviii) observations are enlightening: "In all cases the style of the speeches is Lukan through and through; they are, properly speaking, Lukan compositions. At the same time, in most cases the individuality and distinctiveness of the material points to the conclusion that Luke has been able to draw on and incorporate tradition—not necessarily any specific record or recollection as such, but tradition related to and representative of the individual's views and well suited to the occasion." See also Dibelius, *Acts*, 49–86; Haenchen, *Acts*, 185–89. Therefore, 3:10–14 as well as other redactional additions of Luke (e.g., 3:6; εὐηγγελίζετο, 3:18), indicate that for him the Baptist's message contained not only elements of judgment but also elements of compassion and salvation. As Meier (*Marginal Jew*, 2:41) points out, "John would have been a most unusual spiritual guide within Judaism at the turn of the era if he had not delivered some teaching on morality and daily conduct."

10. In the Lukan narrative a misleading answer to the imprisoned John would have been uncharacteristic of Jesus, because whenever someone asks him directly about his identity he never leads people astray (9:20–21; 22:67–71; 23:3; Acts 9:5; 22:8; 26:15).

John reiterates his implicit prophetic claim in the previous narrative and serves as an indirect response to which John is able to relate.

The scene that centers on John's question ends with a final saying in which Jesus declares the one who is not scandalized by him to be blessed.[11] Jesus' statement is both a blessing and a warning to all the people (ὃς ἐάν), but especially to those who have overheard the exchange between him and John's disciples. The beatitude captures the predicament posed by the previous plot. There is a choice to be made for or against Jesus. Those who accept him are blessed, whereas those who reject him will be excluded from the kingdom. The decisive issue is whether the scandal will lead the characters to accept or reject Jesus.

The story does not mention how John reacts to the beatitude and many commentators have used this silence to impugn the historical reliability of the account or to suggest that the Baptist did not accept Jesus as "the coming one." The manner in which one interprets the "unreported reaction" of the Baptist—or what one may call "the great gap" of John—determines how one understands the role of the Baptist and his characterization in Luke-Acts. I have argued that the absence of John's formal response should be understood within the parameters of an enthymematic argumentation. This literary device, which is part of the rhetorical strategy of the subunit aimed at persuading the audience that Jesus is God's eschatological agent, forms a natural gap in the narrative that does not necessitate a response. Since, in the ongoing narrative, Jesus has been portrayed as performing the actions that are to be associated with a prophetic figure, the implicit conclusion of the enthymeme is that he is indeed "the one who is to come." The final beatitude balances the uncertainty of John, reinforces the narrative's implicit intimation of a lack of mutual knowledge between John and Jesus, and expresses Jesus' hope that the people (John included) will recognize him as the promised agent of God.

The gap created by the absence of a response from John should be interpreted as an implicit acceptance of Jesus. From a narrative perspective, it is more likely that Luke would have understood the reaction of John—someone chosen by God to carry out a divine mission, and praised as the greatest of those born of woman—positively rather than negatively. A negative interpretation would entail a departure from the author's positive point of view of John's role within the plan of God, a

---

11. See ch. 3, 116–10.

deviation not envisioned by the narrative. Therefore, the gap created by the enthymematic form of the saying implies that John was satisfied with Jesus' answer. As far as the narrative is concerned, John's expectations have been fulfilled.

In the second subunit of the passage (7:24–28), Jesus addresses a crowd with a monologue that recapitulates the characterization of John in the previous narrative.[12] Luke conceives this scene as part of an ongoing episode in which, after John's disciples have departed, Jesus interrogates the crowd and speaks about the virtues of the Baptist.

From the words of Jesus there emerges a portrayal of John that is consonant with the preceding narrative, especially with the infancy narratives. Jesus' successive rhetorical questions depict the Baptist as a man of moral integrity, someone who does not waver in the face of difficulties. John is a man of solid character, a person who remains firm and unshaken in the midst of trials. He is an austere man, whose sober and ascetic lifestyle puts to shame those who live surrounded by luxuries and extravagance. Above all, John is a prophet and more than a prophet. He is confirmed as the one who the angel said would come in the spirit of Elijah, the "prophet of the Most High," the forerunner of the Lord. Because of his privileged role in God's plan of salvation, John has been associated in a special way with the coming of the Lord and the dawn of a new eschatological era. For this reason he is more than a prophet and the precursor of Jesus and the kingdom of God. Jesus' high esteem of John denotes his personal admiration for the Baptist and echoes the people's high regard for him.

However, for Jesus the proclamation of a new era takes precedence and, as his praise of John reaches a climax, Jesus reminds his listeners about the preeminence of the kingdom. Although John is the greatest born of woman, the least in the kingdom of God is greater than he. Jesus does not denigrate the stature of John. Rather he uses his importance to bring into focus a higher order. Jesus uses the opportunity to teach that if John is great it is because he has been associated in a unique way with the dawn of the kingdom. Since the kingdom is present in the things that Jesus says and does (7:21–22; cf. 17:21) those who see and hear him are greater than John, who in prison has been temporarily deprived from this present stage of the kingdom.[13]

---

12. See ch. 4, 112–22.

13. The present stage of the kingdom has appeared with Jesus (Fitzmyer, *Luke X–XXIV*, 1157–62).

Luke takes advantage of Jesus' reference to the "kingdom of God," and in the next subunit (7:29–30) summarizes, for the first time in the narrative, how the ministry of John, which enabled the coming of this new era, has been received by different character groups.[14] Whereas the people and toll collectors accepted the baptism of John, the Pharisees and the scholars of the Law rejected it, thereby opposing the plan of God. By virtue of the careful literary parallel that he has forged between John and Jesus, Luke implies that the religious leaders have responded to John in much the same way that they responded to Jesus. Luke's assertion that the religious leaders have rejected the baptism of John exposes their shortsightedness and lack of wisdom. They have failed to recognize the significance of the Baptist, and in doing so they have missed his role in God's plan of salvation.

Luke's narrative commentary in this part of the passage is critical for several reasons. First, 7:29–30 shows how Luke has accommodated this tradition about John and Jesus to suit his theological perspective regarding the "plan of God." This reference to the "plan of God" is Luke's first explicit allusion to a theme that permeates his two-volume work. These verses are crucial for understanding how Luke has adapted this passage, particularly his incorporation of the Baptist into his overall literary work. Wink's conclusion regarding Luke's special contribution to the characterization of John is corroborated by 7:29–30; "Luke's originality lies not so much in his alteration of the traditional picture as in the way in which he has adapted John into his scheme of redemptive history."[15]

Second, the way in which Luke weaves this narrative commentary into the fabric of the pericope is a prime example of his literary skills. Here Luke is at his best, forging the thrust of the tradition in a decisive yet unobtrusive way. The different ways in which scholars (e.g., Fitzmyer and Nolland) attribute these verses to the preceding material or to what follows bear tribute to the ingenuity with which Luke has been able to synchronize his own point of view with that of Jesus within the narrative framework.

Third, as a transitional narrative commentary, 7:29–30 serves a number of literary functions. First, the verses summarize the plot of the previous story and supply a narrative pause from which the responses of

---

14. See ch. 4, 125–51.

15. Wink, *John the Baptist*, 57; see also Keefer, *New Testament as Literature*, 41; Tannehill, *Luke*, 1. 2.

the different characters to the ministries of John and Jesus can be evaluated. Second, the verses serve as an important thematic summary to the role of the Baptist. From this moment on, the role of the Baptist begins to fade, and his importance becomes subsidiary to the more christological focus of the narrative. Third, Luke's remarks about the religious leaders' failure to respond to the ministry of John serve as a prologue to the parable of the children in the marketplace and shape its interpretation into an indictment not only of "the people of this generation" but of the religious leaders as well.

In the final subunit of the pericope (7:31–35), Jesus compares the people of this generation to children sitting in the marketplace.[16] In this parable, the invitation of one group of children to mourn and to dance recalls John's call for a change of lifestyle and Jesus' enthusiastic preaching and healing ministry, whereas the unresponsiveness of the other group of children recalls the shortsightedness of "the people of this generation" (i.e., the religious leaders). After Luke's narrative commentary in 7:29–30, the parable ridicules the behavior of the religious leaders for their unwillingness to accept the different offers of salvation. They have shown themselves to be like annoying children who ask endless questions for the sole purpose of objecting and refusing to do what is required of them.

Jesus criticizes the religious leaders for having derided the lifestyle of John just as they have shunned his. By levying false accusations against John and Jesus, the religious leaders have demonstrated their petty behavior and lack of knowledge. Their charges against John and Jesus are baseless because the preceding narrative has shown that not only John and Jesus have been divinely chosen, but their behavior has been exemplary. Jesus' remarks denote his frustration with how the religious authorities have failed to respond to God's offer of salvation. His ironic rebuttal of the false accusations accentuate one more time the narrative's parallel portrayal of John and Jesus and John's character as a man whose lifestyle bears the marks of a true prophet.

The last verse of the passage (7:35) reiterates that the religious leaders, in their lack of wisdom, have missed the deeper meaning of the ministries of John and Jesus. The allusion to wisdom stands in parallel to Luke's previous reference to the plan of God. In both references the idea reverberates that God's purpose underlies the destiny of human

---

16. See ch. 4, 151–65.

affairs. Just as the rejection of the religious leaders frustrated the plan of God in their lives, those who have accepted the messages of John and Jesus have shown themselves to be wisdom's children. Jesus' final saying emphasizes the vindication of the plan of God despite the foolishness of the religious leaders. This concluding remark reassures us that regardless of the apparent failures of God's plan, its inexorable force will prevail amid the travails of human history. As witnesses to John and Jesus, the children of wisdom, as the "least" in the kingdom of God, reinforce the narrative's claim that God has revealed his wisdom to those who are like them (10:21).

ISSUES RELATED TO JOHN THE BAPTIST IN LUKE-ACTS AND THE OTHER GOSPELS: THE CONTRIBUTION OF 7:18–35

As an important testimony dealing with the Baptist, Luke 7:18–35 (// Matt 11:2–19) is often cited to support different claims about John's role in the Gospel of Luke and in the rest of the gospel traditions. In light of the previous investigation, I will address how the interpretation of this passage contributes to the ongoing discussion on some of these issues. My aim is not to engage in a thorough examination of these topics, each one of which deserves an extensive investigation. Rather, my purpose is to outline the issues and to point out what light my analysis of 7:18–35 sheds on the discussion of these topics.

Luke's Alleged Anti-Baptist Apologetic Motif

Scholars have claimed that some passages in Luke-Acts reveal an anti-Baptist apologetic on the part of Luke.[17] According to them, many redactional alterations betray Luke's apologetic interest just as different literary forms conceal the polemical influences in the life of the community (*Sitz im Leben*) under which some of the traditions would have developed. Within Luke-Acts, signs of this apologetic agenda are supposedly found in following places: (1) Luke's deletion of the phrase ὀπίσω μου (Mark 1:7; Luke 3:6); (2) John's denial that he is the Messiah (Luke 3:15–16; Acts 13:24–25); (3) Luke's reference to the insufficiency of John's baptism (Acts 18:24—19:7); and (4) Luke's omission of the

---

17. For a convenient summary of the issue, see Wink, *John the Baptist*, 23–26; 82–86; see also Brown, *John*, 153–57.

following material: (a) Jesus' baptism *by* John (Mark 1:9; Luke 3:21); (b) the report of John's death (Mark 6:17–29; Luke 9:9); (c) Jesus' intimation of John's role as Elijah *redivivus* (Mark 9:9–13); and (d) the two references to Elijah during the crucifixion (Mark 15:35, 36), which come after Jesus' implicit identification of John with Elijah.[18]

Signs of this polemical concern are supposedly found in the question of John (7:18–23), whereby he is said to be made a witness to Christ by the early church, and in Jesus' remark about John's subordination to the least in the kingdom of heaven (7:28b). In a similar vein, 7:23 is interpreted as an implicit judgment of John for having been "scandalized" by Jesus. Finally, it is claimed that while an original logion of Jesus survives in 7:28a, 7:28b is a later addition of the church to deal with the embarrassment that Jesus appears to be subordinated to John.

In light of the present study some observations regarding the apologetic interpretation of 7:18–23 are in order. First, the final beatitude is not directed at John but at the people in general. Therefore, it should not be interpreted as a condemnation of the Baptist. Second, since the absence of John's reaction to Jesus' reply is an implicit assent to his identity, Bultmann is justified in viewing the Baptist as a witness to Christ.[19] However, from a narrative perspective, this testimony of John is part of a literary pattern whereby Luke alternates favorable and unfavorable responses to the ministry of Jesus. Therefore, it would appear that literary considerations were at work when Luke decided to incorporate this passage about John and Jesus in this part of the Gospel. Luke's use of 7:18–35 has not been determined by a polemical concern but by a desire to boost the section's overriding focus on the identity of Jesus and the different reactions that his ministry elicited.

With regard to the apologetic intent of 7:28b, it should be noted that from a structural standpoint 7:28b is part of an antithetical parallelism that balances the scriptural citation in 7:27. This delicate balance is not the result of a fortuitous editorial addition by which a secondary redactor subsequently attempted to supply a restrictive remark. The literary form of the statement has the appearance of an already fixed

---

18. The apologetic interpretation of these passages is by no means unanimous. A discussion about the merits or lack thereof of each of them is outside the scope of this conclusion. These are listed to illustrate the evidence alluded to in the so-called anti-Baptist agenda in the Gospel of Luke.

19. Bultmann, *History*, 23; for a critique, see Kümmel, *Promise and Fulfillment*, 110.

composition.[20] If 7:28b is supposed to be an apologetic statement, it does not fully achieve its purpose because, in its present context, the verse does not curtail the importance of John. Joan Taylor's observations are relevant in this regard:

> The point does not really concern John at all, who remains "more than a prophet"; there is no one greater than him. The point is about the radical inversions of the kingdom of heaven, in which someone as insignificant as an innocent little baby may be considered "greater" than John (who is still part of the kingdom, and no doubt the greatest one in it); the innocent little baby is the paradigm of excellence. This is hyperbole, designed to confound (cf. *Acts of Philip* 34). It does not relativize John; it dramatically promotes the small, humble, and lowly.[21]

In the parable of the children in the marketplace (7:31–35), John and Jesus are placed on a par with each other without any indication of John's subordination. Both John and Jesus are portrayed as envoys of God whose messages have been rejected by the religious leaders but accepted by children of wisdom. The fact that Luke does not add any remark to minimize the role of the Baptist in this part of the passage indicates that he was not bothered by the portrayal of the ministries of John and Jesus on an equal basis.

A number of literary features in 7:18–35 suggest there that Luke's incorporation of this tradition has not been guided by a polemical intent. This is not to say that at an earlier stage in the composition of this tradition a previous redactor would not have been motivated by an apologetic concern. But in its present context 7:18–35 is part of a literary pattern that is consistent with the efforts of an accomplished writer who promised to provide a reliable account of events in 1:4. The use of this tradition, then, would have been motivated more by compositional (christological) considerations than by an anti-Baptist apologetic. Hence, Luke's use of this passage need not be interpreted as part of an apologetic motif but as part of his stated compositional goal.

---

20. Schulz, *Spruchquelle*, 233.
21. *John the Baptist*, 303–4; see also Wink, *John the Baptist*, 83–84.

John and the Kingdom of God

Another issue for which Luke 7:18–35 is often cited is the debate about whether John the Baptist is included or excluded from the kingdom of God. No other scholar has done more to spark this debate than Hans Conzelmann.[22] According to Conzelmann, the history of salvation is divided into three epochs: the period of Israel, the period of Jesus' ministry, and the period of the church. Within this structure, John belongs to the period of Israel and his ministry marks the dividing line between his period and the era associated with the kingdom. For Conzelmann, Luke's view of John's role in salvation history determines his exclusion from the period of kingdom. Conzelmann appeals to Luke's geographical motifs to support his claim, but it is in 16:16 that he finds the most important evidence for his proposal.[23] For him this verse marks a clear division between the period of Israel and the period of Jesus' ministry, from which John is separated.

Those who, like Conzelmann, consider that John is excluded from the kingdom often cite 7:28–30 to support their position. In their view, these verses mean that although John participates in the saving events, he has fallen short of the eschatological kingdom.

In light of the present study, several observations should be made. While there are differences between John and Jesus in 7:18–35, the passage does not envision a sharp division between them. This tradition has the highest regard for John's role in the history of salvation (the plan of God). The question of John and the answer that Jesus gives imply a tacit recognition of Jesus' identity by the Baptist. In line with the foregoing narrative, the passage characterizes John as the forerunner of the Lord (7:27; see also 1:17, 76), an indication of the close association between John and Jesus in God's salvific plan. John and Jesus are placed on a par in the parable of the children in the marketplace (7:31–35) without any indication of John being inferior to Jesus or of a division between their ministries. As noted above, 7:28b is not meant to downplay the relevance of John. In that verse, τῇ βασιλείᾳ τοῦ θεοῦ stands in contrast to γεννητοῖς γυναικῶν in the previous clause. This contrast indicates

---

22. Conzelmann, *Theology*, 22–27; see also Becker, *Jesus of Nazareth*, 114–15.

23. The meaning of Luke 16:16 (// Matt 11:12–13) is one of the most highly disputed in the NT. The crux of the passage's interpretation lies on the temporal meaning of μέχρι and ἀπὸ τότε, both of which can be understood as including or excluding John.

that the focus of the comparison has to do with categories, not persons.[24] The statement aims to emphasize the superiority of the kingdom, not the inferiority of John. Nonetheless, to the extent that John's imprisonment separates him from the present manifestation of the kingdom, it can be said that the least in the kingdom is greater than he. The reason is that, since the kingdom is present in things that Jesus does and says, those who see and hear Jesus are greater than John: "Blessed are the eyes that see what you see. For I say to you, many prophets and kings desired to see what you see, but did not see it, and to hear what you hear, but did not hear it" (10:23–24).

Luke's overarching view of God's plan of salvation envisions John's ministry as an essential element of the kingdom. As a transitional figure who stands at the crossroads of the Law and Prophets on the one hand and the kingdom of God on the other, John has initiated an era in salvation history.[25] Luke probably considers John, who is more than a prophet, to be of those to whom Jesus refers to when he talks about the fate of the patriarchs and all the prophets in the day of judgment: "There will be wailing and grinding of teeth when you see Abraham, Isaac, and Jacob and all the prophets in the kingdom of God and you yourselves cast out (13:28)." Hence, Luke's broadened eschatological perspective offers the framework for the inclusion of John into the kingdom at a later phase.[26]

Jesus' high regard for John as "greater than a prophet" and the "greatest of all born of women" seems to confirm rather than to deny the Baptist's qualification as a candidate for the kingdom. In Luke-Acts those whom Jesus praises are worthy of emulation and, implicitly, fitting members for the kingdom (e.g., 7:9; 18:14; 21:3–4). Jesus' praise of the Baptist reinforces the narrator's regard for John in the infancy narratives as well as in other passages of Luke-Acts and confirms that he belongs to the new age (Luke 3:1; Acts 1:22). Consequently, this passage does not support the claim that the Baptist is envisioned as excluded from the kingdom or as belonging exclusively to the old age.

---

24. Viviano, "Least in the Kingdom," 53.

25. Fitzmyer, *Luke*, 1:181–87; 2:1114–18.

26. Regarding the eschatological perspective of Luke, see Conzelmann, *Theology*, 95–136; Schnackenburg, *Jesus in the Gospels*, 175–79.

The Relationship between John and Jesus

The historical relationship between John and Jesus continues to be a matter of discussion and debate.[27] While many scholars are willing to admit that Jesus was in some sense a disciple of John, what that relationship entailed remains unsettled. Outside of Luke-Acts, this issue is complicated by the seemingly conflicting reports about the extent to which John and Jesus knew each other. Whereas Matthew and John contain some evidence about their mutual acquaintance (Matt 3:13–17; John 1:15–18; 26–36; 5:33), Mark and Luke are more reserved about the nature of their relationship.[28]

From a literary perspective, the narrative-critical analysis of Luke 7:18–35 (// Matt 11:2–19) helps to shed some light on this discussion by looking at the way Luke conceives and portrays the relationship between John and Jesus. My analysis has shown that in the Gospel of Luke the question of the Baptist is best explained by John's ignorance of Jesus' identity. John's question confirms what the narrative intimates: that although John baptized Jesus, the Baptist did not know Jesus *personally*.

In the Lukan narrative, John's ignorance of Jesus' identity is explained by several facts. First, in the infancy narratives Luke separates John from Jesus after their birth by placing John in the desert (1:80) and Jesus in Nazareth (2:39, 51). Second, Luke's way of presenting the proclamation of John and the baptism of Jesus (3:1–22) further distances John from Jesus, creating a greater gap between them than in any of the other Gospels. On the one hand, whereas Mark 1:9 and in Matt 3:15 Jesus is baptized *by* John, in Matt 3:14–15 John and Jesus talk to each other. Moreover, in John 1:15–18, 26–36 the Baptist speaks at length about Jesus and bears testimony that he is the Messiah. On the other hand, Luke never explicitly links John and Jesus together until 7:18–35—and then only through the disciples of Baptist.[29] Unlike the other Gospel ac-

---

27. Helpful discussions can be found in Meier, *Marginal Jew*, 2:116–71; Taylor, *John the Baptist*, 261–316.

28. In both Mark 1:4–11 and Luke 3:1–22, Jesus' baptism is depicted as one of many among a crowd.

29. Before this instance, John and Jesus have only "met" in their mothers' wombs during Mary's visit to Elizabeth (1:40–45). Despite the ambiguity of Luke's baptism account, it is not impossible that he presumed that John had baptized Jesus as his source had indicated (Mark 1:9). However, even under this assumption, the encounter between John and Jesus seems to have been for John—according to Luke—nothing more than the inconsequential baptism of another person in the midst of a crowd. In Mark 1:9–11,

counts, in Luke John neither baptizes Jesus nor speaks directly to him nor testifies about his identity. Third, Luke suggests that John's imprisonment kept him from witnessing the ministry of Jesus (3:19–20). Fourth, in the rest of Luke-Acts, nothing else is said about any meeting between John and Jesus, even though Luke's account of John is the most extensive in the entire NT.

As a result of this literary portrayal about the way in which John and Jesus interact, the reader of the Lukan narrative is left with the impression that both characters never meet until the Baptist's question in 7:18–23. It is in this passage that John for the first time in the story tries to ascertain if Jesus is "the one who is to come"—a question that confirms the insinuation in the previous narrative that the Baptist was unaware of who Jesus was.

Jesus' encomium of the Baptist in Luke 7:24–28 stands in apparent contrast to John's lack of acquaintance with Jesus. At first sight, these laudatory words seem to witness to Jesus' personal knowledge of John. However, as I have pointed out above, the previous narrative has not linked John and Jesus either explicitly or directly. The most that can be assumed is that Jesus speaks in this way about the Baptist because he has been among the crowd listening to his proclamation (3:7, 22) or has heard what other people have been saying about John (3:15; 5:33). Therefore, according to the narrative, Jesus' encomium does not reflect any personal knowledge of John but rather Jesus' most profound admiration for someone whom he has come to esteem but never spoken to. Jesus' laudatory remarks about John reflect the kind of opinion someone may have about a person whom one greatly respects but has never met personally. Jesus' high regard for John does not mean that they knew each other well. Rather, Jesus' remarks point eloquently to the people's high esteem for John (3:15; 5:33; 9:7; 20:6). Consequently, the tradition about John and Jesus in Luke 7:18–35 suggests that, although Jesus held the Baptist in highest regard, John had not previously known Jesus.[30]

---

the vision which Jesus has is a personal experience not witnessed by John; see Fitzmyer, *Luke*, 1:481; Taylor, *John the Baptist*, 277.

30. As a result of this portrayal, Dunn's (*Jesus Remembered*, 350) characterization of Jesus as emerging "from the circle round John" seems to me more appropriate than that of a "disciple" in the narrow sense; see Meier, *Marginal Jew*, 2:116–17.

The Question of John the Baptist

From a historical perspective, John's lack of knowledge about Jesus provides a better explanation of why he sends two of his disciples to ask Jesus if he is "the one who is to come" than the prevailing interpretation regarding the Baptist's alleged disappointment with Jesus' ministry.[31] Three observations support this view and require that a different explanation be posited for John's question within the Gospel tradition.

First, there are further indications in the gospels that the relationship between John and Jesus was, at best, limited. Besides what I have argued about their mutual knowledge according to the Gospel of Luke, the Gospel of Mark is also circumspect about the extent of the relationship between John and Jesus. Although Jesus is baptized by John (Mark 1:9), the heavenly vision is only experienced by Jesus (1:10–11), implying that John was unaware of Jesus' identity. Mark notes that after the baptism, Jesus withdrew to the desert and Herod put John in prison (1:12–15; 6:17), suggesting that there was no overlap in their ministries.[32] Moreover, in the rest of the narrative there is no further indication that John and Jesus ever crossed paths or spoke to each other again. In the Gospel of John, the evangelist twice portrays the Baptist asserting that he did not previously know Jesus (John 1:31, 33).[33] It was only after the baptism that John recognizes Jesus' identity and testifies about him; but even then Jesus and John never speak to each other, and the evangelist continues to depict Jesus and John separately (1:29 [?], 35–37; 3:22–26).[34]

---

31. I presume the essential historicity of this episode (Matt 11:2–6 // Luke 7:18–23), which is acknowledged by a number of scholars; e.g. Meier, *Marginal Jew*, 2:154; Dunn, *Jesus Remembered*, 447–50.

32. Taylor, *Immerser*, 294.

33. Although the Gospel of John has been relegated for decades to the canons of myth and theology in the quests for the historical Jesus, today many scholars are reassessing the possibility that at least some of the material in John's Gospel may rest on authentic historical memory. This is the case, for instance, with some of the material related to the Baptist, including the Gospel's testimony about the religious leaders' interrogation of the Baptist (1:19, 21a–22, 24–25), the Baptist's teaching about the "one coming after me" (1:26–27), the Baptist's rejection of messianic and prophetic roles (1:20, 21b, 23), the origin of Jesus' first disciples (1:35, 37–48), and the overlap of the Baptist's and Jesus' baptizing ministry (3:22–26; 4:1). See Anderson, *John, Jesus, and History, Volumes 1 and 2*; Moloney, "Fourth Gospel," 42–58.

34. The phrase ὃς ἦν μετὰ σοῦ πέραν τοῦ Ἰορδάνου (3:26) gives no indication about how long John and Jesus were together or about the nature of their relationship. John's reply to his disciples in 3:27–30 rehearses his previous testimony about Jesus

John seems to derive his knowledge about Jesus from the baptismal experience and from what "the one who sent" John to baptize (John 1:33) revealed to him about Jesus, rather than from an established relationship with Jesus. Nevertheless, despite the renewed appreciation for the historical value of John's Gospel, many scholars are still cautious about the reliability of this testimony about Jesus because of the purported Christian overlay. As Moloney notes, "The Baptist's witness to Jesus and the conscious presentation of Jesus to his disciples as the Lamb of God are surely the results of early Christian theologizing."[35] Indeed, historically it would be difficult to explain why John continued his ministry and did not join "the stronger one" as one of his most fervent disciples if—as the Fourth Gospel insists—the Baptist witnessed Jesus' baptismal epiphany. The Gospel of Matthew also has a dialogue between John and Jesus (3:14–15) that implies that the Baptist knew Jesus before the baptism. This testimony, however, is best understood as an isolated attempt by Matthew to explain the early Christian community's embarrassment of Jesus' baptism by John.[36]

Second, several NT passages suggest that the ministry of Jesus may have developed along the lines of John's ministry and not, as some have argued, in contrast to John's ministry. In the Gospel of Luke this affinity is indicated by the symmetry with which the evangelist presents the birth accounts and early public ministries of John and Jesus, but outside the Lukan Gospel there are other passages that support this view: (1) Both John (Mark 1:4–5) and Jesus (or his disciples) preach and practice a ritual of baptism (Matt 28:19; John 3:22; 4:1–2; Acts 2:41); (2) John lives in the desert (Mark 1:4) and Jesus frequents deserted places (Mark 1:12, 35; John 10:40); (3) both John (Mark 2:18: Matt 11:2; Acts 19:1–7) and Jesus had disciples (Mark 3:13–19); (4) both John (Matt 3:8–10, 12, 17) and Jesus (Mark 4:7–8, 26–29; 12:2; Matt 7:16–19; 12:33–35; John 15:1–8) use similar agricultural metaphors; (5) both

---

(1:19–34). John's figurative language provides no concrete information about whether the phrase ἀκούων αὐτοῦ χαρᾷ χαίρει διὰ τὴν φωνὴν τοῦ νυμφίου (3:29) refers to John's conversations with Jesus or his disciples' report about Jesus' (implied) preaching ministry.

35. Moloney, "Fourth Gospel," 45.

36. Dunn, *Jesus Remembered*, 222 n. 213; Taylor, *Immerser*, 288–89. The other variants in Matthew's baptism account, i.e., the opening of the heavens as an observable event and the heavenly voice proclamation to those present "this is my son . . .," can also be understood as the evangelist's modifications.

John (John 3:27–30) and Jesus (Matt 9:15) use nuptials metaphors; (6) John wears clothing befitting an ascetic and itinerant preacher (Mark 1:6; Matt 11:8) and Jesus urges his itinerant disciples not to be concerned about their clothing (Mark 6:8–9); (7) both John (Matt 11:18) and Jesus (Mark 3:22) are accused of being possessed by a demon (Beelzebul); (8) John preaches against Herod (Mark 6:18), and Jesus shows contempt for Herod (Mark 8:15; Luke 13:32; 23:9); (9) the similarities between the ministries of John and Jesus seem to have been so conspicuous that people confused one with the other (Matt 16:14; Mark 8:28; Luke 9:19); (10) John (Matt 21:32) welcomes prostitutes and Jesus (John 8:3–11; Luke 7:36–50) shows compassion towards sinful women; (11) both John (Mark 1:2–8, 14) and Jesus (cf. Matt 19:12) adopted a celibate lifestyle during their public ministries; (12) both John (Matt 3:1–12) and Jesus (Mark 13:28–32) proclaimed God's imminent judgment; (13) John (Luke 5:33; 11:1) and Jesus (Matt 6:5–14) teach their disciples to pray; (14) John (Mark 1:6b; Matt 11:18; Luke 5:33a) and Jesus (Matt 4:1–2; 6:18; John 4:31–33) fast and teach their followers to fast; and (15) the determination to fulfill God's will led John (Mark 6:17–29) and Jesus (Mark 8:31; 9:31; 10:32–34; 14:43—15:39) to their own arrest and execution. These passages do not prove that Jesus modeled his ministry after John, but they do indicate that their words and deeds had much in common. As Meier has cautiously noted regarding some of these intriguing similarities between John and Jesus, "a great deal of argumentation lies between them and any conclusion."[37] Nonetheless, given the limited information we have about the Baptist, these similarities show a remarkable correspondence between the ministries and lives of John and Jesus.[38] In light of this affinity, there is not sufficient evidence to postulate a "break" or "conversion" of Jesus away from the Baptist that would justify the latter's question.[39]

---

37. Meier, *Marginal Jew*, 2:118.

38. On the affinity between the ministries of John and Jesus, see Becker, *Jesus of Nazareth*, 49–53; Meier, *Marginal Jew*, 2:116–30; Dunn, *Jesus Remembered*, 350–52.

39. According to Meier (*Marginal Jew*, 2:124), "To posit early loyalty to John's views on Jesus' part and then a later 'defection' or 'apostasy' is to introduce into the Gospel traditions chronological indicators and massive theological turnabouts that are simply not present. To be sure, there was a definite shift away from some of John's views and practices, a certain spiritual 'leave-taking.' But the idea of a hostile and total break conjured up by words like defection and apostasy lacks solid evidence."

Third, other NT and extra-biblical passages suggest that John's messianic expectations may have been in line with Jesus' ministry and not as many have thought in conflict with it. As I have argued, in the Gospel of Luke the Baptist's identification of Jesus with the expected prophetic figure is less problematic than in Matthew because for Luke there is continuity rather than contrast between the message and the ministry of John and Jesus.[40] Apart from the Gospel of Luke, other texts make it conceivable that the Baptist's proclamation comprised not only an apocalyptic message of judgment, but also a salvific dimension that may have included a more benign view of the Messiah's work: (a) Mark 1:2-3 and parallels prelude the message of the Baptist with a mélange of OT texts that introduces the appearance of John with an oracle of salvation from Isaiah (Exod 23:20; Mal 3:1; Isa 40:3).[41] (b) Matthew portrays the Baptist as a kingdom preacher (Matt 3:2). Matthew's redaction does not mean that the message of John and Jesus were the same, but it does imply that Matthew conceived it as more than a threat of judgment: ". . . Matthew wants to say that their [John's and Jesus'] ministries begin from the same place and *share the same overall vision* of what God is in the process of doing."[42] (c) In book 18 of *Antiquities*, Josephus hails the Baptist as an ethical preacher sought by many: ". . . Herod slew him, who was a good man and one who commanded the Jews to exercise virtue, both as to righteousness toward one another and with piety towards God, and [so] to come to baptism. . . . Now when [many] others came in crowds about him, for they were greatly moved [or pleased] by hearing his words . . ."[43] Josephus' characterization of John and the crowds' enthusiasm for him would seem unintelligible unless the Baptist's proclamation would have encompassed more than a message of coming judgment. (d) Although the Baptist's messianic expectation evidently had an apocalyptic component of judgment (Matt 3:7-12; Luke 3:7-9, 16-17), the publication of the Messianic Apocalypse (4Q521) in recent years encourages the possibility that he may have also envisioned the coming of the Messiah alongside Jesus' ministerial activity.[44] Column 2 of that document reads:

40. See ch. 3, 98-100.
41. Marcus, *Mark*, 1:147-49.
42. Nolland, *Matthew*, 175; emphasis added.
43. Quoted from Whiston, *Josephus*, 581.
44. Unofficial publications of the text have been circulating since 1991, but the official translation in charge of Émile Puech was published only in 1998.

> [The hea]vens and the earth will listen to His Messiah, and none therein will stray from the commandments of the holy ones. Seekers of the Lord, strengthen yourselves in His service! All you hopeful in (your) heart, will you not find the Lord in this? For the Lord will consider the pious (*hasidim*) and call the righteous by name. Over the poor His spirit will hover and will renew the faithful with His power. And He will glorify the pious on the throne of the eternal Kingdom. He who liberates the captives, restores sight to the blind, straightens the b[ent]. And f[or] ever I will clea[ve to the h]opeful and in His mercy ... And the fr[uit ...] will not be delayed for anyone [...] And the Lord will accomplish glorious things which have never been as [He ...] For He will heal the wounded, and revive the dead and bring good news to the poor.... He will lead the uprooted and make the hungry rich ...[45]

The parallel of the Messianic Apocalypse with some texts in the Jesus tradition (Matt 11:4–5; Luke 4:18–19; 7:22; see also Isa 26:19; 29:18; 35:5–6; 42:7; 42:18; 61:1–2) has been already recognized, but the relevance of this text for the question of John has not been fully explored. As some have noted, the text suggests that at the time of Jesus his words and deeds would have been interpreted as the typical works of the expected Messiah.[46] Since, as many scholars acknowledge, John could have lived for some time in the community of the Essenes,[47] it is possible that he may have been familiar with the messianic expectations echoed by this document. The hypothesis cannot be proven, but if John's proclamation entailed more than an apocalyptic message of judgment it is probable that he may have also espoused, in his preaching, the messianic expectation present in this text. If so, it could explain why Jesus, who held John in the highest esteem (Matt 11:14 // Luke 7:28), responded to the Baptist's disciples the way he did (Matt 11:4–5 // Luke 7:22).

Although from a historical perspective this appears to be the best explanation about why the Baptist sends two of his disciples to ask Jesus if he is "the one who is to come," as noted above the Gospel of John is steadfast in its affirmation that the Baptist recognized Jesus and witnessed to his identity (1:29-36; 3:27-30; see also 1:6-8, 15). Despite the difficulties with this material, for the sake of the argument I will consider

---

45. Quoted from Vermes, *Dead Sea Scrolls*, 412–13.
46. Collins, "Messiah," 110.
47. Fitzmyer, *Luke*, 1:388–89, 453–54, 459–60.

here why if the Baptist identified Jesus as the "lamb of God" and the "Son of God" (1:29, 34, 36) later did he ask if Jesus was "the one who is to come" (Matt 11:2–6 // Luke 7:18–23).⁴⁸ If John's alleged ignorance of Jesus could no longer be posited and the prevailing interpretation regarding the Baptist's alleged disappointment with Jesus' ministry no longer offers the best explanation for the Baptist's probe, the motivation for the Baptist's question would have to be found elsewhere. The preceding discussion suggests that John's limited knowledge of Jesus stands at the root of the Baptist's question. If both men had known each other well, John would not have raised the question about Jesus' identity. If John felt compelled to revise his opinion about Jesus, he must have learned something about him that he did not previously know. I propose that under this second scenario the reason for John's perplexity would have to lie not in the character of Jesus' ministry but in his Nazarene origin, an issue found in all four Gospels.

Both Matthew and Luke agree that the question of the Baptist arises after his disciples bring him news about Jesus' activity.⁴⁹ Among the things that John could have heard from his disciples was that Jesus was from Nazareth. The Gospels record that some believed that an aura of secrecy would shroud the origin of the Messiah.⁵⁰ According to this view, the fact that Jesus was from an obscure locale in the region of Galilee would disqualify him as a messianic candidate. Indeed, Matthean infancy narratives (chs. 1–2) may have been inspired, in part, to explain why Jesus could legitimately be the Messiah even though he was known as a Nazarene: he was born in Bethlehem, but his family had to settle in Nazareth because of Archelaus.⁵¹ Likewise, Jesus' messianic proclama-

---

48. Paul N. Anderson's ("Why This Study Is Needed," 38–39) reservations about the Gospel of John's paschal theology seem to imply that the Baptist's identification of Jesus as the "lamb of God" could retain some reminiscences of historical memory; see, however, Meier's (*Marginal Jew*, 2:106–16) discussion regarding the difficulties with the passages depicting Jesus' baptismal theophany and Mary Coloe's ("John as Witness," 53) opinion concerning the Baptist's identification of Jesus in the Gospel of John. In Coloe's (ibid., 53) view: "That the historical John clearly identified Jesus as this coming one is highly questionable."

49. Matthew 11:2 speaks about τὰ ἔργα τοῦ Χριστοῦ and Luke 7:18 talks about περὶ πάντων τούτων, but the narrative function of both phrases is similar: to illustrate what John's disciples told him about Jesus. See ch. 3, 93 esp. n. 39.

50. Isa 7:14–17; Mal 3:1; Dan 7:13; *b. Sanh.* 97a; *1 En.* 46; 48:2–6; *Esdr.* 7:28; 13:32; *2 Bar* 29:3; Justin, *Dial.* 8:4; 110:1; see also Mowinckel, *He That Cometh*, 304–8.

51. Brown, *Birth*, 179–83.

tion in his hometown of Nazareth was met with resistance and caused a scandal (σκανδαλίζω) because his fellow villagers knew where he was from (Mark 6:1–6; Luke 4:16–30).

Although the prejudice against that Palestinian region is latent in all four Gospels (Mark 14:70; Matt 26:71–73; Luke 22:59), the Gospel of John is the one that most vividly depicts the bias against that territory. It is here that we first find Nathaniel vocalizing what appears to have been a common preconception: "Can anything good come from Nazareth?" (John 1:46). Later, the inhabitants of Jerusalem dismiss Jesus' messianic credentials because of his origin: "[W]e know where he is from. When the Messiah comes, no one will know where he is from" (7:27). Still later we learn that others refuse to recognize Jesus as the Messiah because he did not come from the city of David: "The Messiah will not come from Galilee, will he? Does not scripture say that the Messiah will be of David's family and come from Bethlehem, the village where David lived?" (7:41–42). The chief priests and the Pharisees express a similar objection in their response to Nicodemus: "Look and see that no prophet arises from Galilee" (7:52). A final ironic allusion to this bias may be at work in the fourth evangelist's form of the title on the cross: "Jesus the Nazorean, the King of the Jews" (19:19).

If John's knowledge about Jesus was restricted to an epiphany on the day of his baptism with limited interactions before he departed and the Baptist was imprisoned, John could have been ignorant that Jesus was from Nazareth. He may have only learned about this in prison when his disciples arrived to tell him about Jesus' growing fame. If John shared the popular belief about the Messiah's origin, he too may have been scandalized (σκανδαλίζω) by Jesus' provenance (Matt 11:6 // Luke 7:23). This would explain why the Baptist appears to reconsider his previous endorsement of Jesus and dispatches his disciples to ask him about his identity.

To summarize, the conclusion that from a historical perspective John's question is prompted by his lack of knowledge of Jesus and not by an alleged disappointment with Jesus' ministry is supported by additional information in the other gospels as well as by the statements in Josephus and in the Messianic Apocalypse (4Q521). Only Matt 3:14–15 and a few passages in the Gospel of John (1:15, 29–36; 3:27–30) pose some difficulties to this explanation. In this case, if as those passages indicate the Baptist identified Jesus as God's eschatological agent, John's question would have to be explained by his disappointment regarding Jesus' provenance. However, the theological and literary features of the passages that attest to the Baptist's identification of Jesus suggest that these testimonies must be approached with greater critical sensitivity. In light of this evidence, John's limited knowledge of Jesus stands as the *raison d'être* as to why the Baptist sends his disciples to ask Jesus whether he is "the one who is to come."

CONCLUSION

A modern response to the question formulated by Algasia to Jerome about why John asks Jesus if he is "the one who is to come" after he had identified him as the "Lamb of God" (Hieronymus, *Epist.* 121.1) finds a complex answer within the Gospel tradition. A proper response has to take into account some of the advances that scholars have made since the period of modern biblical interpretation regarding the origin and transmission of many NT writings. The Gospels have left us four different testimonies about Jesus whose individual themes and nuances are noteworthy and whose differences can only be harmonize with tentative results. However, in the Gospel of Luke the question of the Baptist is part of a tradition about John and Jesus whose meaning contains three main elements.

First, John asks the question about the identity of Jesus because he had not previously recognized him (7:18–23). After receiving the reports about the activity of Jesus, John sees the promise of fulfillment of his eschatological expectations at hand and sends his disciples to confirm if Jesus is "the one who is to come." John receives his confirmation through mighty deeds and words and, as the most important character in the story, realizes that Jesus is the expected one.

Second, Jesus' encomium of John (7:24–28) reflects his admiration for the Baptist, but there is no evidence of a mutual personal knowledge between them. John is a man of principles, a prophet, the forerunner of the Lord, and the greatest among those born of women. His imprisonment has temporarily deprived him from witnessing the present manifestation of this new era. But, in God's scheme of salvation, John will inherit one of the most privileged places in the kingdom.

Third, Luke's skillful literary use of this tradition is best appreciated in his narrative commentary in 7:29–30. Luke weaves his own point of view with that of Jesus in this narrative commentary and makes the plan of God the theme that controls John's role in the Gospel. This role of John in connection with Jesus, as Müller notes, emphasizes Luke's theocentric perspective at the service of his Christology: "Das bedeutet, daß Johannes der Täufer bei Lukas in einer theozentrischen Perspektive von Anfang an in das Konzept einer narrativen Christologie einbezogen ist."[52] In 7:29–30, Luke transforms the last part of this tradition (7:31–35) into an indictment of the religious leaders. Their lack of wisdom has led them astray and in their childish behavior they have frustrated God's offer of salvation.

By incorporating this story about John and Jesus within his overall literary work, Luke has given us an example of the complexities of composition. He has also given us a glimpse of an essential aspect of the biblical vision of human beings in which characters sometimes appear "unpredictable, in some ways impenetrable, constantly emerging from and slipping back into a penumbra of ambiguity."[53] In this tradition, Luke found an ideal account about an agonizing wait and fulfillment of prophetic expectations, an apt portrayal of the identity of Jesus, a worthy testimony of Jesus' admiration for John, and a reliable assessment of how the religious leaders' lack of wisdom had misled them. As a skilled writer, Luke made the most of it. His compositional concern for the identity of Jesus and the way different characters in the story react to him reached an important threshold in this story. From this moment on, the narrative came a step closer in its attempt to proclaim that Jesus is "the one who is to come."

---

52. Müller, *Charakterzeichnung*, 297; see also Wink, *John the Baptist*, 57–58.
53. Alter, *Biblical Narrative*, 129.

Bibliography

Achtemeier, Paul J. "The Lucan Perspective on the Miracles of Jesus: A Preliminary Sketch." In *Perspectives on Luke-Acts*, edited by Charles H. Talbert, 153–67. PRS Special Studies Series 5. Danville, VA: Assn. of Baptist Prof. of Religion, 1978.

Aletti, Jean-Noël. *L'Art de ranconter Jésus Christ: L'Écriture narrative de l'évangile de Luc.* PD. Paris: Éditions du Seuil, 1989.

Allison, Jr., D. C. "Elijah Must Come First." *JBL* 103 (1984) 256–58.

Alter, Robert. *The Art of Biblical Narrative.* New York: Basic Books, 1981.

———. *The World of Biblical Literature.* New York: HarperCollins, 1992.

Ambrosius, Episcopus Mediolanesis. *Expositio evangelii secundum Lucam: Fragmenta in Esaiam.* CC 14. Turnholt, Belgium: Brepols, 1957.

Anderson, Garwood P. "Seeking and Saving What Might Have Been Lost: Luke's Restoration of an Enigmatic Parable Tradition." *CBQ* 70 (2008) 729–49.

Anderson, Paul N., et al., editors. *John, Jesus, and History.* Vols. 1 and 2. SBL Symposium Series 44. Atlanta: SBL, 2007, 2009.

———. "Why This Study Is Needed, and Why It Is Needed Now." In *John, Jesus, and History*, edited by Paul N. Anderson et al., vol. 1. SBL Symposium Series 44. Atlanta: SBL, 2007.

Aristotle. *The 'Art' of Rhetoric.* Translated by John Henry Freese. LCL 22. Cambridge, MA: Harvard University Press, 1947.

———. *Problems.* Vol. 2, bks. 22–38. *Rhetorica ad Alexandrum.* Translated by W. S. Hett and H. Rackham. LCL 16. Cambridge, MA: Harvard University Press, 1965.

Aune, David E. "The Use and Abuse of the Enthymeme in New Testament Scholarship." *NTS* 49 (2003) 299–320.

———. *Prophecy in Early Christianity and the Ancient Mediterranean World.* Grand Rapids: Eerdmans, 1983.

———. *The New Testament and Its Literary Environment.* LEC. Philadelphia: Westminster, 1987.

Backhaus, Knut. *Die "Jüngerkreise" des Täufers Johannes. Eine Studie zu den religionsgeschichtlichen Ursprüngen des Christentums.* PTS 19. Paderborn: F. Schöningh, 1991.

Bacon, Benjamin W. "The Q Section on John the Baptist and the *Shemoneh Esreh*." *JBL* 45 (1926) 23–56.

Bakke, Odd Magne. *When Children Became People: The Birth of Childhood in Early Christianity.* Translated by Brian McNeil. Minneapolis: Fortress, 2005.

Beare, Francis Wright. *The Earliest Records of Jesus.* Nashville: Abingdon, 1962.

———. *The Gospel According to Matthew: Translation, Introduction and Commentary.* San Francisco: Harper & Row, 1981.

Becker, Jürgen. *Jesus of Nazareth.* Translated by James E. Crouch. 1996. New York: de Gruyter, 1998.

———. *Johannes der Taüfer und Jesus von Nazareth*. BS 63. Neukirchen-Vluyn: Neukirchener, 1972.

Bede Venerabilis. *In Lucae Evangelium exposition*. CC 120. Turnhout: Brépols, 1960.

Bird, Michael F. *Are You the One Who Is to Come?: The Historical Jesus and the Messianic Question*. Grand Rapids: Baker Academic, 2009.

Black, David Alan, and David R. Beck. *Rethinking the Synoptic Problem*. Grand Rapids: Baker Academic, 2001.

Böcher, Otto. "Aß Johannes der Täufer kein Brot (Luk. vii. 33)?" *NTS* (1971–72) 90–92.

Böhlemann, Peter. *Jesus und der Täufer: Schlüssel zur Theologie und Ethik des Lukas*. SNTSMS 99. Cambridge, MA: Cambridge University Press, 1997.

Bonaventure. *Opera omnia: Commentarius in Evangelium S. Lucae*. Quaracchi: Collegium S. Bonaventurae, 1882–1902.

———. *St. Bonaventure's Commentary on the Gospel of Luke, Chapters 1–8*. Translated by Robert J. Karris. Works of St. Bonaventure 8/1. St. Bonaventure, NY: Franciscan Institute Publications, 2001.

Boucher, Madeline. *The Mysterious Parable: A Literary Study*. CBQMS 6. Washington, DC: CBA, 1977.

Bovon, François. *Luke 1: A Commentary on the Gospel of Luke 1:1—9:50*. Hermeneia. Minneapolis: Augsburg Fortress, 2002.

———. *Luke the Theologian*. 2nd ed. Waco, TX: Baylor University Press, 2006.

Bowker, J. *Jesus and the Pharisees*. London: Cambridge University Press, 1973.

Brawley, Robert. *Luke-Acts and the Jews: Conflict, Apology, and Conciliation*. SBLMS 33. Atlanta: Scholars, 1987.

Brodie, Thomas L. *The Birthing of the New Testament: The Intertextual Development of the New Testament Writings*. New Testament Monographs 1. Sheffield: Sheffield Phoenix, 2004.

Broshi, Magen. *Bread, Wine, Walls and Scrolls*. JSPSup 36. New York: Sheffield Academic, 2001.

Brown, Raymond E. *An Introduction to the Gospel of John*. AB Reference Library. New York: Doubleday, 2003.

———. *An Introduction to the New Testament*. AB Reference Library. New York: Doubleday, 1997.

———. *The Death of the Messiah: From Gethsemane to the Grave. A Commentary on the Passion Narratives in the Four Gospels*. 2 vols. AB Reference Library. New York: Doubleday, 1994.

———. *The Birth of the Messiah: A Commentary on the Infancy Narratives in the Gospel of Matthew and Luke*. Rev. ed. AB Reference Library. New York: Doubleday, 1993.

Büchsel, Friedrich. "γεννητός." In *TDNT* 1:672.

Bultmann, Rudolph. *History of the Synoptic Tradition*. Translated by John Marsh. 1958. Peabody, MA: Hendrickson, 1963.

Burnyeat, M. F. "Enthymeme: Aristotle on the Rationality of Rhetoric." In *Essays on Aristotle's Rhetoric*, edited by Amélie Oksenberg Rorty, 88–115. Philosophical Traditions 6. Berkeley: University of California Press, 1996.

Busse, Ulrich. *Das Nazareth-Manifest: Eine Einführung in das lukanische Jesusbild nach Lk 4,16–30*. SBS 91. Stuttgart: Katholisches Bibelwerk, 1978.

Cadbury, Henry J. *The Making of Luke-Acts*. 2nd ed. Peabody, MA: Hendrickson, 1999.

———. *The Style and Literary Method of Luke: The Diction of Luke and Acts*. HTS 6. Cambridge, MA: Harvard University Press, 1919.

———. "Four Features of Lucan Style." In *Studies in Luke-Acts: Essays Presented in Honor of Paul Schubert*, edited by Leander E. Keck and J. Louis Martyn, 87–102. Nashville: Abingdon, 1966.

Calvinus, Ioannes. *Harmonia ex Tribus Euangelistis Composita, Matthaeo, Marco, & Luca: Adiuncto Seorsum Iohanne, quòd Pauca aliis Communia Habeat / cum Iohannis Caluini Commentariis*. 2nd ed. Geneva: Oliua Roberti Stephani, 1560.

———. *Calvin's Bible Commentaries: Matthew, Mark and Luke, Part II*. Translated by John King. Charleston, SC: Forgotten Books, 2007.

Cameron, Peter Scott. *Violence and the Kingdom: The Interpretation of Matthew 11:12*. ANTJ 5. Frankfurt: P. Lang, 1984.

Cameron, Ron. "'What Have You Come Out to See?': Characterizations of John and Jesus in the Gospels." *Semeia* 49 (1990) 35–69.

Caragounis, C. C. "Kingdom of God/Heaven." In *DJG*, 417–30.

Carroll, John T. "Luke's Portrayal of the Pharisees." *CBQ* 50 (1988) 604–21.

Carson, D. A. "Matthew 11:19b/Luke 7:35: Test Case for the Bearing of Q Christology on the Synoptic Problem." In *Jesus of Nazareth: Lord and Christ. Essays on the Historical Jesus and New Testament Christology*, edited by Joel B. Green and Max Turner, 128–46. Grand Rapids: Eerdmans, 1994.

Carter, Warren. "Kernels and Narrative Blocks: The Structure of Matthew's Gospel." *CBQ* 54 (1992) 463–81.

———. *Matthew and the Margins: A Socio-Political and Religious Reading*. JSNTSup 204. Sheffield: Sheffield Academic, 2000.

Collins, John J. "The Works of the Messiah." *DSD* (1994) 98–112.

Coloe, Mary. "John as Witness and Friend." In *John, Jesus, and History*, edited by Paul N. Anderson et al., vol. 2. SBL Symposium Series 44. Atlanta: SBL, 2009.

Conzelmann, Hans. *The Theology of St. Luke*. Translated by Geoffrey Buswell. 1953. New York: Harper & Row, 1961.

Cotter, W. J. "The Parable of the Children in the Marketplace, Q (Lk) 7:31–35: An Examination of the Parable's Image and Significance." *NovT* 29 (1987) 289–304.

Craghan, John F. "A Redactional Study of Lk 7:21 in the Light of Dt 19:15." *CBQ* (1967) 353–67.

Crossan, John Dominic. *In Fragments: The Aphorisms of Jesus*. San Francisco: Harper & Row, 1983.

Culpepper, Alan R. "Seeing the Kingdom of God: The Metaphor of Sight in the Gospel of Luke." *CTM* (1994) 434–43.

Cyrillus, Episcopus Alexandrinus. *Commentarii in Lucam*. CC 44 B. Turnhout: Brépols, 1980.

———. *Commentary on the Gospel of St. Luke*. Translated by R. Payne Smith. Astoria, NY: Studion, 1983.

Dahl, Nils. "A People for His Name." *NTS* 4 (1957–58) 319–27.

Danker, Frederick W. *Jesus and the New Age: A Commentary on St. Luke's Gospel*. Philadelphia: Fortress, 1988.

Darr, John A. *On Character Building: The Reader and the Rhetoric of Characterization in Luke-Acts*. LCBI. Louisville: John Knox, 1992.

Davies, W. D., and Dale C. Allison. *A Critical and Exegetical Commentary on the Gospel According to Saint Matthew*. 3 vols. ICC. Edinburgh: T. & T. Clark, 1988–97.

Demetrius. *Du Style*. CUF. Paris: Belles Lettres, 1993.

Dibelius, Franz. "Zwei Worte Jesu; II: Der Kleinere ist im Himmelreich grösser als Johannes (Mt 11,11)." *ZNW* 11 (1910) 190–92.

Dibelius, Martin. *Die urchristliche Überlieferung von Johannes dem Täufer*. FRLANT 15. Göttingen: Vandehoeck & Ruprecht, 1911.

———. *The Book of Acts: Form, Style and Theology*. FCBS. Minneapolis: Fortress, 2004.

———. *Studies in the Acts of the Apostles*. Translated by Mary Ling. London: SCM, 1956.

Dillon, R. J. "Previewing Luke's Project from His Prologue (Luke 1:1–4)." *CBQ* 43 (1981) 205–27.

Doble, Peter. *The Paradox of Salvation: Luke's Theology of the Cross*. SNTSMS 87. New York: Cambridge University Press, 1996.

Donahue, John R. "Tax Collectors and Sinners: An Attempt at Identification." *CBQ* 33 (1971) 39–61.

Du Plessis, I. J. "Contextual Aid for an Identity Crisis: An Attempt to Interpret Luke 7:35." In *A South African Perspective on the New Testament: Essays by South African New Testament Scholars Presented to Bruce Manning Metzger during His Visit to South Africa in 1985*, edited by J. H. Petzer and P. J. Hartin, 112–27. Leiden: Brill, 1986.

Dunn, James D. G. *Jesus Remembered*. Christianity in the Making 1. Grand Rapids: Eerdmans, 2003.

———. *The Acts of the Apostles*. NC. Valley Forge, PA: Trinity, 1996.

Dupont, Jaques. "L'Ambassade de Jean-Baptiste." *NRT* (1961) 805–21; 943–59.

Easton, Burton. *The Gospel According to St. Luke: A Critical Exegetical Commentary*. New York: Scribner, 1926.

Ernst, Josef. *Johannes der Täufer. Interpretation-Geschichte-Wirkungsgeschichte*. BZNW 53. Berlin: de Gruyter, 1989.

Faierstein, Morris M. "Why Do the Scribes Say That Elijah Must Come First?" *JBL* 100 (1981) 75–86.

Farmer, W. R. *The Synoptic Problem: A Critical Analysis*. 2nd ed. Macon, GA: Mercer University Press, 1976.

Fitzmyer, Joseph A. "The Composition of Luke, Chapter 9." In *Perspectives on Luke-Acts*, edited by Charles H. Talbert, 139–52. PRS Special Studies Series 5. Danville, VA: Assn. of Baptist Prof. of Religion, 1978.

———. *A Wandering Aramean: Collected Aramaic Essays*. SBLMS 25. Missoula, MT: Scholars, 1979.

———. *The Gospel According to Luke: Luke I–IX*. AB 28. Garden City, NY: Doubleday, 1981.

———. *The One Who Is to Come*. Grand Rapids: Eerdmans, 2007.

———. *Luke the Theologian: Aspects of His Teaching*. 1989. Eugene, OR: Wipf & Stock, 2004.

Flender, Helmut. *St. Luke: Theologian of Redemptive History*. Philadelphia: Fortress, 1967.

Foerster, Werner. "δαίμων, δαιμόνιον, κτλ." In *TDNT* 2:1–20.

Fohrer, Georg, and Ulrich Wilckens. "σοφία, κτλ." In *TDNT* 7:465–526.

Foster, Robert. "Why on Earth Use 'Kingdom of Heaven'?: Matthew's Terminology Revisited." *NTS* 48 (2002) 487–99.

France, R. T. *The Gospel of Matthew*. NICNT. Grand Rapids: Eerdmans, 2007.

Gagnon, Robert A. J. "Luke's Motive for Redaction in the Account of the Double Delegation in Luke 7:1–10." *NovT* 36 (1994) 112–45.

Gathercole, Simon. "The Justification of Wisdom (Matt 11.19/Luke 7.35)." *NTS* 49 (2003) 476–88.

George, Augustin. "Israël dans l'oeuvre de Luc." *RB* 75 (1968) 481–525.

Gnilka, Joachim. *Jesus of Nazareth: Message and History*. Peabody, MA: Hendrickson, 1997.
Goguel, Maurice. *Au Seuil de L'Évangile: Jean-Baptiste*. BH. Paris: Payot, 1928.
Goodacre, Mark. *The Case against Q: Studies in Markan Priority and the Synoptic Problem*. Harrisburg, PA: Trinity, 2001.
———. *The Synoptic Problem: A Way through the Maze*. TBS 80. London: T. & T. Clark, 2001.
Goulder, Michael. "Is Q a Juggernaut?" *JBL* 115 (1996) 667–81.
———. "Self-contradictions in the IQP." *JBL* 118 (1999) 506–17.
Grangaard, Blake R. *Conflict and Authority in Luke 19:47 to 21:4*. SBL 8. New York: P. Lang, 1999.
Green, Joel B. *The Gospel of Luke*. NICNT. Grand Rapids: Eerdmans, 1997.
Grundmann, Walter. "δεῖ." In *TDNT* 2:21–25.
Haenchen, Ernst. *The Acts of the Apostles: A Commentary*. Philadelphia: Westminster, 1971.
Hahn, Scott W. "Kingdom and Church in Luke-Acts: From Davidic Christology to Kingdom Ecclesiology." In *Reading Luke: Interpretation, Reflection, Formation*, edited by Craig G. Bartholomew, Joel B. Green, and Anthony C. Thiselton, 294–326. SHS 6. Grand Rapids: Zondervan, 2005.
Harnack, Aldolf von. *The Sayings of Jesus: The Second Source of St. Matthew and St. Luke*. Translated by J. R. Wilkinson. 1907. New Testament Studies 2. New York: Putnam, 1908.
Hartmann, Michael. *Der Tod Johannes des Täufers: Eine exegetische und rezeptionsgeschichtliche Studie auf dem Hintergrund narrativer, intertextueller und kulturanthropologischer Zugänge*. SBB 45. Stuttgart: Katholisches Bibelwerk, 2001.
Hauck, F. "μακάριος." In *TDNT* 4:367–70.
Hawkins, John C. *Horae Synopticae: Contributions to the Study of the Synoptic Problem*. 2nd ed. Oxford: Clarendon, 1968.
Heil, John Paul. *The Meal Scenes in Luke-Acts: An Audience-Oriented Approach*. SBLMS 52. Atlanta: SBL, 1999.
Hieronymus. *Epistola CXXI*. PL 22. Paris: Migne, 1845.
Hoffman, Paul. *Studien zur Theologie der Logienquelle*. NTAbh 8. Münster: Aschendorff, 1972.
Holladay, Carl R. *A Critical Introduction to the New Testament: Interpreting the Message and Meaning of Jesus Christ*. Nashville: Abingdon, 2005.
Hollenbach, Paul W. "John the Baptist." In *ABD* 3:887–99.
Jeremias, Jacob. "Paarweise Sendung im Neuen Testament." In *New Testament Essays: Studies in Memory of Thomas Walter Manson 1893–1958*, edited by A. J. B. Higgins, 136–43. Manchester: Manchester University Press, 1959.
Jeremias, Joachim. *Jesus' Promise to the Nations*. SBT 24. Naperville: Allenson, 1958.
———. *The Parables of Jesus*. 3rd ed. London: SCM, 1972.
Jervell, Jacob. *Luke and the People of God: A New Look at Luke-Acts*. Minneapolis: Augsburg, 1972.
———. *The Theology of the Acts of the Apostles*. NTT. Cambridge, MA: Cambridge University Press, 1996.
Johnson, Luke Timothy. *The Gospel of Luke*. SacPag 3. Collegeville, MN: Liturgical, 1991.
———. *The Literary Function of Possessions in Luke-Acts*. SBLDS 39. Missoula, MT: Scholars, 1977.

Josephus. *The Complete Works*. Translated by William Whiston. Nashville: T. Nelson, 1998.
Karris, Robert J. "Poor and Rich: The Lukan *Sitz im Leben*." In *Perspectives on Luke-Acts*, edited by Charles H. Talbert, 112–25. PRS Special Studies Series 5. Danville, VA: Assn. of Baptist Prof. of Religion, 1978.
———. *Eating Your Way through Luke's Gospel*. Collegeville, MN: Liturgical, 2006.
Kazmierski, Carl R. *John the Baptist: Prophet and Evangelist*. Zacchaeus Studies: New Testament. Collegeville, MN: M. Glazier, 1996.
Kee, Howard C. "Jesus: A Glutton and a Drunkard." *NTS* 42 (1996) 374–93.
Keefer, Kyle. *The New Testament as Literature: A Very Short Introduction*. Oxford: Oxford University Press, 2008.
Kennedy, George A. *New Testament Interpretation through Rhetorical Criticism*. Chapel Hill: University of North Carolina Press, 1984.
———. *Progymnasmata: Greek Textbooks of Prose Composition Introductory to the Study of Rhetoric*. SBLWGRW 10. Atlanta: SBL, 2003.
Kilgallen, John J. "John the Baptist, the Sinful Woman, and the Pharisee." *JBL* 104 (1985) 675–79.
Kilpatrick, G. D. "Scribes, Scholars of the Law, and Lukan Origins." *JTS* 1 (1950) 56–60.
Kingsbury, Jack Dean. "The Figure of Jesus in Matthew's Story: A Literary-Critical Probe." *JSNT* 21 (1984) 3–36.
———. *Conflict in Luke*. Minneapolis: Augsburg Fortress, 1991.
Klein, Hans. *Das Lukasevangelium*. KEK I/3. Göttingen: Vandenhoeck & Ruprecht, 2006.
Kloppenborg, John S. *Excavating Q: The History and Setting of the Sayings Gospel*. Minneapolis: Fortress, 2000.
———. *Q Parallels: Synopsis, Critical Notes & Concordance*. FF Reference Series. Sonoma, CA: Polebridge, 1988.
———. *The Formation of Q: Trajectories in Ancient Wisdom Collections*. Philadelphia: Fortress, 1987.
Kodell, Jerome. "Luke's Use of *LAOS*, 'People,' Specially in the Jerusalem Narrative (Lk 19,28—24,53)." *CBQ* 31 (1969) 327–43.
Kraeling, Carl H. *John the Baptist*. New York: Scribner, 1951.
Kümmel, Werner Georg. *Introduction to the New Testament*. Translated by Howard Clark Kee. 1973. Nashville: Abingdon, 1975.
———. *Jesu Antwort an Johannes den Täufer: Ein Beispiel zum Methodenproblem der Jesus-forschung*. Wiesbaden: Franz Steiner, 1974.
———. *Promise and Fulfillment: The Eschatological Message of Jesus*. Translated by Dorothea M. Barton. 3rd ed. SBTFS 23. London: SCM, 1961.
Kurz, William S. *Reading Luke-Acts: Dynamics of Biblical Narrative*. Louisville: Westminster John Knox, 1993.
Lagrange, Marie Joseph. *Évangile selon Saint Luc*. 4th ed. EBib. Paris: Gabalda, 1927.
Leaney, Robert. "ΝΟΜΙΚΟΣ in St. Luke's Gospel." *JTS* 2 (1951) 166–67.
Levine, Amy-Jill. "Luke's Pharisees." In *In Quest for the Historical Pharisees*, edited by Jacob Neusner and Bruce D. Chilton, 113–30. Waco, TX: Baylor University Press, 2007.
Linton, Olof. "The Parable of the Children's Game: Baptist and Son of Man (Matt. xi. 16–19 = Luke vii. 31–35): A Synoptic Text-Critical, Structural and Exegetical Investigation." *NTS* 22 (1975–76) 159–79.
Loisy, Alfred. *L'Évangile selon Luc*. Paris: Émile Nourry, 1924.
Lührmann, Dieter. *Die Redaktion der Logienquelle*. WMANT 33. Neukirchen-Vluyn: Neukirchener, 1969.

Lupieri, Edmondo F. *Giovanni Battista fra Storia e Leggenda*. BCR 53. Brescia: Paideia, 1988.
Luz, Ulrich. *Matthew 1–7: A Commentary*. Translated by Wilhelm C. Linss. 1985. Minneapolis: Augsburg Fortress, 1989.
———. *Matthew 8–20: A Commentary*. Translated by James E. Crouch. Hermeneia. Minneapolis: Augsburg Fortress, 2001.
Marcus, Joel. *Mark: A New Translation with Introduction and Commentary*. 2 vols. AB 27, 27A. New York: Doubleday, 2000; New Haven, CT: Yale University Press, 2009.
Marshall, I. Howard. "Son of Man." In *DJG*, 775–81.
———. *The Gospel of Luke*. NIGTC. Grand Rapids: Eerdmans, 1978.
Matera, Frank J. "Jesus' Journey to Jerusalem (Luke 9.51—19.46): A Conflict with Israel." *JSNT* 51 (1993) 57–77.
———. *New Testament Christology*. Louisville: Westminster John Knox, 1999.
———. *New Testament Theology: Exploring Diversity and Unity*. Louisville: Westminster John Knox, 2007.
McComiskey, Douglas S. *Lukan Theology in the Light of the Gospel's Literary Structure*. PBM. Waynesboro, GA: Paternoster, 2004.
McKnight, Scot. "Matthew, Gospel of." In *DJG*, 526–41.
Meier, John P. "Dividing Lines in Jesus Research Today: Through Dialectical Negation to a Positive Sketch." In *Gospel Interpretation: Narrative-Critical & Social-Scientific Approaches*, edited by Jack Dean Kingsbury, 253–72. Harrisburg, PA: Trinity, 1997.
———. *A Marginal Jew: Rethinking the Historical Jesus*. 4 vols. AB Reference Library. New York: Doubleday, 1991–2009.
Meinertz, M. "'Dieses Geschlecht' im Neuen Testament." *BZ* (1957) 283–89.
Metzger, Bruce. *A Textual Commentary on the Greek New Testament*. 2nd ed. New York: UBS, 1994.
Meyer, Rudolf. "ὄχλος." In *TDNT* 5:585–90.
Meyer, Rudolf, and Konrad Weiss. "Φαρισαῖος." In *TDNT* 9:11–48.
Michel, Otto. "τελώνης." In *TDNT* 8:88–105.
Minear, Paul S. "Jesus' Audiences According to Luke." *NovT* 16 (1974) 81–109.
———. "Luke's Use of the Birth Stories." In *Studies in Luke-Acts: Essays Presented in Honor of Paul Schubert*, edited by Leander E. Keck and J. Louis Martyn, 11–30. Nashville: Abingdon, 1966.
Miquel, Esther. *Amigos de Esclavos, Prostitutas y Pecadores: El Significado Sociocultural del Marginado Moral en las Éticas de Jesús y de los Filósofos Cínicos, Epicúreos y Estoicos. Estudio desde la Sicología del Conocimiento*. ABE 47. Navarra: Verbo Divino, 2007.
Moloney, Francis. "The Fourth Gospel and the Jesus of History." *NTS* 46 (2000) 42–58.
———. *The Gospel of Mark: A Commentary*. Peabody, MA: Hendrickson, 2002.
Moore, Ernest. "ΒΙΑΖΩ, ΑΡΠΑΖΩ and Cognates in Josephus." *NTS* 21 (1974–75) 519–43.
Morgan, Teresa. *Literate Education in the Hellenistic and Roman Worlds*. CCS. Cambridge, MA: Cambridge University Press, 1998.
Mowinckel, Sigmund. *He That Cometh*. Translated by G. W. Anderson. Nashville: Abingdon, 1954.
Müller, Christoph Gregor. *Mehr als ein Prophet. Die Charakterzeichnung Johannes des Täufers im lukanischen Erzählwerk*. HBS 31. Freiburg: Herder, 2001.
Müller, Ulrich B. *Johannes der Täufer, jüdischer Prophet und Wegbereiter Jesu*. Leipzig: Evangelische Verlagsanstalt, 2002.
Murphy, Catherine M. *John the Baptist: Prophet of Purity for a New Age*. Collegeville, MN: Liturgical, 2003.

Mussner, Franz. "Der nicht erkannte Kairos (Matt 11,16–19 = Lk 7,31–35)." *Bib* 40 (1959) 599–612.

Neirynck, Frans. "La Rédaction Matthéenne et la structure du premier Évangile." In *De Jésus aux Evangiles*, 41–73. BETL 25. Leuven: Leuven University Press, 1967.

Neusner, Jacob. *The Rabbinic Traditions about the Pharisees before 70. Part III: Conclusions*. Leiden: Brill, 1971.

Nolland, John. "The Role of Money and Possessions in the Parable of the Prodigal Son (Luke 15:11–32): A Test Case." In *Reading Luke: Interpretation, Reflection, Formation*, edited by Craig G. Bartholomew, Joel B. Green, and Anthony C. Thiselton, 178–209. SHS 6. Grand Rapids: Zondervan, 2005.

———. *Luke 1—9:20*. 3 vols. WBC 35A. Colombia: T. Nelson, 1989–93.

———. *The Gospel of Matthew: A Commentary on the Greek Text*. NIGTC. Grand Rapids: Eerdmans, 2005.

O'Rourke, John J. "Asides in the Gospel of John." *NovT* 21 (1979) 210–19.

O'Toole, Robert F. *The Unity of Luke's Theology: An Analysis of Luke Acts*. GNS 9. Wilmington, DE: M. Glazier, 1984.

Origen. *Homilies on Luke*. Translated by Joseph T. Lienhard. FC 94. Washington, DC: Catholic University of America Press, 1996.

Osiek, Carolyn, et al. *A Woman's Place: House Churches in Earliest Christianity*. Minneapolis: Fortress, 2006.

Parsons, Mikeal C. *Luke: Storyteller, Interpreter, Evangelist*. Peabody, MA: Hendrickson, 2007.

Percy, Ernst. *Die Botschaft Jesu: Eine traditionskritische und exegetische Untersuchung*. Lunds Universitets Arsskrif 5. Lund: C. W. K. Gleerup, 1953.

Perrin, Norman. *Rediscovering the Teaching of Jesus*. New York: Harper & Row, 1967.

Phillips, Thomas E. "'Will the Wise Person Get Drunk?' The Background of the Human Wisdom in Luke 7:35 and Matthew 11:19." *JBL* 127 (2008) 385–96.

Plummer, Alfred. *A Critical and Exegetical Commentary on the Gospel According to S. Luke*. 5th ed. ICC. Edinburgh: T. & T. Clark, 1901.

Poirier, John C. "Jesus as an Elijianic Figure in Luke 4:16–30." *CBQ* 71 (2009) 349–63.

Powell, Mark Allan. *What Is Narrative Criticism?* GBS. Minneapolis: Fortress, 1990.

———. "The Religious Leaders in Luke: A Literary-Critical Study." *JBL* 109 (1990) 93–110.

Puech, Émile. *Qumran Cave 4. XVIII: Textes hébreux (4Q521–4Q528, 4Q576–4Q579)*. DJD 25. Oxford: Clarendon, 1998.

Quintilian. *The Orator's Education*. Vol. 2: *Books 3–5*. Edited and translated by Donald A. Russell. LCL 125. Cambridge, MA: Harvard University Press, 2001.

Rawson, Beryl. *Children and Childhood in Roman Italy*. Oxford: Oxford University Press, 2003.

Reid, B. A. "Violent Endings in Matthew's Parables and Christian Nonviolence." *CBQ* 66 (2004) 237–55.

Rengstorf, Karl Heinrich. "σημεῖον." In *TDNT* 7:208–61.

Resseguie, James L. *Narrative Criticism of the New Testament: An Introduction*. Grand Rapids: Baker Academic, 2005.

Robbins, Vernon K. "From Enthymeme to Theology in Luke 11:1–13." In *Literary Studies in Luke-Acts: Essays in Honor of Joseph B. Tyson*, edited by Richard P. Thompson and Thomas E. Phillips, 191–214. Macon, GA: Mercer University Press, 1998.

———. "Progymnastic Rhetorical Composition and Pre-Gospel Traditions: A New Approach." In *The Synoptic Gospels: Source Criticism and the New Literary Criticism*, edited by Camille Focant, 111–47. BETL 110. Leuven: Leuven University Press, 1993.

Robinson, A. T. "Elijah, John, and Jesus: An Essay in Detection." *NTS* 4 (1957–58) 263–81.
Robinson, James M., et al. *The Critical Edition of Q*. Hermeneia. Minneapolis: Fortress, 2000.
Roth, S. John. *The Blind, the Lame, and Poor: Character Types in Luke-Acts*. JSNTSup 144. Sheffield: Sheffield Academic, 1997.
Sabugal, Santo. *La Embajada Mesiánica de Juan Bautista (Mt 11:2–6=Lc 7:18–23): Historia, Exégesis Teológica, Hermenéutica*. Madrid: Systeco, 1980.
Saldarini, Anthony J. *Pharisees, Scribes, and Sadducees in Palestinian Society: A Sociological Approach*. Wilmington, DE: M. Glazier, 1988.
Sanders, E. P. *Jesus and Judaism*. Philadelphia: Fortress, 1985.
———. *Tendencies of the Synoptic Tradition*. SNTSMS 9. Cambridge, MA: Cambridge University Press, 1969.
Sanders, Jack T. *The Jews in Luke-Acts*. Philadelphia: Fortress, 1987.
Sanders, James A. "From Isaiah 61 to Luke 4." In *Christianity, Judaism and Other Greco-Roman Cults: Studies for Morton Smith at Sixty*, edited by Jacob Neusner, 1:75–106. SJLA 12. Leiden: Brill, 1975.
Satterthwaite, Philip E. "Acts against the Background of Classical Rhetoric." In *The Book of Acts in Its First-Century Setting*, edited by Bruce W. Winter, 1:337–79. Grand Rapids: Eerdmans, 1993.
Schanz, Paul. *Commentar über das Evangelium des heiligen Lucas*. Tübingen: Franz Fues, 1883.
Schmid, Josef. *Das Evangelium nach Matthäus*. RNT 1. Regensburg: Friedrich Pustet, 1965.
Schmidt, Thomas E. *Hostility to Wealth in the Synoptic Gospels*. JSNTSup 15. Sheffield: Sheffield Academic, 1987.
Schnackenburg, Rudolph. *God's Rule and Kingdom*. 2nd ed. New York: Herder, 1968.
———. *Jesus in the Gospels: A Biblical Christology*. Translated by O. C. Jean Jr. 1993. Louisville: Westminster John Knox, 1995.
Schneider, Carl. "μάστιξ." In *TDNT*. 4:518–19.
Schnelle, Udo. *The History and Theology of the New Testament Writings*. Translated by M. Eugene Boring. 1994. Minneapolis: Fortress, 1998.
Schrenk, Gottlob. "δίκαιος." In *TDNT* 2:182–225.
Schulz, Siegfried. "Gottes Vorsehung bei Lukas." *ZNW* 54 (1963) 104–16.
———. *Q. Die Spruchquelle der Evangelisten*. Zürich: Theologischer, 1972.
Schürmann, Heinz. *Das Lukas Evangelium: Kommentar zu Kap. 1,1—9,50*. 3 vols. HTKNT 1. Breisgau: Herder, 1969.
Schüssler Fiorenza, Elisabeth. *Jesus: Miriam's Child, Sophia's Prophet. Critical Issues in Feminist Christology*. New York: Continuum, 1995.
Scobie, Charles Hugh Hope. *John the Baptist*. Philadelphia: Fortress, 1964.
Scott, Martin. *Sophia and the Johannine Jesus*. JSNTSup 71. Sheffield: Sheffield Academic, 1992.
Seesemann, Heinrich. "πειρασμός." In *TDNT* 6:23–36.
Sheeley, Steven M. *Narrative Asides in Luke-Acts*. JSNTSup 72. Sheffield: Sheffield Academic, 1992.
Spencer, Patrick E. *Rhetorical Texture and Narrative Trajectories of the Lukan Galilean Ministry Speeches: Hermeneutical Appropriation by Authorial Readers of Luke-Acts*. LNTS 341. New York: T. & T. Clark, 2007.
Squires, John T. *The Plan of God in Luke-Acts*. SNTSMS 76. New York: Cambridge University Press, 1993.

Strathmann, H. "λαός." In *TDNT* 4:50–57.
Talbert, Charles H. *Literary Patterns, Theological Themes and the Genre of Luke-Acts.* SBLMS 20. Missoula, MT: Scholars, 1974.
Tannehill, Robert C. "Israel in Luke-Acts: A Tragic Story." *JBL* 104 (1985) 69–85.
———. *The Narrative Unity of Luke-Acts: A Literary Interpretation.* 2 vols. FF. Philadelphia: Fortress, 1986, 1990.
Taylor, Joan E. *The Immerser: John the Baptist within Second Temple Judaism.* Grand Rapids: Eerdmans, 1997.
Tenney, Merrill C. "The Footnotes of John's Gospel." *BSac* 117 (1960) 350–64.
Theissen, Gerd. "Das 'schwankende Rohr' in Mt 11,7 und die Grundungsmünzen von Tiberias." In *Lokalkolorit und Zeitgeschichte in den Evangelien. Ein Beitrag zur Geschichte der synoptischen Tradition*, 26–44. NTOA 8. Göttingen: Vandenhoeck & Ruprecht, 1989.
Tuckett, C. M. *Q and the History of Early Christianity: Studies on Q.* Edinburgh: T. & T. Clark, 1996.
Tyson, Joseph B. "Conflict as a Literary Theme in the Gospel of Luke." In *New Synoptic Studies: The Cambridge Gospel Conference and Beyond*, edited by William R. Farmer, 303–27. Macon, GA: Mercer University Press, 1983.
———. "The Jewish Public in Luke-Acts." *NTS* 30 (1984) 574–83.
Vermes, Geza, translator and editor. *The Complete Dead Sea Scrolls in English.* 4th ed. New York: Penguin, 2004.
Vinson, Richard B. "A Comparative Study of the Use of Enthymemes in the Synoptic Gospels." In *Persuasive Artistry: Studies in New Testament Rhetoric in Honor of George A. Kennedy*, edited by Duane F. Watson, 119–41. JSNTSup 50. Sheffield: Sheffield Academic, 1991.
Viviano, Benedict T. "The Least in the Kingdom: Matthew 11:11, Its Parallel in Luke 7:28 (Q), and Daniel 4:14. *CBQ* 62 (2000) 41–54.
Vögtle, Anton. "Wunder und Wort in Urchristlicher Glaubenswerbung (Mt 11,2–6=Lk 7,18–23)." In *Das Evangelium und die Evangelien: Beiträge zur Evangelienforschung.* KBANT. Düsseldorf: Patmos, 1971.
Wallace, Daniel B. *Greek Grammar beyond the Basics; An Exegetical Syntax of the New Testament.* Grand Rapids: Zondervan, 1996.
Webb, Robert L. *John the Baptizer and Prophet: A Socio-Historical Study.* 1991. Reprint, Eugene, OR: Wipf & Stock, 2006.
Weiss, Johannes. *Die Predigt Jesu vom Reiche Gottes.* 2nd ed. Göttingen: Vandenhoeck & Ruprecht, 1900.
Wellhausen, Julius. *Einleitung in die drei ersten Evangelien.* Berlin: Georg Reimer, 1905.
Wendling, E. "Synoptische Studien, III: die Anfrage des Täufers und das Zeugnis über den Täufer." *ZNW* 10 (1909) 46–58.
Wink, Walter. *John the Baptist in the Gospel Tradition.* SNTSMS 7. Cambridge, MA: Cambridge University Press, 1968.
Yamasaki, Gary. *John the Baptist in Life and Death: Audience-Oriented Criticism of Matthew's Narrative.* JSNTSup 167. Sheffield: Sheffield Academic, 1998.
Zeller, Dieter. "Die Bildlogik des Gleichnisses Mt 11,16f./Lk 7,31f." *ZNW* 68 (1977) 252–57.
Ziesler, J. A. "Luke and the Pharisees." In *From Politics to Piety: The Emergence of Pharisaic Judaism*, edited by Jacob Neusner, 161–72. 2nd ed. New York: KTAV, 1979.

Index of Subjects

Adversaries (opponents, antagonists), 108, 141n49, 145n62, 153, 158–59
Allegory (allegorical interpretations), 3n5, 6n21, 16n86, 23, 33n187, 151n85, 152n89
Angel(s), 2, 4, 7n26, 92–93, 95, 115, 116, 117, 121, 123, 139, 147
Apocalyptic, 10, 99, 156n105, 191
Apologetic motif, 181–83
Apothegm, 33, 109
Ascetic (austerity), 50, 52n30, 92, 114–15, 123, 156–60

Baptism, 96n47, 98, 139–45, 175n7, 186, 188–89, 193n48
Beatitude (blessed), 106–12, 177, 182
Blasphemy (Scandal), 106–9 esp. n. 91

Characterization(s), 92n38, 99, 105n83, 115–18, 137–39, 145n62, 187n30, 191
Children, 151–65
Christian Communities 40–41, 43, 94n40, 119n126
Compassion, 47, 67–69, 94, 175, 176n9
Conflict, 56, 71, 73–74, 75, 107–9, 143–45
Confrontation, 16, 67, 73, 75n112, 142, 145
Contradiction, 40, 107, 169
Controversies, 16, 17, 43, 150

Disciples 91–94, 101–6, 188–95
Divine, 146–49, 162–63
Doubt, 7, 8, 12, 21, 23, 26, 38, 100, 175

Editorial activity (transpositions, additions, and omissions), 46, 58, 60, 63n68, 70nn94–95, 82, 83n12, 131, 171–73
Ekphrasis (Ecphrasis), 39n220, 47, 115n114
Elijah, 17, 52–53, 102n70, 115–17, 126
Enthymeme, 39, 109–10, 177
Envy, 5, 6, 108n96
Eschatological, 94n43, 95n44, 96n47, 97, 98, 99, 100, 123, 176, 185
Essenes, 18, 192
Evil forces (demons, devil, Beelzebul), 72, 96, 157–59, 190

Fasting, 161, 190
Fine garments (clothing), 114–15, 190

Galilean ministry, 61–63, 67–73
Good news, 99n54, 105, 118n125
Gospel of John, 51n27, 188, 189, 192–94
Gospel of Matthew, 50, 52, 125, 175, 176, 189

Harmonization, 6n21, 8, 21, 59, 83n14, 85n18, 195
Healing, 102–5
Herod Antipas, 70, 71, 72, 73, 113n109, 190, 191
Historical Jesus, 9, 19, 34, 188n33,
Historical-critical methods, 2, 9–21, 40–41
Holy Spirit, 140, 141
Hostility, 51n26, 74, 76, 143–45

Identity of Jesus, 62–64, 67–73, 94–104, 173–76
Ignorance, 4, 12, 21, 36, 94, 97, 100, 186, 193
Illnesses (infirmities, diseases), 46, 102–05, 112
Incredulity, 3n8, 107
Indictment, 23, 55, 60, 149, 150, 156, 180, 196
Infancy narratives, 41, 92–93, 95–96, 113, 116–19, 136, 139, 141, 147
Israel, 56, 64, 65, 66, 95, 136–37, 151, 154n98, 184

Jesus
  Baptism, 96, 98n49, 148, 182, 186, 189, 193n48.
  Birth, 95, 97, 147
  Lord, 31, 94n41, 95
  Messiah, 14, 15, 27n154, 33, 52n33, 95, 99, 106n88, 118, 146, 191–92, 193n50, 194
  Ministry, 21, 47, 62–73, 91–97, 102–3
  Parallels to John, 189–90
  Relationship to John, 186–90
  Savior, 95, 96
  Son of God, 72, 73, 96, 193
  Son of Man, 160n117
Jewish religious leaders, 54, 63, 64, 68–75, 141–67
John the Baptist
  beheading (death), 16, 119n130
  birth, 73n105, 92–93
  eating and drinking habits, 157–62
  forerunner (precursor), 52n33, 53, 56n45, 116–18
  greatness, 119–20
  imprisonment, 45n8, 91, 93, 98, 114n111, 122n139, 123, 176n10, 185, 188
  message (proclamation), 99, 118n125, 175–76, 191–92
  prophet, 116–18
  Relationship to Jesus, 100, 119, 186–87
Journey to Jerusalem, 53, 62n64, 72–73
Judgment, 65n79, 66, 67, 94, 96n47, 98, 99, 140, 176, 191–92

Kingdom of God, 119–23, 178–79, 184–85

Lamb of God, 1, 189, 193
Law (Mosaic), 3, 4, 8, 21, 51–54, 126–27, 138n44, 139–40, 159
Least, 119–23
Literary context, 40, 61–79, 133, 170
Literary skills, 47, 80–81, 179

Messengers, 103–6, 112, 164n131
Messianic Apocalypse, 191–92
Messianic expectation, 10, 11, 12, 13, 18, 21, 23, 31, 34, 95n44, 96, 106n106, 191–92
Metaphor, 16n86, 32n180, 99, 102n69, 156
Mighty deeds (mighty works, works of wonder), 12, 16, 32, 70n96, 102–6, 108n94, 176, 195
Moral exhortations, 3, 5, 7, 138, 146, 176n9
Moses, 2, 164

Narrative comment, 88, 131–34, 136, 149, 153, 179, 195

Index of Subjects

Narrative-critical, 2, 29, 41, 81, 168–69
Narrative styles, 66, 80n1, 89, 90, 132, 176n9
Negative reactions, 29, 64, 174

Parable, 16n86, 33, 69, 74, 76, 77, 114, 130, 138n42, 151–56
Patristic writers, 2–8
"People of this generation," 151–53
People (multitudes, crowds), 112–13, 136–38
Pharisees, 108, 138, 141–45
Plan of God, 145–48
Polemic, 78, 119n126, 181–83
Poor (downtrodden, outcasts), 7, 35, 50, 67, 104–6 esp. n. 83
Positive reactions, 55, 64, 67, 140
Prayer, 69, 73, 92, 113, 136, 190
Progymnasmata, 82, 92, 102, 103, 109, 115, 134, 158
Prologue, 41, 92, 147–48
Prophetic (figure, expectations, claims), 39, 95–97, 99, 106, 108, 116–18

Q, 42–44

Redactional (stylistic) tendencies, 40, 44, 46, 47, 50–51, 54n41, 61, 70n94, 78, 97–98, 125–27, 176
Rejection, 54–56, 64, 137–38, 143–45, 152–53
Repentance (conversion), 34, 66, 77, 96, 118, 101, 118, 140, 143n54, 148
Rhetorical, 36, 39, 64, 80–82, 88–89, 109, 112–17, 134–35, 151–53
Righteousness, 52, 139–40

Salvation, 95, 98–100, 105, 146, 156, 161–62, 184–85
Scholars of the Law, 141–45
Sectarian disciples, 15, 19, 24, 41, 92n37, 119n126
Sinners, 138–42, 159–63
"Stronger one," 94, 96n47, 97, 118
Stürmmerspruch, 126–31
Subordination, 4, 6, 8, 15, 97, 120, 123, 182, 183
Superiority, 4, 5, 18, 37, 108, 119, 185
Synkrisis, 38, 39, 115n114
Synoptic problem, 22, 42–43

Temple, 17, 95, 136, 145
"The one who is to come," 93–97
Theological (perspective, theme), 15, 46, 129, 131, 135, 136, 139n46,
Toll collectors, 138–41
Tradition(s), 9, 12, 15, 19, 34, 43, 58, 80n1, 126, 128, 131, 156n104, 192

Warning, 9, 34, 106–9, 177
Wealth and riches, 50
Wilderness (desert), 13, 113–15, 158, 188, 189
Wisdom, 149, 150, 154n98, 159, 162–65
Witnesses, 94n40, 104, 112, 165, 181
Words and deeds, 47n14, 67, 69–70, 72, 174, 190, 192

Index of Authors

Achtemeier, Paul J., 69, 100, 108
Aletti, Jean-Noël, 67, 71, 73, 96
Algasia, 1, 195
Allison, D. C., Jr., 51–52
Alter, Robert, 81–82, 87, 88, 101, 110, 196
Ambrosius, 3–4, 156
Anderson, Garwood P., 78
Anderson, Paul N., 188, 193
Aristotle, 109, 113, 120
Aune, David E., 81, 109, 147

Backhaus, Knut, 46, 59, 78
Bacon, Benjamin W., 62–63, 74–76
Bakke, Odd Magne, 154
Beare, Francis Wright, 66, 128
Becker, Jürgen, 99, 110, 184, 190
Bede Venerabilis, 5–6
Bird, Michael F., 110
Black, David Alan, 43
Böcher, Otto, 157
Böhlemann, Peter, 37, 119, 121
Bonaventure, 6–7
Boucher, Madeline, 152
Bovon, François, 28–29, 50, 59, 64, 83, 86, 90, 94, 99, 110, 132, 145, 155–59, 164
Bowker, J., 141
Brawley, Robert, 96, 101, 108, 112, 137–38
Brodie, Thomas L., 42, 102
Broshi, Magen, 161
Brown, Raymond E., 62, 117, 119, 154, 155, 159, 163, 181, 193

Büchsel, Friedrich, 119
Bultmann, Rudolph, 16, 33, 43–44, 54, 58–59, 87, 99, 119, 130, 170, 180, 182
Burnyeat, M. F., 109
Busse, Ulrich, 67, 106, 108

Cadbury, Henry J., 47, 54, 80–82, 146
Calvin, John, 7–8
Cameron, Peter Scott, 126–28
Cameron, Ron, 109
Caragounis, C. C., 51, 121, 127
Carroll, John T., 141
Carson, D. A., 162
Carter, Warren, 65, 75
Collins, John J., 192
Coloe, Mary, 193
Conzelmann, Hans, 47, 54, 56, 98–99, 117–18, 122, 145, 184–85
Cotter, W. J., 151, 153
Craghan, John F., 84, 94, 102
Crossan, John Dominic, 128
Culpepper, Alan R., 103–4
Cyril of Alexandria, 4–5

Dahl, Nils, 136
Danker, Frederick W., 81
Darr, John A., 36, 92, 97–98, 100, 110, 115, 141, 158
Davies, W. D., 51
Demetrius, 109
Dibelius, Franz, 120

Dibelius, Martin, 9–10, 16, 23, 34, 43–44, 46, 87, 92, 98, 100, 127, 148, 151, 157, 164, 170, 176
Dillon, R. J., 147
Doble, Peter, 139
Donahue, John R., 138
Du Plessis, I. J., 88
Dunn, James D. G., 106–7, 110, 160–61, 176, 187–90
Dupont, Jaques, 12–13, 94, 104, 105

Easton, Burton, 128
Ernst, Josef, 15–17, 43, 46, 50, 53, 58–59, 92, 99, 126–27, 158

Faierstein, Morris M., 52
Fitzmyer, Joseph A., 27, 42–43, 46, 49–52, 54–56, 59, 62–65, 67–68, 70, 72–73, 80–81, 88, 93, 95–96, 99, 105–8, 112–14, 117–18, 120, 122, 126, 128, 131–32, 138, 141, 143–46, 151, 154–57, 159–61, 164–65, 178–79, 185, 187, 192
Flender, Helmut, 105
Foerster, Werner, 159
Fohrer, Georg, 164
Foster, Robert, 51, 127
France, R. T., 43, 51, 65, 75–77

Gagnon, Robert A. J., 50, 63, 155
Gathercole, Simon, 162
George, Augustin, 136, 137
Gnilka, Joachim, 141
Goguel, Maurice, 10–11
Goodacre, Mark, 42
Goulder, Michael, 42
Grangaard, Blake R., 74, 141
Green, Joel B., 29–30, 62, 69–70, 72, 87–88, 90, 94, 101–3, 105, 116, 134, 139, 143, 154, 164
Grundmann, Walter, 147

Haenchen, Ernst, 92, 176
Hahn, Scott W., 121

Harnack, Aldolf von, 23, 34, 128
Hartmann, Michael, 62
Hauck, F., 107
Hawkins, John C., 128
Heil, John Paul, 74, 142, 157, 160, 162
Hoffman, Paul, 16, 44, 46, 47, 50, 51, 53, 58–59, 66, 126–27, 153
Holladay, Carl R., 62
Hollenbach, Paul W., 94

Jerome, 1, 80, 195
Jeremias, Jacob, 94
Jeremias, Joachim, 33, 105, 151, 154, 162, 164
Jervell, Jacob, 137
Johnson, Luke Timothy, 78, 99, 105, 137, 173
Josephus, 191, 94

Karris, Robert J., 50, 115, 160–61
Kazmierski, Carl R., 17–18, 99–100
Kee, Howard C., 161
Keefer, Kyle, 77, 81, 179
Kennedy, George A., 82, 109
Kilgallen, John J., 153
Kilpatrick, G. D., 141
Kingsbury, Jack Dean, 74, 76, 107, 112, 137, 141, 143–45
Klein, Hans, 30, 59, 62, 93, 120, 131, 136
Kloppenborg, John S., 42, 53–54, 126, 128, 151
Kodell, Jerome, 136
Kraeling, Carl H., 11
Kümmel, Werner Georg, 34–35, 42, 46, 62–63, 70, 182
Kurz, William S., 81, 110

Lagrange, Marie Joseph, 23, 132
Leaney, Robert, 141
Levine, Amy-Jill, 141
Linton, Olof, 151, 154, 156
Loisy, Alfred, 23–24

Index of Authors

Lührmann, Dieter, 44, 46, 49, 55, 58, 60, 87, 128
Lupieri, Edmondo F., 107
Luz, Ulrich, 51, 52, 53, 56, 61, 65, 66, 67, 75, 76, 77, 126, 127

Marcus, Joel, 191
Marshall, I. Howard, 26, 46-47, 50, 54, 58-59, 85, 93, 113-15, 117, 119, 128, 144, 147, 159-60, 164
Matera, Frank J., 51, 55, 62, 65, 67, 71, 75-77, 82, 96, 140, 145-46
McComiskey, Douglas S., 72
McKnight, Scot, 51, 52, 121, 127
Meyer, Rudolf, 105, 137, 141
Meier, John P., 19, 42, 54, 99, 126-27, 130, 140-41, 151, 155-57, 163-65, 176, 186-88, 190, 193
Meinertz, M., 152
Metzger, Bruce, 83, 85-86
Michel, Otto, 138
Minear, Paul S., 136, 147
Miquel, Esther, 159
Moloney, Francis, 70, 188-89
Moore, Ernest, 51
Morgan, Teresa, 82
Mowinckel, Sigmund, 193
Müller, Christoph Gregor, 38, 73, 82, 92, 99, 143, 196
Müller, Ulrich B., 20
Murphy, Catherine M., 21
Mussner, Franz, 151, 154, 165

Neirynck, Frans, 75
Neusner, Jacob, 141
Nolland, John, 27-28, 46, 50-51, 53, 58-59, 62-63, 65, 76, 88, 90, 98, 112, 114-115, 117-20, 122, 128, 131-32, 139, 143-44, 152, 155-56, 158, 163-65, 179, 191
O'Rourke, John J., 132

O'Toole, Robert F., 47, 55, 59, 68, 71-72, 145
Origen, 2-3
Osiek, Carolyn, 155

Parsons, Mikeal C., 47, 64, 68, 80, 82, 155
Percy, Ernst, 32, 70
Perrin, Norman, 151, 162
Phillips, Thomas E., 162-64
Plummer, Alfred, 24, 83, 85-86, 102, 132, 151, 153, 164
Poirier, John C., 105-6, 117
Powell, Mark Allan, 81, 141, 144
Puech, Émile, 106, 191

Quintilian, 109

Rawson, Beryl, 155
Reid, B. A., 51
Rengstorf, Karl Heinrich, 108
Resseguie, James L., 81
Robbins, Vernon K., 82, 109
Robinson, A. T., 52
Robinson, James M., 42, 46, 50, 58-59, 63, 128, 158
Roth, S. John, 37, 89, 101, 103-5, 110, 113, 137

Sabugal, Santo, 15, 43, 46, 94, 100, 102, 104, 107
Saldarini, Anthony J., 141
Sanders, E. P., 43, 47, 138, 160
Sanders, Jack T., 141, 145
Sanders, James A., 106
Satterthwaite, Philip E., 82
Schanz, Paul, 22
Schmid, Josef, 65
Schmidt, Thomas E., 50, 115
Schnackenburg, Rudolph, 32, 70, 185
Schneider, Carl, 102
Schnelle, Udo, 42, 62, 75
Schrenk, Gottlob, 139

Schulz, Siegfried, 145, 183
Schürmann, Heinz, 25–26, 46, 54, 59, 105, 114, 128, 131–32, 151, 158
Schüssler Fiorenza, Elisabeth, 164
Scobie, Charles Hugh Hope, 13
Scott, Martin, 164
Seesemann, Heinrich, 159
Sheeley, Steven M., 54, 132, 134
Spencer, Patrick E., 39, 101, 113, 115, 117, 120, 144, 153, 156
Squires, John T., 55, 108, 145–46, 147–48
Strathmann, H., 105, 136–37

Talbert, Charles H., 70, 72, 80, 108
Tannehill, Robert C., 35–36, 64, 71, 74, 87, 89, 99, 100, 104–5, 112, 117–18, 137, 145, 179
Taylor, Joan E., 18–19, 99, 110, 120, 140, 143, 183

Tenney, Merrill C., 132
Theissen, Gerd, 113
Tuckett, C. M., 42
Tyson, Joseph B., 137, 143

Vermes, Geza, 192
Vinson, Richard B., 109
Viviano, Benedict T., 119–20, 185
Vögtle, Anton, 34

Wallace, Daniel B., 120
Webb, Robert L., 17, 96, 99, 117, 140
Weiss, Johannes, 128
Weiss, Konrad, 141
Wellhausen, Julius, 31
Wink, Walter, 14, 52, 78, 98, 102, 116–17, 118, 122, 128, 179, 181, 183, 196

Zeller, Dieter, 151
Ziesler, J. A., 141

Index of Scripture and Other Ancient Writings

OLD TESTAMENT

Exodus
12:26	156
23:20	50, 117, 191

Deuteronomy
6:20	156
17:6	94
18:15	108
18:18	108
19:15	94
21:18–21	161
21:20	161
32:25	152

Joshua
4:6	156
4:21	156

Judges
2:10	152

1 Samuel
2:21	163
2:26	163

1 Kings
12:22	116

2 Kings
2:11	117

Job
11:2	119
11:12	119
14:1	119
15:14	119
25:4	119
28	164

Psalms
8:3	5
16:8	114
78:8	152

Proverbs
1:20–33	164
8:1—9:6	164
8:32	165
23:20–21	161

Isaiah
1:2–4	154
7:11	108
7:14–17	193
16:10	156
26:19	192
29:18–19	105
29:18	192
30:1	154
35:5–6	105, 192
38:4	116
40:3–5	98
40:3	191
42:7	192

Isaiah (cont.)

42:18	105, 192
43:8	105
61:1–2	192
61:1	36, 105–6

Jeremiah

1:4	116
2:31	152
7:34	156
16:9	156
25:10	156
48:33	156

Ezekiel

1:3	116
26:13	156

Daniel

7:1	160
7:13	193

Joel

2:12–13	5

Jonah

1:1	116

Micah

1:1	116

Zechariah

1:1	116

Malachi

3:1	50, 117–18, 191, 193
3:23–24	117
3:24	154

APOCRYPHA AND SEPTUAGINT

Baruch

3:4	164

1 Esdras

7:28	193
13:32	193

2 Maccabees

15:9	127

Sirach

1:1	127
1:24	164
4:11	165

Wisdom of Solomon

7:22—11:1	164

NEW TESTAMENT

Matthew

1:1–2:23	75
3:1—4:11	75
3:1–17	98
3:1–12	190
3:1	95
3:2	51–52, 191
3:7–12	141, 191
3:7	144
3:8–10	189
3:11	35, 76
3:12	189
3:13–17	186
3:13	98
3:14–15	97, 169, 186, 189, 194
3:15	140, 186
3:17	189
4:1–2	190
4:12–25	75
4:12	76

Index of Scripture and Other Ancient Writings

Matthew (cont.)

Reference	Pages
4:13	67
4:17	51
4:23	75–76
4:24–25	69
5:1—7:29	46, 76
5:1—7:29	75
5:1—7:27	69
5:17–19	51
5:17	127
5:20	51
5:46	138
6:5–14	190
6:18	190
7:12	127
7:16–19	189
8:1—9:38	76
8:1—9:34	46, 75
8:1–4	68, 76
8:5–13	62
8:11	162
8:14–15	68
8:16–17	68
9:1–8	68
9:2–8	76
9:9–13	69
9:10–13	76
9:10–11	138
9:14–17	69
9:14	76
9:15	190
9:18–26	63, 76
9:27–31	76
9:35—11:1	75
9:35	75, 76
10:1–42	65–66, 76
10:1–4	69
10:3	138
11:1	65–66
11:2–19	2, 42–45, 52, 60, 64–67, 75, 77–78, 81, 87, 125, 131, 163, 168, 170–71, 181, 186
11:2–11	171
11:2–6	11, 44, 46, 87, 102, 171, 188, 193
11:2	45, 51, 59, 76, 91, 94, 127, 189, 193
11:3	52, 83
11:4–6	47
11:4–5	192
11:4	102, 104
11:5–6	43, 171
11:5	63, 76
11:6	60, 170–71, 194
11:7–19	9
11:7–15	44, 48, 87, 171
11:7–11	48, 61, 170–71
11:7–10	49
11:7–8	60
11:7	49, 112–13
11:8	114, 190
11:10	50, 60
11:11	49, 50, 83, 122, 124
11:12–19	172
11:12–15	50–51, 53–54, 56, 60–61, 124–26, 128, 131, 135, 171–72
11:12–13	19, 51, 126, 172, 184
11:13	122, 127
11:14	46, 51–52, 119, 126, 192
11:15	126
11:16–24	53
11:16–19	44, 57, 87, 170–72
11:16	57, 58, 65, 153
11:18–19	58, 156–58
11:18	157, 190
11:19	22, 76, 86, 138, 161, 170, 171
11:20—16:12	75
11:20–24	65–67, 76
11:22	65
11:24	65
11:25–27	65–66
11:28–30	65–66
12:1–8	69, 76
12:9–14	69, 76
12:14	65

Isaiah (cont.)		Mark	
12:18	65	1:2–8	190
12:20	65	1:2–3	191
12:22–29	76	1:2	62
12:30–37	76	1:3	118
12:36	65	1:4–11	186
12:38–42	76	1:4–5	189
12:41	65	1:4	189
12:42	65	1:5	141
13:1–23	76	1:6	128, 157, 190
13:9	126	1:7	181
13:11	77	1:7–8	31
13:13	65, 77	1:9–11	11, 186
13:16	47	1:9	98, 128, 182, 186, 188
13:24	77	1:10–11	188
13:31	77	1:12–15	188
13:33	77	1:12	189
13:43	126	1:14—9:41	70
13:44	77	1:14	190
13:45	77	1:16–20	68
13:47	77	1:16	67
13:51	77	1:21—3:19	69
13:52	77	1:21–28	68
13:53–58	67	1:29–31	68
13:54–58	76	1:35–39	68
13:57	65	1:40–45	68
14:33	65	2:1–12	68
16:13–20:34	76	2:13–17	68
16:14	190	2:15	138
16:16	65	2:17	162
17:13	126	2:18–22	68
18:17	138	2:18	128–29, 189
19:12	190	2:23—3:6	68
21:1—25:46	76	3:5	142
21:9	76	3:7–12	69
21:31–32	22, 54, 125, 129–31, 135, 138	3:13–19	189
		3:22	190
21:32	52, 190	3:28–30	159
22:24	127	3:31–35	70
25:29	126	4:1—9:40	70
26:1—28:15	76	4:7–8	189
26:6–13	63	4:9	126
26:71–73	194	4:26–34	70
28:16–20	76	4:26–29	189
28:19	189	4:35—6:44	70

Mark (cont.)

6:1–6	67, 70, 194
6:8–9	190
6:14–16	32
6:17–29	70, 128–29, 182
6:17	188
6:18	190
6:45—8:26	70, 105
7:16	126
7:31–37	105
8:15	190
8:28	126, 190
8:31	190
9:9–13	128–29, 182
9:11–13	70
9:31	190
10:32–34	190
12:2	189
13:28–32	190
14:3–9	63
14:43—15:39	190
14:70	194
15:35	128, 182
15:36	128

Luke

1:1	150
1:1–4	61–62, 73, 78, 92
1:3	64
1:4	174, 183
1:5—2:52	55, 61–62, 73
1:6	139
1:7	93
1:10	136
1:11–20	147
1:13–17	147
1:13	92–93
1:14–17	93
1:15–17	114–15
1:15	74, 119, 157, 159
1:17	51–52, 70, 95, 116–18, 126, 137, 139, 141, 153–54, 158–59, 184
1:18	93
1:20	148
1:21	136
1:24	147
1:25	93
1:26–28	146
1:30–33	95
1:32	119
1:33	121
1:36–37	93
1:36	93
1:39–56	38
1:40–45	186
1:41	93
1:43	95, 118
1:44	93, 97, 114
1:45	107, 146
1:48	120, 152
1:50	152
1:52–53	120
1:59–64	93
1:60–64	147
1:60	92
1:63	92
1:66	93
1:67	93
1:68	137
1:69	95
1:75	139
1:76–77	35, 93, 114, 159
1:76	70, 93, 95, 116, 118, 184
1:77	137, 141
1:80	93, 97, 113, 115, 158, 163, 186
2:9–14	95, 147
2:10	137
2:11	94, 146
2:17	95
2:20	139
2:23	117, 149
2:25	139
2:26–32	147
2:26	94, 96
2:29–32	95
2:31–32	137

Luke (cont.)		3:19–20	45, 70, 73–74, 98, 143, 187
2:34–35	74, 95, 147	3:20	91–92, 175
2:34	107	3:21—4:30	62
2:38	95	3:21—4:13	62
2:39	97, 186	3:21–22	98
2:40	163	3:21	98, 137, 140, 182
2:46	154	3:22	37, 96, 148, 187
2:49	147	4:1–13	159
2:51	97, 186	4:1	113
2:52	163	4:2–4	161
3:1—4:13	62	4:2	158
3:1–22	186	4:3	96, 158–59
3:1–20	61, 114	4:4	117
3:1–18	73, 98, 176	4:6	158
3:1	185	4:8	117
3:2–3	93	4:9	96, 159
3:2	92, 113, 115–16, 158	4:12	117
3:3–18	116, 155	4:13—9:50	96
3:3	133, 140	4:13–37	68
3:4–6	98, 147	4:13	149, 158
3:4	62, 93, 113, 115, 117–18, 158	4:14—9:50	47, 61–62, 70–71, 129, 173
3:6	146, 176, 181	4:14–30	39
3:7–18	141, 143	4:14–15	62, 67, 141
3:7–15	93	4:16—9:50	103
3:7–14	140	4:16—7:17	72, 94, 155
3:7–9	94, 191	4:16–30	62, 67, 70, 76, 103, 106, 108, 111, 176, 194
3:7	105, 112, 137, 140, 148, 187	4:17–30	142
3:8–9	99	4:18–21	70, 146
3:8	154, 176	4:18–19	47, 67–68, 72
3:10–14	98, 118, 176	4:18	37, 120
3:10	105, 112, 137	4:21	148
3:11	115	4:22	68, 71, 97, 100, 112, 175
3:12–13	160	4:23–27	71
3:12	133, 138, 140	4:24–27	116
3:15–16	181	4:28–29	74
3:15	92, 96, 100, 118–19, 137, 187	4:28	68, 149
3:16–17	94, 96, 118, 191	4:31—7:17	105
3:16	25, 36, 92–93, 96, 140	4:31–6:19	69
3:17	99	4:31–32	141
3:18	99, 118, 137, 175–76	4:33–36	159
		4:33–35	103

Index of Scripture and Other Ancient Writings

Luke (cont.)

Reference	Pages
4:34	96, 159
4:35	72
4:36–37	141
4:36	68, 71, 97, 158, 175
4:38–39	68, 103
4:40–42	105
4:40–41	68, 102
4:40	46, 68
4:41	37, 72, 96, 159
4:42–44	68
4:42	113, 137
4:43	121, 147, 148
4:44	141
4:48	30
5:1–11	68
5:1	105, 112, 137, 141
5:3	112, 137
5:8	94, 138
5:9	68
5:10	152
5:15	137, 141
5:12–16	68, 70
5:12–14	105
5:12	94
5:13	103
5:15–16	103
5:15	46, 104–5, 108, 112
5:16	113
5:17–26	68, 70, 105, 148
5:17–25	103
5:17	141
5:19	112, 137
5:20	142
5:21	71, 74, 97, 108, 142, 156, 175
5:24	72, 160
5:25	139
5:26	137, 139
5:27—6:5	74
5:27–39	74, 160
5:27–32	69, 142
5:27–28	138
5:27	133, 138
5:28	138
5:29–39	160
5:29–32	36
5:29	133
5:30	71, 74, 97, 108, 133, 138, 142, 156, 175
5:31	160
5:32	140, 144
5:33–39	69, 142
5:33	73–74, 92, 94, 115, 119, 142–43, 161, 187
5:38–39	149
6:1–5	69, 74, 108, 142, 160–61
6:2	71, 74, 97, 133, 142, 156, 175
6:3–4	117
6:5	72, 94, 160
6:6–11	69, 142
6:6–10	108
6:7	74, 142
6:8	142
6:10	103, 142
6:11	74, 108, 142, 149, 161
6:12–16	69
6:17–49	39
6:17–19	69, 108, 137
6:17	112
6:18–19	102–3
6:18	46, 105, 158
6:19	112
6:20—8:3	64, 69–70
6:20—7:1	105
6:20–49	28, 64, 69
6:20–38	146
6:20–23	70
6:20–22	107
6:20	35, 116, 120–21
6:21	155
6:22	72, 152, 160
6:25	155
6:35	153
6:43–44	99
6:46	72, 94

Luke (cont.)

6:47–49	74, 152
6:48	114
6:49	133
7:1–17	28, 64
7:1–10	50, 62–64, 66, 69, 77, 93, 103, 108, 175
7:1	137
7:3	64, 133
7:6	160
7:9	112, 133, 137, 185
7:11–17	63–64, 66, 69–70, 77, 87, 93, 103, 105, 108, 148, 175
7:11	64, 91, 112, 137
7:13	83, 94, 155
7:16–17	104, 108
7:16	63–64, 108, 116, 137, 139
7:17–23	39
7:17	72, 91
7:18—8:56	72
7:18–35	1, 8–9, 18, 21–22, 28, 31, 33, 37–38, 40–44, 60–65, 67, 69–70, 72–74, 77–78, 81–88, 90, 105, 109, 125, 129, 131, 158, 162, 167–71, 173–74, 183–84, 186–87
7:18–30	108
7:18–28	55, 83, 148, 157, 171
7:18–23	4, 11, 12, 14–15, 27, 33–35, 37–38, 40, 43–46, 70, 87, 90, 109, 112, 136, 170–71, 174, 182, 187–88, 193, 195
7:18–20	151
7:18–19	90
7:18	38, 45–46, 83, 87–93, 100, 108, 112, 175, 193
7:19–20	3, 47, 61, 87–88
7:19	13, 17, 24, 33, 36, 37, 45–46, 71, 89
7:20–21	47
7:20	30, 46, 61, 89–90, 92, 101, 112
7:21–22	32, 88, 90, 176, 178
7:21	37, 46, 61, 88–90, 102, 104–6, 108, 112
7:22–23	47, 88, 110, 171–72
7:22	7, 30, 32, 36–37, 63, 72, 74, 83, 89–90, 92, 102, 104–5, 120, 146, 174, 192
7:23	28, 60, 88–90, 102, 107–9, 170–71, 182, 194
7:24–35	36, 38–39, 87, 115
7:24–30	11, 43–44, 48, 71, 87, 157, 174
7:24–29	9
7:24–28	4, 16, 30, 49, 54, 61, 88–91, 136, 143, 170–71, 178, 187, 195
7:24–27	49, 114
7:24–26	3, 30, 39, 88, 158
7:24–25	60
7:24	13, 38, 49, 88–89, 91–92, 105, 112–14, 134, 151, 152
7:25–28	134
7:25	3, 89, 91, 113–14, 152
7:26–28	159
7:26–27	35
7:26	6, 8, 83, 88–89, 91, 113, 116, 119, 152
7:27–28	117
7:27	28, 30, 39, 50, 52, 60, 88–89, 91, 117–18, 126, 182, 184
7:28	1, 2, 9, 12, 26, 28, 37, 39, 49, 75, 88–89, 91–92, 119, 121–22, 124, 132, 134, 142, 165, 182–84, 192
7:28–30	56, 184
7:29–35	61, 63–64, 73–75, 83, 120, 172, 174
7:29–30	4, 7, 18, 22, 24–30, 38–39, 50, 54–56, 60–61, 64, 88–91, 122, 124–25, 128–33, 139, 143, 148, 150–51, 157, 171–73, 179, 195–96

Index of Scripture and Other Ancient Writings

Luke (cont.)

7:29	8, 91–92, 105, 132–40, 152, 160, 164–65
7:30–35	163
7:30–34	64
7:30	91, 129, 140–41, 143, 146, 148, 153–54, 156
7:31–35	1, 4, 7, 19, 44, 55, 57, 61, 64, 71, 87–91, 122, 124, 145, 151, 162, 165, 170–72, 180–81, 196
7:31–32	27–28, 39, 43, 90, 151, 154
7:31	1, 30, 57, 59, 88, 90–91, 134, 151–52
7:32–34	90
7:32	30, 57–59, 88, 90–91, 153, 155
7:33–35	30
7:33–34	28, 39, 43, 58, 74, 89–91, 94, 151, 156–58, 162
7:33	13, 92, 101, 143–44, 157–58
7:34	9, 32, 64, 72, 133, 138–40, 159–60, 162
7:35	3, 5, 20, 22, 27–28, 37, 39, 43, 59, 64, 89–91, 133, 151, 162–63, 171–72, 180
7:36—8:3	67
7:36–50	28, 63–64, 66, 69, 74, 87, 153, 160, 167
7:36	133
7:37–38	64
7:38	155
7:39	64, 72, 108, 116, 137, 145
7:44–46	64
7:47	146
7:49	64, 71, 101, 108
8:1–3	63, 69
8:1	105, 121
8:2	103, 158–59
8:3—9:50	69
8:4—9:50	72
8:4–18	28, 39, 64
8:4–15	70, 74, 76
8:8	99, 126
8:10	121
8:12	158
8:16–18	70
8:19–21	70
8:22–25	70
8:25	71, 101
8:26–39	70
8:27–39	159
8:27–33	103
8:28	72, 96, 159
8:29	158
8:37	68
8:40–42	70
8:40	137
8:41–42	145
8:41	137
8:42–48	70, 138
8:43	103
8:47	103
8:49–56	70
8:50	133, 137
8:51	153
8:52	155
9:1–6	70, 105
9:1	103, 159
9:2	103, 121
9:6	103
9:7–9	70
9:7–8	72, 116
9:7	73, 92, 119, 174, 187
9:8	72
9:9	71, 73, 92, 101, 182
9:10–17	70, 74, 160
9:11	103, 121, 137
9:18–21	70
9:18	71, 101
9:19	72, 92, 101, 116
9:20–21	176
9:20	71–72, 101
9:22	70–72, 137, 145, 147, 160
9:23–27	70

Luke (cont.)		11:15	158
9:24	71	11:16	108
9:26	72, 160	11:18	158
9:27	121	11:19	158
9:28–36	70	11:20	121
9:31	148	11:24	158
9:35	72, 96	11:26	158
9:37–43	70	11:27–28	107
9:38–42	159	11:27	107
9:41	152	11:29–32	152
9:42	103, 158	11:29	108
9:43–45	70, 72	11:30	160
9:43	137–38	11:31	164
9:44	72, 138, 145, 147–48, 160	11:37–54	160
9:46–48	70, 119	11:37	133
9:47–48	155	11:38	145
9:48	37, 120, 165	11:39–54	134
9:49–50	70, 159	11:39–43	133
9:51—19:46	53, 72	11:45	133, 141
9:50	70	11:46	133, 141, 152
9:58	160	11:49	164
9:60	121	11:50–51	152
9:62	121	11:52	133, 141
10:9	103, 121	11:53–54	145, 149
10:11	121	12:1	133–34
10:16	133, 144	12:4	117
10:17–20	159	12:8	160
10:18	158	12:10	159–60
10:21	35, 148, 153, 165, 181	12:31	121
10:23–24	35, 122, 185	12:32	120–21, 148, 165
10:23	47, 107	12:37–38	107
10:25–28	146	12:40	160
10:25	133, 141, 145	12:43	107
10:29	133, 140	12:45	161
10:38–42	160	12:48	117
11:1	73, 92, 174	12:50	133, 145–46
11:2	121, 146	13:6–9	99
11:5	160	13:13	139
11:6	160	13:14	103, 145
11:8	160	13:16	158, 159
11:13	155	13:17	137
11:14–26	159	13:18–21	121
11:14–20	159	13:18	121, 152
11:14	105, 137, 138	13:20	121, 152

Luke (cont.)

13:28–29	121
13:28	122, 185
13:31	133, 145
13:32	159
13:33	147
13:34	155
13:36	149
14:1–24	160
14:1–3	145
14:1	133
14:2	158
14:3–4	103
14:3	133, 141
14:12–14	162
14:14–15	107
14:15	121, 133
14:21	36
14:35	126
15:1–32	160
15:1–2	139, 145
15:1	138, 160
15:2	133
15:7	140, 144
15:18	46
15:21	46
15:26	46
15:51	159
16:5	46
16:8	152, 165
16:13–14	145
16:14–18	53
16:14–15	53
16:14	133, 162
16:15	133, 134, 140
16:16–18	54
16:16–17	53
16:16	19, 51, 53–54, 73, 92, 119, 121, 126–29, 131, 135, 174, 184
16:18	53
16:19	115, 158
17:2	120, 165
17:15	103, 139
17:20	121, 133, 145
17:21	121, 178
17:22	160
17:24	160
17:25	145, 147, 152
17:26	160
17:30	160
18:8	160
18:9	140, 144
18:10–14	139, 160
18:10–11	133
18:10	133, 138
18:11	133, 138
18:13	133, 138
18:14	133, 185
18:16–17	121, 155
18:16	46, 121
18:17	121
18:18	145
18:21	146
18:22	133
18:23	133
18:24–25	121
18:29–30	121
18:31–33	145, 147
18:31	117, 160
18:35–43	103, 106
18:36	133
18:43	139
19:1–10	160
19:3	137
19:7	137
19:10	160
19:11	121
19:30–34	46
19:31	101
19:34	101
19:37	47
19:39	145
19:41	155
19:46	62, 117
19:47—21:38	62
19:47–48	137, 138
19:47	145

Luke (cont.)

19:48	149
20:1–18	145
20:1–8	73, 144, 174
20:3–7	64
20:4	92, 133
20:6	92, 116, 159, 187
20:7	119
20:9–19	145
20:10	99
20:17	117
20:18	30
20:19–20	149
20:19	137
20:20–25	145
20:26	145
20:27–38	145
20:27	149
20:39	145
20:40	145
20:46–47	134
20:47	117
21:1—23:56	62
21:3–4	185
21:9	147
21:15	164
21:22	117
21:24	148
21:26	114
21:27	160
21:31	121
21:34	161
21:37	117, 147
21:36	148, 160
21:38—22:2	137, 138
22:2–6	145
22:2	137, 149
22:3–4	149
22:3	158–59
22:7–38	160
22:16–18	121
22:16	121, 148
22:18	121
22:22	147, 150, 160
22:23	148
22:24–27	119
22:26	37, 120, 165
22:29	121
22:30	121
22:31	149, 158–59
22:37	146
22:42	146
22:48	160
22:51	103
22:53	149, 159
22:59	194
22:62	155
22:63–65	145
22:66–71	145
22:67–71	176
22:67	101
22:69	160
22:70	101
23:2	137, 145
23:3	101, 176
23:5	145
23:6	133
23:8	108
23:10	145
23:13	68
23:24–25	138
23:27	137–38, 155
23:28	155
23:29	107
23:34	137–38
23:37	101
23:39	101
23:42	121
23:47	139–40
23:48	137–38
23:50–52	137
23:50	139
23:51	121, 133
23:55	145
23:56—24:53	62
24:7	145, 147, 160
24:19	116
24:21	148

Index of Scripture and Other Ancient Writings

Luke (cont.)	
24:25–27	147
24:26	147
24:27	117
24:28–35	160
24:41–43	160
24:44–46	117
24:44	148
24:46	147

John	
1:6–8	192
1:15–18	186
1:15	192, 194
1:19–34	189
1:19	188
1:20	188
1:21–22	188
1:21	6, 8, 188
1:23	98, 188
1:24–25	188
1:26–36	186, 192, 194
1:26–27	188
1:29–38	98
1:29–34	1
1:29	11, 188, 193
1:31	188
1:33	188–89
1:34	3, 193
1:35–37	188
1:35	188
1:36	11, 40, 169
1:37–48	188
1:46	194
3:1–9	30
3:22–26	188
3:22	189
3:26	5, 188
3:27–30	169, 188, 190, 192, 194
3:28–31	4
3:29	189
4:1–2	189
4:1	188
4:31–33	190
4:46–53	62
5:33	186
7:27	194
7:41–42	194
7:52	194
8:3–11	190
10:40	189
12:36	165
15:1–8	189
19:19	194
20:24–29	28

Acts	
1:3	121, 149
1:5	56, 75, 92, 141, 174
1:6–7	121
1:6	149
1:7	146, 150
1:9–11	149
1:16	146, 149
1:20	146
1:21–22	74, 174
1:21	149
1:22	62, 92, 122, 133, 141, 185
2:3	149
2:7	47
2:22	108
2:23	133, 138, 147, 149–50
2:25	114
2:28	149
2:33	47
2:36	138
2:39	46, 154
2:40–41	146
2:40	152
2:41	189
2:43	108
2:47	146
3:11–26	137
3:12	47
3:14–15	138
3:14	140
3:18	147, 149–50

Acts (cont.)		7:21	158
3:20	146, 150	7:22	164
3:21	149	7:27	108
3:22–23	116	7:36	108
4:1–21	145	7:37	116
4:1	137	7:41–42	108
4:2	109, 138	7:52	108, 140, 150
4:4	137	7:54	109
4:12	47, 146, 149	8:3	145
4:13	94	8:5	105
4:14	103	8:6	108
4:16	108	8:7	103, 158
4:19–20	94	8:12	121
4:20	47	8:13	47, 108
4:21	139	8:25	105
4:26–28	146	8:33	152
4:28	133, 147, 150	9:1–2	145
4:29	138	9:3–6	149
4:30	108	9:5	101, 176
5:3	158	9:6	147, 149
5:12	108	9:16	147, 149
5:14	137	9:23	145
5:16	103, 158	9:34	103
5:17–18	145	9:39	155
5:17	137	10:3–7	149
5:19–20	149	10:10–16	149
5:26–40	145	10:22	139
5:28	109	10:24	160
5:29	149	10:30–32	149
5:34	133, 141	10:33	108
5:38–39	146	10:37	56, 62, 74, 92, 133, 141, 174
5:38	133	10:38	103, 158
5:40	46	10:41	147, 150
5:42	105	10:42	105, 147, 150
6:2	46	11:5–10	149
6:3	163–64	11:13–14	149
6:7	137	11:16	56, 75, 92, 174
6:8	108	11:18	139
6:9–14	138	11:20	105
6:10	163–64	11:28	149
6:11	109	12:3–4	145
6:12—8:1	145	12:7–11	149
7:10	163–64	12:23	149
7:12	133		

Acts (cont.)

13:2–3	94
13:2	46
13:7	46
13:10	158
13:12	47
13:15	127
13:22	146
13:23–25	56, 92
13:24–25	75, 92, 141, 174, 181
13:24	133
13:27	147, 149
13:29	146
13:33	154
13:36	133, 147, 152
13:38–39	133, 140
13:42	137
13:45	137, 145
13:47	150
13:48	150
13:50	145
14:2	137, 145
14:3	108
14:5	145
14:7	105
14:16	152
14:19	145
14:22	121, 149
14:26	149
15:5	133
15:12	108
15:21	152
16:9–10	149
16:10	46, 147
16:30	149
16:31	146
17:3	147, 149
17:5–9	145
17:5	137
17:12	137
17:18	105, 158
17:25	103
17:26	146, 150
17:31	147, 149–50
18:5–6	145
18:9	149
18:12–13	145
18:24—19:7	56, 92, 181
18:25	75, 92, 133, 141, 174
19:1–7	92, 110, 189
19:3–4	133, 141
19:3	92
19:4–5	75, 174
19:4	92, 101
19:8	121
19:11	47
19:12	103, 158
19:13	105, 158
19:15	158
19:16	158
19:21	149–50
19:31	160
20:25	121
20:27	133, 146
20:28	150
20:35	107, 149
21:14	146, 149
21:20	137, 139
21:27–31	145
21:31	155
22:6–8	149
22:8	101, 176
22:10	150
22:14	47, 140, 146, 149–50
22:17–21	149
22:22–23	109, 148
22:24	102–3
22:26	133
23:6	133
23:11	147, 149
23:12–15	145
23:16	133
23:17	46
23:18	46
23:23	46
24:1–9	145
24:19	149
25:2–3	145

Acts (cont.)

25:7	145
25:10	149
25:24	138
26:2	107
26:5	133
26:9	149
26:13–18	149
26:15	101, 176
26:16	47, 147, 150
26:18	158
26:22	149
26:23	149
27:12	133
27:23–24	149
27:24	147, 149
27:42	133
28:8–9	103
28:23	121
28:24–28	145
28:27	103
28:31	121

Romans

3:21	127

Galatians

4:4	119

Ephesians

5:8	165

Colossians

4:14	80

1 Thessalonians

5:5	165

2 Timothy

4:11	80

Philemon

24	80

Hebrews

11:36	102

1 Peter

1:10–11	28

Revelation

2:7	126
2:11	126
2:17	126
2:29	126
3:6	126
3:13	126
3:22	126
13:19	126

OT PSEUDEPIGRAPHA

2 Baruch

29:3	193
48	164

1 Enoch

	160
42	164
46	193
48:2–6	193

4 Ezra

	160
5:10	164

NT APOCRYPHA AND PSEUDEPIGRAPHA

Acts of Philip

34	183

Index of Scripture and Other Ancient Writings

EARLY PATRISTIC WORKS

Justin Martyr

Dialogue with Trypho

8:4	193
110:1	193

Jerome

Epistulae

121.1	1, 195

JOSEPHUS

Antiquities

18	191

QUMRAN SCROLLS

1QS

11.21	119

11QPsa

18	164

4Q521

2	191, 194

RABBINIC LITERATURE

Babylonian Sanhedrin

97a	193

OTHER WRITINGS

Aelius Theon

Progymnasmata

78	102
79	103
84	91
87	158
96	109
103	134
118–20	115

Aristotle

Rhetorica

1.2.1357a.13–14	109
2.22–26	109
2.23.1397b.12–29	120
3.17.1418a.6–1418b.17	109
3.18	113

Demetrius

De elocutione

30–33	109

Quintilian

Institutio oratoria

5.10.1–4	109
5.14.1–3	109

Rhetorica ad Herenium

4.23–24	113

www.ingramcontent.com/pod-product-compliance
Lightning Source LLC
Chambersburg PA
CBHW051637230426
43669CB00013B/2344